OUR BUSINESS OUR WAY

Stories and Lessons from Family Businesses

OUR BUSINESS OUR WAY

Stories and Lessons from Family Businesses

Editors
VIVEK RAJVANSHI
SHIRSHA GUHA

BLOOMSBURY
NEW DELHI • LONDON • OXFORD • NEW YORK • SYDNEY

BLOOMSBURY INDIA
Bloomsbury Publishing India Pvt. Ltd
Second Floor, LSC Building No. 4, DDA Complex,
Pocket C – 6 & 7, Vasant Kunj,
New Delhi 110070

BLOOMSBURY, BLOOMSBURY QUEST and the Diana logo are
trademarks of Bloomsbury Publishing Plc

First published in India 2025
This edition published in 2025

ISBN: 978-93-69522-34-7
2 4 6 8 10 9 7 5 3 1

Printed and bound in India by Sanat Printers

To find out more about our authors and books, visit
www.bloomsbury.com and sign up for our newsletters

Contents

Preface

There are countless books about businesses, but most focus on the journeys of individual entrepreneurs or on large, well-known corporations. What often goes untold are the stories of lesser-known family-run enterprises that may not make headlines but have quietly built remarkable legacies through perseverance, strong values, and a clear vision. Their challenges, opportunities, and achievements are unique and deeply inspiring.

This book brings together the real stories of sixteen remarkable family-run enterprises that have built enduring legacies. They have stood strong against the test of time, and many of them have grown after facing major shocks such as the COVID-19 pandemic, internal family conflicts, and intense market competition. These businesses didn't just survive. They evolved–shifting from B2B to B2C markets, professionalising their structures, setting clear processes, and improving operational efficiency. And at the heart of it all, they continued to carry forward something far deeper than profits–a proud legacy for the next generation.

Documenting Your Business Journey

I once told a young family business owner, 'You may think you're just running a company, but in truth, you're shaping a community. Every decision you make, every risk you take or avoid, doesn't just affect your family. It reaches your employees, your customers, your suppliers, and even their families.' Over time, he began to see what I meant. His business was a living network of people connected by shared effort and trust.

One of the most meaningful exercises for business owners is to write their journey. Through this, they will discover that the process itself is incredibly rewarding. As you document your journey, you begin to uncover insights and lessons that might otherwise remain hidden.

Writing your story also encourages you to engage with others, not just senior family members, but also long-serving employees, advisors, and even old friends. You may find yourself searching through old records, photographs, and memories, feeling both pride and nostalgia for the business's remarkable progress.

These conversations and reflections deepen your appreciation for the people behind the business and often strengthen bonds within the family. Sharing the story also inspires the next generation to take pride in their heritage and contribute to its growth with renewed respect and enthusiasm.

One contributor wrote to me after completing the first draft of their story that the experience of writing about their business and themselves had given shape to what had always been a pool of scattered thoughts in their mind. They said that they had always respected their legacy but had never had the chance to truly honour it until then. They shared that they deeply cherished the writing process, that it had given them clarity, and that their vision now felt stronger than ever.

Another contributor of a story wrote that writing the story of their own business had been an incredibly rewarding experience, as it had helped them confidently define their role and clarify the business goals they had been striving to articulate, and, more importantly, had deepened their appreciation for their legacy and the skills they had inherited.

I hope that after reading this book, you will also feel inspired to start writing your own family business story, not just as a record of success, but as a celebration of your journey, your values, and your legacy.

Initial Idea of the book

As one of the Programme Directors of the Postgraduate Certificate in Family Business (PGCFBM) at IIM Calcutta in 2025, I encountered many fascinating stories about family businesses and their unique challenges. What struck me most was the participants' deep enthusiasm, pride in their business legacy, and deep understanding of their businesses.

During one of the capstone project presentations, I was sitting with Mr Saurabh Jain (whose story is also featured in this book), and I asked him, 'Why don't you write your story?'

After the session, I shared the idea more broadly with the participants, announcing that if there was sufficient interest and at least one volunteer willing to contribute to editing, we could move forward with a book project. Ms Shirsha Guha (whose story is also featured in this book) graciously agreed to edit the book with me, marking the beginning of this journey.

Acknowledgements

I would like to express my gratitude to Dr Alok Kumar Rai, Director, IIM Calcutta, for his encouragement and support during the writing of this book. I am also deeply grateful to Prof. Rajesh Babu, Dean (Executive Education), IIM Calcutta, for his generous support of this project and for facilitating the photographs included in this book.

Most of all, my heartfelt thanks to my wife, Rupali, whose unwavering support has always encouraged me to take on and complete projects like this. A big thank you to my daughter, Suhani, and my son, Aditya, for the many rounds of discussions we had while I was drafting my chapter. Their questions and perspectives, as well as their input on editing other chapters, have meant more to me than they know.

Together with my family, I am also deeply grateful to all the contributors for their stories. Their experiences not only made it possible to complete this project successfully, but also helped me uncover many hidden gems of life, insights and situations I could share and reflect on with my children, sparking conversations that might never have taken place otherwise. These narratives highlight important lessons that everyone, whether directly involved in a family business or not, ought to understand. My special thanks to the co-editor of this book, Ms Shirsha Guha, for her excellent support, which played a vital role in bringing this project to fruition. I would like to thank my friends, Ms Rashmi Soni and Mr Amit Verma, for their valuable input and ideas for the cover page of the book.

Shirsha and I would like to express our sincere gratitude to Mr Rahul Srivastava, Managing Director – Bloomsbury Publishing India, for believing in this project and supporting its publication. Our heartfelt thanks to Mr Ankur Halder from Bloomsbury, who coordinated every stage from our initial conversations to the final manuscript. We are also grateful to Ms Jyoti Mehrotra and her team at Bloomsbury for their invaluable assistance with formatting and their many thoughtful suggestions that helped refine the writing.

Vivek Rajvanshi

I would like to thank Professor Vivek Rajvanshi for inspiring this book and being the driving force behind it, but most of all for providing me with the opportunity to be a part of this book. The experience has been life-changing. I would like to thank all the contributors to this book, who shared these very personal and emotional insights into their lives, families and businesses. It has been the privilege of my career to work with all of you and learn from each of your unique experiences.

Finally, I would like to acknowledge the love and support that my parents have shown me and for giving me the platform from which I have been able to achieve whatever I have today. My heartfelt gratitude knows no bounds.

Shirsha Guha

1

Building a Legacy for Generations

VIVEK RAJVANSHI

Over the course of my work, I have had the privilege of interacting with more than fifty participants deeply involved in their family businesses. What began as structured sessions often evolved into lively, insightful conversations filled with personal stories about their business journeys. For me, these exchanges were intellectually stimulating, capturing practical experiences which often can't be learnt through theory.

In this chapter, I shift my focus from the technical aspects of financial management and strategy to the guiding principles that can help family businesses become more professionally managed and successful. There is no ready-made formula for this. However, through numerous discussions with family-run enterprise members, several meaningful insights have emerged. While the list is long, I have captured a few key lessons that, I believe, hold lasting value for anyone aiming to build a resilient and forward-looking family business.

Entrepreneurial Ventures to Legacy Enterprises

A family business can be thought of as a business where the family not only owns the company but also plays an active role in managing it. Such enterprises, instead of focusing mainly on profits, focus equally (or even more) on continuity, reputation, and harmony across generations. Decisions are often shaped by emotional connection to the enterprise and its members.

Naturally, family businesses begin as entrepreneurial new ventures and gradually evolve into multi-generational enterprises. Over time, their priorities shift from an entrepreneurial approach to one focused on sustainability and long-term value creation.

As the next generation steps in with fresh ideas and new perspectives, new challenges and opportunities emerge. It becomes important to balance innovation with traditional values.

Guiding Principles to Professionalise Family Businesses

Although each business is unique, family businesses in general differ in features and challenges from startups and other businesses. The following guiding principles may be used to understand family business better and to develop a framework for long-term success:

- Balancing growth with profitability
- Understanding business cycles and managing risks
- Measuring performance against competitors
- Setting clear short- and long-term goals
- Decision about expansion and diversification
- Creating a transparent succession plan
- Developing a family business constitution

The Growth vs. Profit Dilemma

A common question that all businesses face is whether they should prioritise growth or focus on protecting margins. Chasing revenue growth can help build scale and brand presence, but it often comes at the expense of profit margins and negatively impacts free cash flows. Only a few businesses, mostly well-funded start-ups, can afford to burn cash in pursuit of market dominance. Focusing solely on profits, on the other hand, keeps a business stable but small, leaving it vulnerable to larger and more aggressive competitors.

Family businesses understand this dilemma well. Older generations have long mastered the art of balancing stability with profitability.

When the next generation steps in with fresh ideas and bold plans, that inherited wisdom becomes a compass. While seeking market expansion, it is essential to set minimum margins, below which business survival may become challenging. Simultaneously, focusing on profit margins, a floor for growth in revenues should be maintained. Periodically review the strategy to ensure that both growth and profit margins remain above the lower limits. We will discuss benchmarking in detail, along with industry practices, in the next sections.

Understanding Business Cycles and Risks

Business risk refers to the likelihood that a company's revenues, future profits, etc., may fall short of expectations due to changes in the business environment. Every business, whether big or small, faces risks, and understanding and managing these risks is key to long-term success. At its core, business risk is reflected in the variability of earnings. The more unpredictable the profits, the higher the business risk.

Business risk arises from several factors, including fluctuations in demand, shifting customer preferences, competitive pressures, regulatory changes, and technological disruptions. When family businesses face high risk, the stakes are personal. A setback can shake not just profits, but also the family's way of life and the legacy built over generations.

Family businesses that take a cautious and balanced approach often enjoy stability, harmony across generations, and smooth succession. However, excessive caution can hinder a business's progress. When emotional attachment outweighs rationality, decisions may lean too much toward survival rather than growth, limiting the ability to take healthy risks.

A business cycle refers to the recurring highs and lows in economic activity—periods of boom followed by slowdown or recession. For a family business, understanding these economic upturns and downturns not only clarifies where the firm stands in the cycle but also reveals how resilient the business truly is. With a clear sense of risk across the cycle, family business leaders can make informed decisions on how much leverage to take, how much cash to keep in reserve, and how aggressively to pursue growth and expansion.

To stay resilient, family enterprises should maintain sufficient liquidity through investments in cash-equivalent assets and build strength with measured diversification, stable governance, and robust risk management practices.

Managing internal shocks, on the other hand, requires clear systems and well-defined structures. Every family business should develop a contingency plan, providing a clear and actionable roadmap for unexpected events. The firm should anticipate internal risks and prepare for them in advance. This ensures that both the family and the business remain stable, even in times of crisis.

Debt, too, should be handled with balance. Borrowing can fuel growth, but only if the business has the capacity to repay comfortably and withstand tough times. When risks are high, avoid piling on debt. But when the business is steady, a reasonable level of borrowing can actually strengthen growth and stability.

Benchmarking Against Industry Peers

If your business provides comfortably for your family, does that automatically mean it's performing well? Is evaluating success based only on past financial results truly enough?

In one case, the business owner proudly said, 'We're doing well! We are not only managing our expenses, but we live a luxurious life and enjoy great respect in society, what more do we need?' However, upon examining the company's financials, the picture told a different story. The average return on equity, over a reasonable period, was actually lower than the interest available from a simple bank fixed deposit. Curious, we compared the numbers with those of their competitors, and discovered that the competitors were performing significantly better. It was a wake-up call for the enterprise to take charge and identify where the problem is.

While long-standing family practices and financial history can offer valuable insights, they rarely tell the whole story. But, without proper benchmarks, such evaluations lack context. Benchmarks introduce the realities of the market, showing how similar businesses perform and help identify both the strengths and weaknesses of the enterprises.

Finding the right comparisons, however, is not always easy. Family-run enterprises are often privately held, making it challenging to identify direct peers. Still, establishing a set of comparable businesses, even if not perfect, is vital for understanding where your business stands and how it can improve.

When selecting companies to compare your business with, consider those that generate revenue from similar businesses and face comparable risks. Once you have the data, look closely at where your business performs differently from others. These insights will reveal your strengths, expose weaknesses. Performing at or above industry standards builds confidence among owners and investors, making the business stronger and more resilient.

Setting and Achieving Goals

Business owners, sometimes, are so deeply involved and seem satisfied in daily business operations that when asked about their long-term goals, they respond with pride: 'Look at what we've achieved over the years. Isn't that success enough?' After all, why set goals when everything seems to be going well and the business feels stable?

However, the truth is that without clear goals, you may be running fast but with no idea where the road leads.

Setting clear goals, whether operational or strategic, provides direction, instils discipline, and creates a framework for accountability. When setting goals, it is essential to involve all key family members and, when appropriate, external advisors. Goals should follow the SMART framework: *Specific, Measurable, Achievable, Relevant,* and *Time-bound.* Rather than chasing too many objectives at once, it is wiser to identify three to four key focus areas, monitor progress regularly, and make changes whenever needed.

For family businesses, however, goal setting must go beyond growth and profitability. It should also encompass wealth management, family governance (including defining the roles for committees, advisors, and family members), training of the next generation, and leadership transition planning.

On the operational side, short-term goals, typically spanning one to three years, focus on managing profitability, cash flow, and working capital, as well as enhancing customer retention, driving sales growth, responding to crises, and improving overall operational efficiency.

Long-term goals, in contrast, span several years and are often guided by the family's vision for future generations. These include plans for expansion and diversification, HR policies, building brand and reputation, and ensuring wealth preservation and smooth succession.

Finally, budget planning for both the upcoming financial year and the medium term (two to five years) should align with goal setting. A well-structured budget helps assess available cash flows, plan capital expenditures, and allocate resources effectively, ensuring that both short- and long-term objectives remain financially sustainable.

Diversification in Business

Diversification in a business refers to expanding into new products, services, markets, or industries beyond the firm's traditional core activities, with the objective of reducing risk and creating new growth opportunities. However, it is noted that family businesses often hesitate to diversify, instead focusing on preserving wealth and legacy. Businesses often find that diversification can divert focus from their core business and divert management attention.

The key lies in balance, strengthening the core while carefully exploring new opportunities. One practical approach is to use surplus capital or monetise underutilised assets to fund diversification. Family businesses can also leverage their reputation, trust, and brand strength to expand into related sectors.

In one case, a company relied entirely on a single overseas supplier for the supply of raw materials. Due to geopolitical issues, the company experienced import problems, resulting in a significant loss of business. The lesson was clear that when everything depends on one person, one market, or one product, the risk multiplies.

A well-planned diversification strategy acts as a protective cushion against market disruptions. In doing so, it helps ensure that the family's legacy not only endures but continues to grow across generations.

Succession Planning

Succession always sparks curiosity. Who will lead the business after the current leader? How will things change with a shift in leadership? Will the next generation take the business to greater heights, or struggle to maintain its success?

These questions don't arise only in the mind of the current owners, but also among employees, investors, and other stakeholders who have a vested interest in the future of the enterprise.

Normally, the inspiration to join the family business comes from senior family members a father, grandfather, or uncle. Business-related talks often fill family dinners or casual conversations. Even if the younger generation doesn't contribute much at first, simply listening becomes a powerful form of learning. These moments of observing business dynamics at an early age lay the foundation of practical wisdom that others may take years to acquire.

When the business faces tough times, younger members often see the real-life impact of managing liquidity, cutting costs, and even making painful decisions such as layoffs or selling emotionally attached assets like gold or family property. But when the business recovers, they also witness the pride of revival. They learn that with strategy, resilience, and a bit of luck, any downturn can be reversed. Such lived experiences build a deep, strong confidence.

Family members understand each other's strengths and weaknesses, complementing one another while carrying forward the same values. For parents, there is no greater satisfaction than watching their children work side by side, blending family life with business success. However, as a part of succession planning, handing over a business, or distributing assets or units can lead to strained relationships, or worse, long-term rivalries. Sometimes, when disputes remain unresolved, businesses may split, which can often be a painful experience, especially for the older generation.

Even seemingly fair separations can later trigger resentment if one side prospers more than the other. Therefore, having clarity and transparency about the future structure of the business, whether it will remain united or evolve into independent divisions, is essential. When roles are well-defined and expectations are aligned, potential conflicts are easier to manage or avoid.

Family Business Constitution: Role and Benefits

Some family businesses choose to document their shared vision, values, and principles in a family constitution. Though not legally binding, this guiding document serves as a moral and strategic compass for how the family manages both its business and relationships. While still uncommon in India, it is widely practised in several regions/societies and has proven to be a powerful tool for strengthening family enterprises.

A family constitution outlines the family's short- and long-term goals, defines the roles and responsibilities of family members involved in the business, and establishes procedures for conflict resolution.

Creating such a document requires collaboration and openness. All family members and key stakeholders should come together to articulate their collective values, mission, and vision. The document should define governance structures and establish a clear succession framework. External advisors, such as lawyers, consultants, can help facilitate these discussions whenever required.

A well-crafted family constitution brings clarity, transparency, and balance. It helps create structures based on trust and ensures that decisions are fair and conflicts are resolved with mutual respect. It plays an equally important role in succession planning and supporting sustained business performance. After all, the ultimate goal of every family business is a happy and harmonious family, isn't it?

The Role of the Next Generation in Growth and Development

When younger family members join the business, they carry a dual responsibility: to honour the family's legacy while also driving innovation and growth.

Stepping into leadership roles brings its own challenges. Working with employees and managers who are older and more experienced, introducing new ideas can meet resistance. Many long-serving managers believe that 'what worked for years still works today'. Young leaders in such situations should strive to strike a balance between respecting experience and having the confidence to innovate. It is important to remember that trust is earned through humility, consistency, and tangible results.

The most successful transitions occur when the younger generation takes the time to learn from their elders. The senior members' deep understanding of markets, customers, suppliers, and industry dynamics is an invaluable asset. These insights not only enhance the business acumen of younger members but also help them appreciate the values and relationships that have sustained the enterprise over the years.

My mantra for them would be:

Learn first, lead next. Respect tradition, drive innovation.

—xxx—

SAINT JAMES
SCHOOL OF MEDICINE

Your Future. Our Promise.

Shirsha Guha is a second-generation business owner of Saint James School of Medicine (SJSM). The institution was founded in 1999 by her father, Dr Kallol Guha, and is located on the beautiful island of St. Vincent in the Caribbean.

A little-known fact is that the Caribbean, also known as the West Indies, has been a hub for medical education for U.S. and Canadian doctors since the 1970s. Saint James has distinguished itself as one of the most successful medical schools in the region.

The family business today spans multiple geographies. The head office is located in Chicago, while the campus is in St. Vincent. Shirsha's own life mirrors this global spread. Having grown up in Denmark, the Caribbean, India, and later the United States, she now resides in India, where she leads the school's operations in India.

The journey of Saint James is more than just a business venture. It is the story of her father's vision, risk-taking, and persistence in creating a medical institution that not only transformed their own lives but also opened opportunities for hundreds of aspiring doctors across the world.

2

The Story of Saint James School of Medicine: A Vision and a Dream

SHIRSHA GUHA

Our story began in 1969, when my father, Dr Kallol Guha, hitchhiked his way from Kolkata to Denmark with only $3 dollars in his pocket. This long and arduous journey took over 2 months and traversed countries like Iraq, Turkey, Bulgaria, Romania, Austria and Germany, until he finally reached his destination in Denmark. Many ask whether he did this to find a job, or more money, but he will tell you that he made this journey in search of an education.

My father, as he likes to tell the story, was a student who was poor at academics. He was forced into a higher grade at a very young age, and he never quite caught up with his studies. The Indian schooling system did not cater to stragglers, and he struggled on for years, eventually earning a bachelor's degree and even pursuing an additional degree in agriculture. But his yearning for a modern higher education outweighed everything and in 1969, he and an artist friend, dropped everything and embarked on this audacious journey, in search of a different, if not better life.

They set off first on a train from Kolkata to Bombay, then on a boat to Basra, Iraq, and subsequently by train to Istanbul, Turkey. Afterwards, they began hitchhiking through Europe. They were inspired by various travellers they had met in Kolkata during their college days, who came from far-off countries like the United States and the UK. Without much money in their pockets, my father's artist friend would sketch and paint at various stops, and the money they made from selling these paintings was used to buy food and supplies. Those times were different, visas were granted at borders, countries were welcoming to young people, and there were always a handful of fellow students and young people also travelling in a similar way, although almost none from India.

Food was not guaranteed in this way, of course; sometimes they bought food, and sometimes they relied on the hospitality of villagers and farmers in

1969, Odense, Denmark.
My father and his travel companion Biswajit Ganguly

the countryside through which they travelled. They slept in deserted houses and buildings, churches, in vineyards, often out in the open. It's an incredible story of adventure and uncertainty that still amazes me every time I think about it. Growing up, my father often regaled us with stories of his journey and even wrote a book about it in both Bengali and English.

When my father and his friend finally reached Denmark, his first stop was the University to ask whether there was a programme he could join. He was first directed to the University of Odense. In Odense, he washed dishes to earn money for living expenses, and then he was directed yet again to Copenhagen University. There, he would meet his future guide and mentor, Dr Barker Jorgensen, who was an important man in the Physiology department at the University. My father had no background in Physiology to speak of, but Dr Jorgensen, on hearing the story of my father's incredible journey, saw something special in him and accepted him as a PhD student in his laboratory. My father still sometimes tells us of the struggles he had with learning simple concepts that were so lacking from his education in India, but were a matter of course in the Danish system. Slowly and methodically, he taught himself the missing pieces and, in 1976, earned his PhD in Endocrinology under Dr Jorgensen's guidance. Thereafter, he spent another five years working on a DSc (Doctor of Science) at the University of Kuopio in Finland under the guidance of another great scientist, Dr Vanha-Perttula. These two men would instil in my father deep values of discipline and endurance that, to this day, shape his thinking.

Of course, none of this would have been possible without the unwavering support of my mother, Sukla, who met my father in 1968, in Kolkata, just a year before he left for Denmark. Besides looking for a university programme to join, my father worked to save money to buy a plane ticket for my mother to join him. In 1971, from the meagre savings he collected from his modest stipend as a PhD student, he finally saved up enough and sent her a ticket, which she used to fly to Denmark. At a time when there was no email, or cell phone, and not even a proper international calling system, I am equally amazed at the faith that my mother had in my father, to take this very daring step and join him, a student with little or no income, in a foreign country. The only communication between them up to that time was by letters that took months to reach one another. After arriving in Denmark, between 1971 and 1981, she held various clerical positions until she secured a permanent placement at the renowned shipping company, Scandutch.

I became a part of this amazing story when I was born in 1976. That same year, my father moved to Finland to start his DSc. I remember well the gloomy days in Denmark, when it was just me and my mother. I was in daycare from the time I was three months old, as my mother had to return to work almost immediately to make ends meet. She would drop me off at daycare and later at kindergarten in the mornings, and we would go home together at the end of the day. It must have been so lonely and difficult for her all those years managing on her own with a young child, but her faith was unwavering, and she never complained.

For a middle-class young Bengali couple from Kolkata, life in Denmark in the 1970s must have been tough, but this shaped them both in ways they could never imagine.

Once my father was awarded his DSc in 1981, he was offered a job as a professor of Physiology at Ross University School of Medicine, located on the tiny island of Dominica in the West Indies. No one had ever heard of this university or the country, but yet again, my father embarked on another journey into the unknown and landed in Dominica. So began twenty years of teaching in medical school in the Caribbean. A few months later, when I was five years old, my mother and I joined him.

My father taught Histology and Physiology at Ross University School of Medicine. He loved teaching with every ounce of his being. You could see his eyes light up and his voice quiver with excitement whenever he talked about his subject matter. My brother, Kaushik, was born in Dominica in 1981, and we spent many long happy years of childhood in Dominica. My mother gave up working, and dedicated her time to raising her children, because as she puts it, she had done her job of getting my father his PhD and DSc. And there's no doubt about that whatsoever.

Starting afresh in the US and the Fledging University

After almost twenty years as a professor, my father took yet another daring decision, once again an unprecedented move, to quit the safety of his work as a professor and to establish a medical school of his own, this time on another Caribbean island, Bonaire. My parents moved to Chicago, in the United States, and started the operations from a small basement apartment on Devon Avenue. My mother once again supported my father without question, and they worked side by side to start off the operations. This was uncharted territory for all of us. My father was an academic, not a businessman. He poured his life savings into the school, and my mother supported him unconditionally. For a couple who had lived cautiously all their lives, this was a life-changing leap of faith.

Thus began the story of Saint James School of Medicine.

My First Steps

Medicine was woven into our daily lives from the very beginning. Even as a child, I helped my father arrange his teaching slides, sort transparencies, and file grades for his students. The most exciting times for me was visiting

Oct 2024, Shirsha Guha, speaking at the 25th Anniversary Celebrations of Saint James School of Medicine.

the Anatomy Lab, where the cadavers were housed. This is where students would work on the cadavers and they would be stored in formaldehyde in various stages of dissection. While others might have found this gruesome, I was fascinated, and felt completely at ease. For me, the medical school environment was as natural as my own home.

I had started school in Dominica at age five and continued there till high school, but as my brother and I got older, the complete lack of educational facilities beyond high school made my parents decide that my mother, my brother and I, would move back to India to complete our education.

In 2001-02, I had just finished university in Kolkata and was labouring under a PhD programme in New Delhi. Living alone in a large city was challenging, and I soon realised I was not progressing either personally or academically. My parents had just started Saint James, and they encouraged me to come and join them in the US. Since I was not making much headway in India, I thought it was worth taking a chance and moving to the US to work alongside them.

Building the Business Together

My brother and I arrived in America in 2003, and for me, this was a welcome change. After years of being scattered across different cities and countries, our family was finally together again. The security and comfort of living in a house with my parents enfolded me completely, and I embraced this new chapter wholeheartedly.

At that time, my father and I managed the office together, while my mother spent long hours on the phone speaking with students and parents. My brother was young and still wanted to continue his studies, and so while he enrolled in University, I dived headlong into the medical school operations. Our small team consisted of just four people: my parents, one IT assistant, and later an administrative aide. We were a lean but determined unit.

My father was the driving force behind everything, and he had the energy of a hundred. His enthusiasm was infectious. In those early days, I wore many hats: salesperson, IT troubleshooter, registrar, and admissions advisor. Slowly but steadily, student enrollments grew, and revenue began to flow. By 2004, we had secured approval for a US private student loan, which increased our enrollment to over one hundred students.

Expanding Operations and Campus Growth

I frequently travelled to the Caribbean campus, setting up processes with faculty, coordinating with students, and meeting government officials. My father and I rotated between managing the US office and visiting the Caribbean campus. As operations expanded, our team also grew. These were the fledgling days of the company, and looking back, I am amazed at what we achieved with such limited resources.

2024, The brand-new campus of Saint James School of Medicine at Golden Vale, St Vincent

Oct 2024, Dr Kallol Guha, cutting the ribbon with the Prime Minister of St Vincent, Hon. Ralph Gonsalves, inaugurating the new campus of Saint James School of Medicine

In those early days, digital marketing was in its infancy. I vividly remember spending hours with our IT Manager studying the brand-new Google marketing dashboard to experiment with keywords and bidding strategies. It was a thrilling time of discovery.

Over the years, Saint James School of Medicine grew steadily. My father continued to drive growth and expansion. He had an uncanny ability to perceive risk. He would discuss and plan for situations that seemed far-fetched, but eventually came true, leaving us all lost for words. In fact, now it's an accepted fact in our organisation, that we work based on his intuitions of risk, and it has paid off time and time again. From a modest office in 2003, we have now expanded into a building of over 10,000 square feet in Chicago, employing more than twenty-five on-site staff. In St Vincent, our dedicated campus in two locations, now has more than 40 faculty and staff members, and our hospital network in the United States is over 25 strong, altogether serving over 800 students at any given time, with 100s of graduates who are practicing physicians and surgeons in the US and Canada.

The Student Loan Episode: A Hard Lesson

In July 2004, our fortunes rose when we were approved for a private US student loan programme through a well-known student loan agency which doubled our enrollments almost overnight. Representatives from the bank visited our Chicago office, showering us with merchandise and we all went out for a celebratory lunch. At that moment, we were on top of the world and it felt like we had truly 'made it'.

But this success was short-lived. Within two years, the bank discontinued the programme, leaving many of our students stranded without the necessary finance to continue their education. We scrambled to arrange alternative funding, sometimes at our own expense. It was a harrowing experience for both the school and our students. Though we managed to salvage the situation eventually, the episode taught us a crucial lesson: student financing was a fickle friend. Since then, despite significant growth, on principle we have kept our students' loan dependency as low as possible, which in turn serves to reduce student loan debt for our graduates.

Reconciling Personal Ambitions

Having grown up so close to the medical school environment, becoming a doctor felt like a natural path for me. However, I didn't quite succeed in the required examinations when the time came, and instead, I pursued a bachelor's and master's degree in Microbiology and Molecular Biology. At the time, this disappointment came as a huge blow and derailed my ambitions. I wondered where life would take me.

Many have comforted me saying, even though I never became a doctor myself, I now contribute to producing hundreds of doctors each year, a testament to how the universe works in mysterious ways.

Academic Roots in Business

Although at the time, I didn't realise it, my academic and research background proved invaluable in managing a medical school. I quickly integrated with faculty, deans, and students, contributing to curriculum design, academic committees, and overall programme execution. My father and I have this in common, and I was able to understand and match many of his ideas regarding teaching and academics that he works on.

Both my father and I, even now, enjoy giving occasional lectures, not only to share knowledge but also to build direct connections with students. These sessions open channels of communication, making it easier for students to approach us with concerns. Aside from my father, I remain the only senior member of our office administration with an academic background, and this perspective has been a valuable asset in bridging the gap between business operations and academics.

Challenges: Starting Out in India

Approximately ten years ago, I relocated to Kolkata, India, to establish an Indian subsidiary of our US-based company. It was a long-cherished dream of my father's to have business operations in the country of his birth.

Over the years, my parents seemed to grow more and more attached to their Indian roots. My father revisited Bengali literature and music, immersing himself in them. The plan to open an India office was a bit of a hurried decision, and not well researched, but like most things, we took the plunge and I, like a good daughter, took up the challenge.

The original plan had been that the Indian office would build a brand presence for Saint James in India and recruit students from India, while the US office would provide back-end support. However, for various reasons, the back-end support didn't work out. Though my father supported the general concept of the Indian office, he soon lost interest in the day-to-day affairs, and the rest of the office in the US followed suit. It was a slow detachment, and for years, I tried to run the operations largely on my own. In a new country, with an unfamiliar business environment, and without active support from the head office and my family, the task was daunting. I was held solely accountable for the success, or lack thereof, of the venture. I tried everything I could, but nothing seemed to be working. My role in the company was questioned, even by family members, which made the journey more isolating.

Despite these obstacles, I made a concerted effort to establish both myself and the company in India. I travelled extensively, liaising with universities, educational institutions, and hospitals to build a network and promote our presence. Slowly and steadily, I began to make some headway.

Building Strategic Partnerships

COVID-19 and the subsequent restrictions on travel significantly affected our India operations. I had no choice but to downsize to a bare minimum while trying to keep up our network. In 2024, when we were just reestablishing ourselves, a significant breakthrough came through a relationship I had forged with one of the largest universities in Bangalore. This partnership opened new doors for us, and the university's Dean introduced us to an EdTech company, which was exploring opportunities in foreign medical education. Based simply on his recommendation, they joined hands with us. This partnership allowed us to achieve, within a few months, what we had struggled to do for over five years. We made significant progress in a short time, although the learning curve was steep and successes were hard-won.

This served to open everyone's eyes to the challenges of establishing a new educational brand in India, as well as the upside: the potentially unlimited opportunities if pursued strategically.

Thanks to the partnership, our medical school achieved a higher level of visibility and credibility in India that would have otherwise taken years to attain, and we established a mutually beneficial support system to rely on, which would pave the way for future successful ventures as well. It was also heartening to see the renewed enthusiasm among my colleagues as well as my family, regarding working in India; a long-cherished dream was finally taking shape.

The Importance of Family Communication

My natural strengths lie in people management, relationship-building, and academics. However, in India, I had to wear multiple hats: financial planner, operations manager, and strategist, often with limited resources. I was accustomed to working in a collaborative team, sharing ideas, and jointly tackling challenges. Without that synergy, I became overly cautious, which slowed growth and delayed new initiatives. I was accustomed to the unwavering support of my parents, but as time and distance took their toll, our communication also became sparse.

As in many family businesses, one of the biggest challenges we faced was communication. Clear, respectful, and structured communication is essential to running a family enterprise; however, in our case, it was often lacking.

The physical distance between us only deepened the chasm. While I managed the India office, my father and brother were in Chicago overseeing US operations. The time zone differences made regular discussions challenging, and over time, communication within our family deteriorated. At its very lowest point, this breakdown led to the temporary shutdown of our India operations.

The strain also took a heavy personal toll. I felt sidelined, discouraged, and disheartened. I missed my parents, especially working closely with my father. Watching my role shrink within the company I had worked so hard to build was heart-wrenching. The tension seeped into our personal relationships, leaving me feeling isolated from my own family.

My parents, nearly eighty, were deeply disturbed by the conflicts, but despite their best efforts, we were unable to resolve the issues. It was heartbreaking to see my father and my mother caught in the middle of this seemingly impossible situation.

The Turning Point

I realized that we needed to do something about this impasse; it was all of our futures on the line. I tried various suggestions from colleagues and friends, but nothing seemed agreeable to everyone concerned. Finally, in 2024, on my insistence, we engaged a family business consulting firm based in Chicago. I knew that my father and brother would be more comfortable with a US-based consultant. Though there was hesitation, largely due to financial and time considerations, we eventually agreed to give it a try.

The consultants helped us establish processes for professional communication and governance, both of which we had previously neglected. Most of all, they provided a platform for us to communicate clearly and concisely about both business and family matters. Since then, we have made deliberate efforts to improve communication, especially within the family. Structured meetings, mediated discussions, and better-defined roles began to yield results. We became more aware of being respectful and patient during discussions. We found a forum to discuss and address our concerns, whether personal or business-related. This clarity within our family communication trickled down to our company structure as well, and slowly we saw distinct changes in company-wide communication.

Management, Strategy and Finance

My brother, Kaushik, an MBA in finance, has always been our go to person for our company's finances. His expertise ensures that we maintain financial discipline, while my focus remains on academics and operations. As in any company, everyone recognizes that profitability is the lifeblood of the business. A profitable venture creates a positive work atmosphere, instils confidence among employees, and provides the foundation for long-term growth. Whether profits are reinvested in the company, distributed as dividends, or shared with employees through bonuses, they serve as a signal of success and stability.

One of the unique strategic challenges of our journey has been building a brand in a market unfamiliar with the Caribbean model of medical education. In India, the idea of studying medicine in St Vincent, a small island in the Caribbean, was almost unheard of. Many people initially confused the Caribbean with Africa or South America, which made the task of positioning our school a formidable challenge. At the same time, established competitors such as universities in Russia and China had already captured the Indian medical education market. Introducing Saint James as a viable and prestigious alternative required significant effort in awareness building, outreach, and credibility creation.

Perhaps the greatest challenge we have faced, one that resonates with many family businesses, is striking the right balance between short-term cash flow management and long-term investments. Day-to-day operations demand consistent liquidity, yet long-term survival depends on sustained investment in brand building and infrastructure. Our approach has always been cautious, reflecting the mindset of many Indian family-run businesses that hesitate to take on large bank loans or external debt.

This caution delayed some of our growth decisions. For example, although we had been operating successfully for more than twenty-five years, it was only three years ago that we finally invested in a permanent campus of our own in St Vincent. The first phase of this investment was a $3 million investment. Despite our company always being financially solid, we agonised for years over this decision before finally taking the plunge. The upcoming phases are projected to cost an additional $10 million, for which we are raising funds. This reflects our risk-averse nature and underscores the delicate balance needed between preserving financial security and funding growth opportunities.

Like many Indian family enterprises, our tendency to be risk-averse and our reluctance to borrow money have sometimes constrained our ability to expand. To a large extent, my brother's influence, with his background in Finance, has helped us recognise that breaking out of this mindset is essential if we want to scale further and compete globally. Balancing prudence with ambition remains a central theme in our financial strategy, a lesson that continues to shape our family's approach to entrepreneurship.

Looking Ahead: Generational Dynamics and Continuity

Generational dynamics are central to the survival and success of a family business. Ensuring that the older generations feel respected and included, while inspiring younger generations to feel welcome and valued, is an essential responsibility. At the same time, balancing the egos, aspirations, and personalities of multiple family members, each bringing their own strengths and weaknesses, requires both patience and sensitivity.

My identity, whether I like it or not, is deeply tied to this company. Having built it alongside my father more than twenty years ago, I cannot imagine my life without it. My hope is that one day my children will join and experience the same sense of pride and fulfilment that I do. And so, my motivation to resolve conflicts and establish good governance practices within the company extends beyond the present. At one time, I worried that my children, or my brother's children, would inherit these unresolved tensions. I didn't want them to ever feel isolated and uncertain of their place in the family business or the world.

I'm happy to see that now with time, discussions within our family often focus on the next generation and how to effectively incorporate them from an early age into the company, how do we motivate them to do this, and how do we best prepare them for that role. These are positive signs that we are moving in the right direction, and that our children will inherit a company they can take pride in.

Piece of Advice for Family Business Entrepreneurs

If I had to give one piece of advice to family business entrepreneurs, it would be to address conflict resolution early on. Whether it's the use of an elder in the family, a consulting firm like the one we used, or a trusted person outside the company that everyone respects, conflict resolution is a key part of any family enterprise. Respectful and clear communication is also key, but when communication fails due to conflict, the entire fabric of the organization can unravel very quickly. Many families and family-run businesses have fallen apart simply because they failed to address and prepare for this eventuality.

The Priceless Value of a Family Business

Balancing the duality of family and work in a family run business is never easy. Still, the advantages far outweigh the struggles. For me, the business

Oct 2024. The Original Four: L-R: My brother, Kaushik Guha, Shirsha Guha, my mother, Sukla Guha and my father, Dr. Kallol Guha, at the inauguration of the new campus in Golden Vale, St Vincent

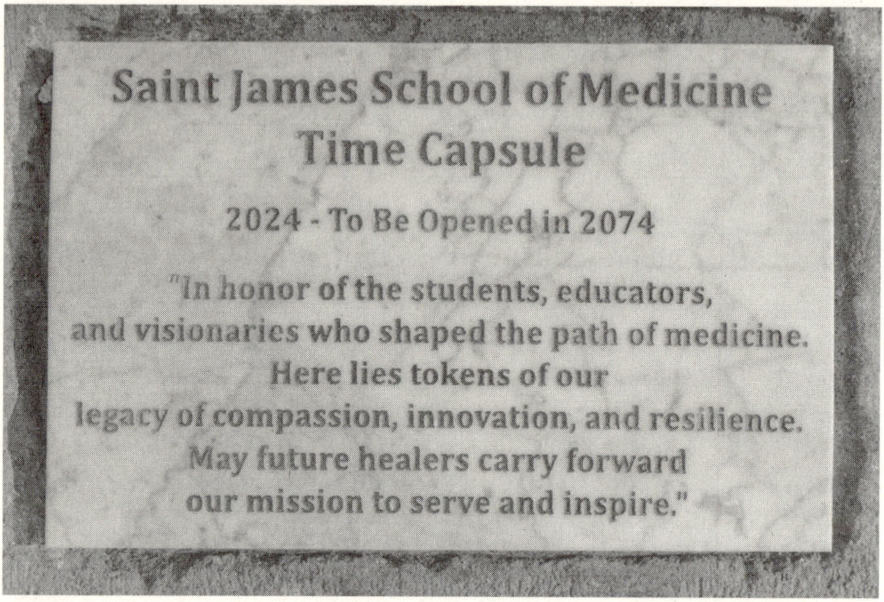

2024. Commemorative Stone placed over a time capsule buried at the new campus, a tribute to the students, educators, and visionaries who shaped the path of medicine

1989. Dr Barker Jorgensen, August Krogh Institute, Copenhagen, Denmark. Mentor and guide to my father, and the man to whom my father attributes his life's successes

has brought security, pride, identity, leadership, and cooperation, gifts that many don't experience even after decades in a corporate career. Despite the inevitable ups and downs, the sense of belonging that a family business instills is unique. It gives you purpose, motivation, and the will to rise each morning with a renewed sense of direction. That is something no salary or position in a conventional workplace can ever replicate, and I'm always grateful for being given that gift, and hope to pass it on to the next generation.

—xxx—

PANORAMA®

Happiness Since 1981

Panorama Electronics Pvt. Ltd., the flagship company of the ₹ 600 crore diversified Panorama Group, began its journey in 2008 with a focus on Homeland Security and IT Infrastructure solutions. Over the years, they have built deep expertise in delivering specialised, turnkey IT-enabled solutions, ranging from Safe and Smart Cities to Integrated Traffic Management Systems (ITMS), Data Centres, and Cybersecurity solutions. Their clientele includes State and central government bodies, Public Sector Undertakings, and large corporations across India.

The Panorama Group itself stands as a symbol of innovation, integrity, and resilience. With a legacy spanning more than 45 years, it has evolved from being a trusted name in consumer electronics to a diversified enterprise with interests across multiple industries.

As a second-generation entrepreneur, Joydeep Chowdhury's story reflects his personal journey, one that narrates the company's humble beginnings, growth, and diversification over the decades, as well as his vision for the future. He sees himself as both a custodian of this proud legacy and a catalyst for its continued evolution and growth, ensuring that Panorama's spirit of progress and purpose endures for generations to come.

3

Inside an Entrepreneur's Mind

JOYDEEP CHOWDHURY

The Story of a First-Generation Entrepreneur

The Chowdhurys hail from a zamindar lineage, though by the time my father, Mr Balaram Chowdhury, was born, not much of that zamindari remained. 'Chowdhury' was a title given to zamindars, though, in truth, we are Chatterjees by origin.

My father was one of six siblings. His father, the Late Duni Lal Chowdhury, my grandfather, served in the Indian Railways, where he was widely known as the "Bara Babu" of Howrah Station. Beyond his official duties, he had an unshakable passion for electronics. After office hours, he would spend his evenings repairing radio sets, not for money, but out of love. His fascination was so deep that he even learned the technical craft from a guru and went on to design components that improved shortwave radio reception, especially to catch Shillong Radio, which was immensely popular in those days.

My father grew up watching him come home from duty, freshen up, have a cup of tea, roll up his sleeves, and lose himself in his small workshop, fixing radios late into the night. Those evenings left an imprint, a spark that would one day define his own path.

When my grandfather passed away in 1962, my father was still a student, in Class XI. A talented badminton player, he had won the Under-19 State Championship three times by then. But his true calling lay elsewhere, in carrying forward his father's passion for electronics.

With just ₹200 borrowed from his mother and her blessings, he started repairing radios in a tiny 100 sq. ft. family-owned shop. Simultaneously, he pursued a diploma in Radio Engineering, learning hands-on under Mr Kishori, a well-known engineer in that field. Eventually, Mr Kishori hired him as a consultant for technical guidance.

A few years later, he secured an agency for Philips radios, and business started to grow. With savings from that venture, he purchased a larger 800 sq. ft. retail outlet in a prime location and began selling television sets made by North Indian manufacturers. What began as retail soon evolved into manufacturing, and prosperity followed.

The Birth of 'Panorama'

In 1981, my father established a manufacturing facility for black & white televisions, later expanding into colour televisions under the brand 'Panorama.' The unit produced about fifty sets a day, but demand was soaring. Within three years, he rented a second facility, doubling production to 100 sets daily, and still, the entire output was sold in advance.

In 1984, he acquired a larger plot on VIP Road, then a quiet suburb of Kolkata, and set up a fully organised television manufacturing unit. Older generations in the city still recall the glowing 'Panorama Colour TV' neon sign that crowned the building.

By 1992, Panorama had become one of the leading television brands in Eastern India, commanding over 20 per cent of the market share with a vast distribution network, approximately 1,200 dealers, and sixteen company-owned service centres. My father personally oversaw the after-sales service, offering what he proudly called 'Domkol Service', a fire-brigade-style rapid response when most others took a week to attend customer complaints. Thanks to his obsession with service quality, Panorama never faced a single consumer court case.

Popular PANORAMA black and white TV in let 80's

Press ad of our entire PANORAMA Product range

Ups and Downs

For Panorama, the early years brought remarkable growth. After launching its Black & White TV line in 1981, sales climbed rapidly, averaging 400 units per month. However, the anti-Sikh riots of 1984, following the assassination of Mrs Indira Gandhi, disrupted the market, wiping out several small manufacturers. That vacuum allowed Panorama to surge ahead, selling over 1,000 units per month.

In 1986, during the Cricket World Cup, Panorama launched its colour TV range, sparking another boom. The company sourced its components from suppliers in Delhi or imported them, deliberately avoiding the lower-quality kits offered by ECIL.

But between 1988 and 1992, the television industry hit turbulent times. About thirty-five manufacturers operated in West Bengal, and most shut down as the market contracted. The 1991 economic reforms, introduced by Dr Manmohan Singh under Prime Minister P.V. Narasimha Rao, liberalised the Indian economy, inviting foreign competition. Soon, global giants like Sony entered India's consumer electronics space.

A New Beginning: The Era of Distribution of Global Brands

In 1994, Sony approached my father, offering him the distribution rights for Sony TVs and music systems in West Bengal. My father agreed, but on one condition: he wanted full control of after-sales service to ensure the quick turnaround his customers were accustomed to. The Japanese team agreed.

Thus began a new chapter. The distribution was handled through another group company, Neosa Electronics Pvt Ltd, and by 2001, it became the largest distributor in India, representing major consumer electronics and home appliance brands.

Expanding Horizons: The Mobile Revolution

As India entered the mobile phone era, the electronics landscape underwent yet another transformation. Riding that wave, we diversified into mobile phone distribution, partnering with some of the largest brands in the country.

Today, apart from our legacy brand Panorama, we handle over twelve major brands across consumer electronics, home appliances, and mobile phones, with a combined turnover of ₹450 crores, a testament to decades of steady growth and adaptation.

A Heart Beyond Business

Beyond business, my father's generosity and humility have always stood out. His connection with football began serendipitously in 1986, during a trip to Hong Kong, where he met the Mohun Bagan football team, honoured as the National Club of India. The team, led by Padma Shri Sailen Manna, as 'Save the Mission', had travelled to China for a tournament but, after failing to qualify, faced financial and logistical struggles while trying to return home.

One of the players, Arjuna Awardee Subrata Bhattacharya, somehow reached my father, calling his friend's office, knowing he was in Hong Kong.

Upon hearing their plight, my father immediately hosted the entire team for lunch, arranged for their train tickets from Kowloon to the airport, and ensured they returned home comfortably.

A journalist travelling with the team published a story about a Bengali businessman who came forward to support the Mohun Bagan team abroad. Upon his return, my father was invited by the General Secretary of Mohun Bagan, Mr Dhiren Dey, to demonstrate their gratitude. Later, he was asked to join the club as an office bearer.

He went on to serve as Cricket Secretary, later as Assistant General Secretary (1989–2005), and was eventually elected Vice President in 2016.

Diversification: The IT & Healthcare Story

In 1997, my father, along with a few partners, ventured into the information technology sector, investing in an offshore software development company. The company started with an extraordinary opportunity: a multi-million-dollar contract from one of the largest banks in the United States. The early years were highly successful; the firm, Earthbase Technologies, was profitable within its first three years. Later, Earthbase decided to reinvent itself by developing a city-based online portal, one of the first of its kind in India. All company surpluses were invested into this ambitious project, and talks with a venture capital firm for ₹20 crores in funding were nearing closure when disaster struck.

The dot-com bubble burst in March 2000, erasing valuations across the tech sector. Investor confidence evaporated overnight, and the deal was called off. Unable to raise funds to sustain the development, the portal project was shelved. The company briefly pivoted to handle software development for U.S. and European clients, as well as web-based projects for Indian government departments, before eventually winding down its operations.

The Healthcare Business Episode

Around 2001, my father made another strategic investment, this time in the healthcare sector. Along with his long-standing friend and business partner, he co-invested in Suraksha Hospital, a 180-bed multi-speciality facility in Salt Lake, Kolkata. However, a few years later, labour union issues created operational challenges. In 2008, the management decided to sell the hospital to AMRI Hospitals. The exit was successful, and all stakeholders made healthy returns on their investment.

Following the sale, the management decided to focus on expanding Suraksha's diagnostic and outpatient services, which were performing well. This led to the growth of Suraksha Diagnostics, a brand that became synonymous with quality and trust in Eastern India's healthcare sector.

In 2016, the company raised its first round of institutional funding, followed by a second round in 2021. Eventually, Suraksha Diagnostics was listed on the NSE & BSE Mainboard in 2024, marking a proud milestone in its growth story. We had already exited before the IPO through a block deal, securing strong returns on our original investment.

Story of the Second-Generation Entrepreneur: The Origin Story

The Call from RBI

It was sometime in August 2006 when I received a call from the Reserve Bank of India, Kolkata. They wanted us to visit and assist them with a critical issue that had been troubling them for some time. Naturally, curiosity took over.

Across the country, hundreds of currency chest branches, run by both public and private sector banks, held vast amounts of cash to supply local branches and ATMs in their regions. Security at these locations was always a top concern. Apart from the armed guards, the only real safeguard was a hotline installed in the Branch Manager's office, directly connected to the nearest police station. In an emergency, the manager would simply pick up the phone, and it would ring at the police station for help.

But there was a catch: no one really knew if the hotline would work when it was truly needed. What they wanted was a simple, more reliable and more intelligent solution.

The problem we were asked to solve felt like a riddle. A quiet doubt lingered in my mind: Could we actually design a system that would solve their problem without disrupting their existing operations?

Over the next few days, we buried ourselves in desk research, trying to understand how similar security systems were handled globally. Then, within a few days, the RBI called again. They had arranged a visit to one of the currency chest branches. Their urgency was evident, and so was our anxiety. What if we failed to come up with a viable concept? It would be a major embarrassment, especially since our recommendation to the RBI had come from someone highly respected in law enforcement circles.

Inside the Currency Chests

The day of the visit remains etched in my memory. It was the first time I had ever seen so much cash in one place, hundreds of crores stacked neatly, counted, and stored in large, sealed trunks. I couldn't resist asking the Branch Manager, 'How much cash do you handle every day?' He smiled and said, 'A couple of hundred crores a day, a couple of thousand every month.' It was mind-boggling.

After several discussions, we came up with an idea, a sensor-based alarm system. The concept was simple yet powerful: motion sensors (to detect movement), magnetic door contacts (to detect unauthorised entry), and an electronic control panel that would trigger a hooter or siren during a security breach. It was practical, scalable, and could be easily integrated into existing operations. When we presented the concept to the RBI, they were impressed. But they had one more question: could the system also alert the local police station automatically during an intrusion? Yes, we could integrate a modem that would dial the police station whenever an alarm was triggered.

Prototype & Pushback

We were asked to build a prototype, and after nearly two months of relentless work, we finally had a working model. We were invited to demonstrate the prototype to a high-level committee, and for a brief moment, it felt like our hard work had paid off. One of the committee members asked, 'Can the system also inform the local police station in case of an emergency?' Here, there was a catch. The call would be a blank call, with no voice message or identification details. And that, as it turned out, was a deal-breaker. The committee collectively insisted that the system must have voice communication capability, including identification of the specific chest branch in distress. The entire concept was rejected outright because of that single missing feature. It was a tough lesson, one that stayed with me for years. "*No matter how innovative your idea is, it has no real value unless it truly solves the customer's problem.*"

From Distribution to Creation

At that time, I was deeply involved in relaunching and expanding Panasonic's Consumer Electronics and Home Appliances business across Eastern India. I had also played a role in convincing Panasonic's top management to introduce new product lines, many of which went on to perform remarkably well in the market.

Then, I made a big decision: to personally step away from the consumer electronics distribution business altogether. The thrill of building something new, innovative, and impactful felt far more fulfilling. By then, the consumer business had a solid foundation and capable managers who could run it independently. It was time for me to move on.

Even though we hadn't yet developed a market-ready prototype, we needed to keep the new initiative alive, both intellectually and financially. To generate initial revenue and establish a formal structure for the venture, we decided to launch it under Panorama Electronics Pvt Ltd, one of our existing group companies.

Our first sale occurred when we sold two Door Frame Metal Detectors to the Asiatic Society of India, located on Park Street, Kolkata, which marked the beginning of our success.

Yet, somewhere deep inside, the unfulfilled dream of developing our own product, the very assignment that had once failed, haunted me every night. The urge to build something original, something that truly solved the RBI's problem, grew stronger by the day.

My colleague came across an Italian company named Syac S.p.A., known for providing IT-enabled security solutions for the banking and financial sector. Meeting the team from Syac turned out to be a turning point. Within a month, we finally designed a solution that not only met the RBI's expectations but, in our eyes, went far beyond. We presented it again to the RBI officials in Kolkata.

'Aisa Ho Sakta Hai?'

Two weeks later, we appeared before the committee again. As we presented our concept, a palpable buzz filled the room. Some members looked genuinely amazed, one even murmured, 'Aisa ho sakta hai?' ('Is this even possible?'). Our solution was futuristic: a high-tech, IT-driven system, the first of its kind for the Indian banking sector.

We were given one month to set it up. We worked at lightning speed. Then came D-Day.

The sensors, motion detectors, door contacts, hooters, and PIRs were seamlessly integrated with a Digital Video Recorder (DVR) and a centralised software system. Whenever an alarm was triggered, the control room automatically received an audio-visual alert with a live video pop-up of the concerned branch.

The demonstration ended in stunned silence. No applause, just that quiet, powerful acknowledgement that something revolutionary had just been shown. The Committee unanimously decided to procure the system.

Hi-tech security for banks

CAMERA COVER

New security system for currency chests

City banks plan novel security system

CITY BANKS

System to detect security breach

MONEY HONEY

Cops and banks get linked

Press coverage of Banking Security System (ISS)

But now came the real challenge: how would the banks procure it?

RailTel, a Mini Ratna PSU under the Ministry of Railways, was brought in as a consultant since the project involved network connectivity. RailTel agreed and submitted a formal proposal to serve as the technical consultant for what would soon be called the Integrated Security Solution (ISS) for Currency Chests. Finally, the Request for Proposal (RFP) was released in early 2007. RailTel conducted the technical evaluation and shortlisted three bidders. When the envelopes were opened, Panorama Electronics was declared the L1 bidder, the lowest and winning bidder.

The project was completed within six months, successfully and efficiently. It became a benchmark in the banking sector, giving us confidence, a reputation, and momentum to explore even bigger opportunities ahead.

Kolkata's First Eye in the Sky

Around 2007, we installed the first surveillance camera in Kolkata, near the Metro Channel, a milestone moment for us and for the city. Around the same time, another call came, this one from Visva Bharati University in Santiniketan. The infamous theft of Rabindranath Tagore's Nobel Prize medal in 2004 had left the institution shaken. Since then, the university has been looking to strengthen its campus security, especially for the museum and vaults that house Tagore's priceless handwritten manuscripts and paintings. For us, it was not just another assignment; it was a matter of cultural pride. We were helping protect the legacy of one of India's greatest minds.

Roads and rush on radar

Road run with auto signals, CCTV

Use of tech helps traffic police overcome manpower challenge

TOP COP KEEPS AN EYE FROM CONTROL ROOM

ELECTION IMPACT

Press coverage of Traffic Camera System

Then came the breakthrough.

In 2011, we bagged our biggest surveillance project yet, a ₹14 crore contract to set up an integrated city-wide video surveillance system in Kolkata. The scope was massive: installation of 400 high-resolution (2-megapixel) cameras, an advanced Video Management System, and the computer and storage infrastructure to manage the enormous video data. The system would be supported by a dedicated citywide fibre optic network, linking every camera to a central Traffic Control Room that would operate 24/7.

Inauguration of City Surveillance System by our Honourable Chief Minister

Inauguration of our City Surveillance System by Hon'ble Chief Minister, Mamata Banerjee

That project opened doors to new opportunities. We began participating in similar surveillance and safety projects in other cities and district towns, while also upgrading the existing systems in Kolkata.

Fast forward to 2024, and we achieved another milestone, our largest project to date, valued at approximately ₹52 crores, under the Safe City (Nirbhaya Fund) initiative. The project aims to extend coverage to 6,750 cameras across Kolkata, significantly enhancing urban safety and public monitoring.

From scratch, we built this business to a top line of ₹101 crores in the last financial year, with an EBITDA margin of 8%, and a net worth of ₹32 crores. From zero to this, it has been a journey of resilience, innovation, and unshakable belief in creating something meaningful and lasting.

The tender win rate had always been a concern. Despite being well-placed both technically and commercially, our bids were occasionally rejected due to minor documentation discrepancies. Even in cases where we received a Letter of Acceptance (LOA), projects were sometimes stalled or cancelled because of funding constraints.

Recognising the complexities inherent in the project business, I decided to diversify into product development. To support this new direction, we began assembling a dedicated R&D team with expertise in electronics, communication, and software.

Over the last two years, we have developed certain products in IIoT (Industrial Internet of Things) for the Power and Transportation business vertical. We are also developing some AI-driven software solutions for image processing and advanced image-based analytics.

Joining the Family Business

It was right after my final year engineering exams when I received a call from my father. 'Now that you've completed your engineering, it's time to come back immediately and join the business.'

There was a sense of urgency in his voice that left little room for discussion. My graduation ceremony was still twenty days away, but I didn't wait. I packed my bags, said goodbye to my friends and classmates, and returned to Kolkata to begin a new chapter.

Barely a couple of days after I got back, still recovering from jet lag, my father told me he wanted me to join a software company where he was a co-promoter and investor along with four others. The company was professionally managed, with a CEO, CTO, and around 140 software developers. It had been set up as an offshore development centre to handle Y2K legacy conversion for one of the largest banks in the United States, Chase Manhattan Bank.

The pilot contract was worth $3 million, with the understanding that if we could deliver it successfully, it would lead to a $30 million rollout project across all Chase branches in the US. This was 1997, and the air was electric with opportunity.

I still remember my first day at Earthbase, the company. I was called into the CEO's office, where another gentleman was seated on the sofa. He introduced himself as Mr Sumit Bandhopadhyay, a former founding member of Sun Microsystems in the US. He had recently joined as our CTO after Earthbase acquired his company, Thematech, which specialised in web development projects for government departments and public sector organisations in India.

'Java is the future,' he said with conviction. Then he made a surprising suggestion: he wanted me to teach Java to the company's developers. Java was still relatively new in India at the time, and very few had practical experience with it. Although I was hesitant at first, being fresh out of college, I accepted. That became my first official assignment, my first job, as a trainer.

Over time, I was moved into active development, working as a coder on portal and web-based projects. Soon, I began supervising a small team of developers, gaining hands-on experience in project execution and delivery.

After about two years, I was promoted to Project Coordinator, where I managed several of our web development projects within the Thematech division. Gradually, I started overseeing the company's software export business and was designated Chief Project Coordinator, my first leadership role.

However, after a few years, differences of opinion with the COO made it difficult to continue. I eventually decided to step away from the company, a difficult but necessary decision.

Building Dreams

In 2019, WBHIDCO (West Bengal Housing & Industrial Development Corporation), a state-owned enterprise responsible for developing the New Town township in Kolkata, issued an Expression of Interest (EoI) for IT and IT-enabled companies. The offer was to acquire plots at special promotional prices in the newly conceptualised Bengal Silicon Valley, envisioned as a hub for technology and innovation.

We applied for three parcels of land and submitted our proposal. To our delight, we were allocated all three plots for which we had applied.

The COVID-19 pandemic hit, and with it came one of the toughest phases of my entrepreneurial journey. Projects were stalled, new business evaporated, and revenues plunged. Cash flows dried up almost overnight, and survival became the only goal. It was, without doubt, the lowest point in my business life.

I knew that with a limited customer base and a six to nine-month sales cycle, long-term stability would come only through Annual Maintenance Contracts (AMCs) and service-based income. That foresight helped us weather the storm. Even in that bleak year, we managed to stay afloat, and remarkably, still posted a profit.

Last year, I made the decision to begin construction on what will soon become our Development and Operations Centre, an 80,000 sq. ft. (G+8 floor) Gold-rated green building, designed to be both energy-efficient and future-ready. Our goal is to make it fully operational by 2027. For me, it will truly be a dream realised. An office shelters ideas, ambitions, and people who bring those ideas to life. I realised building a model workspace would attract better talent and creative minds.

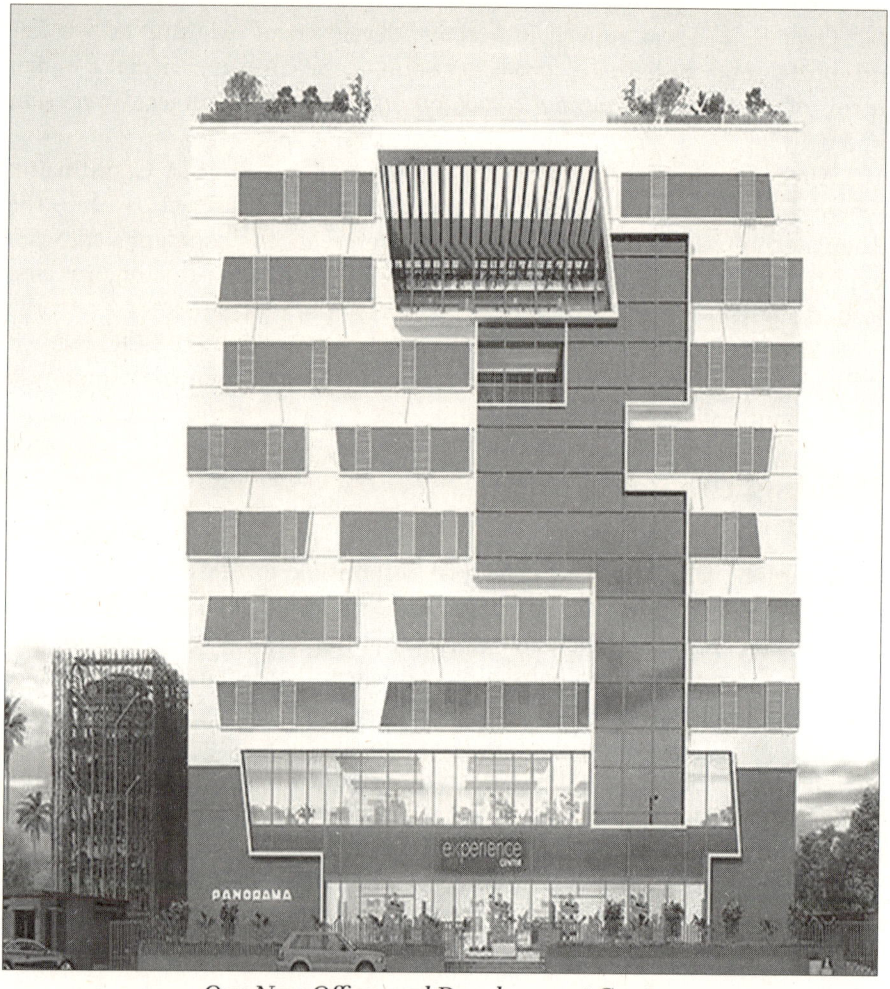

Our New Office and Development Centre

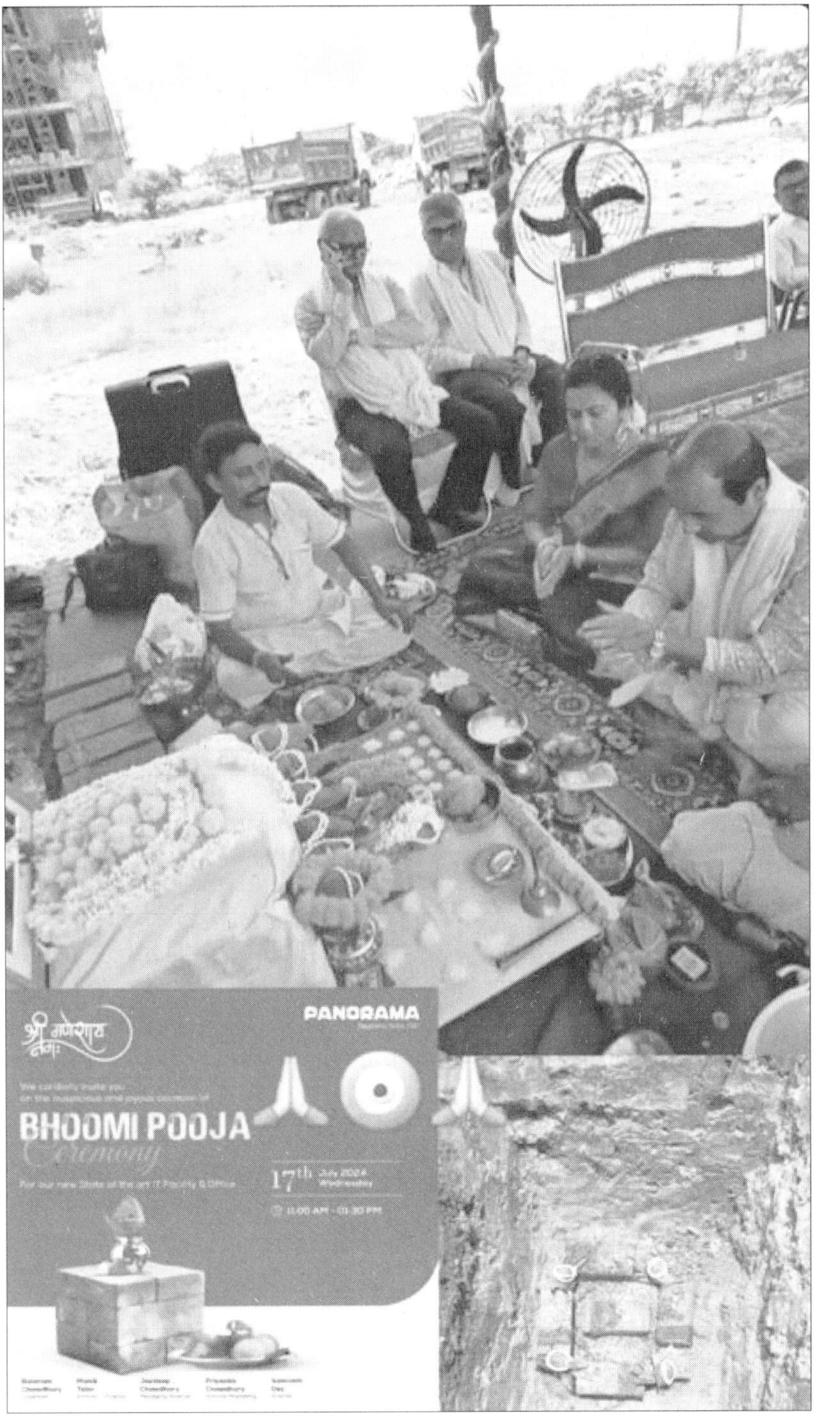

Our New Office's Bhoomi Puja

The Chemical Gamble: A Lesson Learnt

It was sometime in 2017 when an acquaintance of my father approached him with a new business proposal, the idea of entering the construction chemicals industry, primarily focusing on waterproofing products, bonding agents, and sealants.

Fortunately, we already had the necessary infrastructure in place to set up the plant, and within six months, production commenced. The initial plan was to market the products to real estate developers, with a focus on bulk project sales.

To expand beyond real estate, I decided to enter the retail market with a new brand , 'Nanofix'. We developed a fresh product line, specifically tailored for retail consumers, and launched around sixty SKUs over time.

Gradually, we expanded our reach, opening branches in Assam to serve the entire North-East, as well as Odisha, Bihar, and West Bengal. At one point, our team had nearly 100 employees, with about forty in sales and marketing. Sales grew steadily, and by early 2020, we had recorded our first profitable quarter, just before the world was hit by the COVID-19 pandemic.

Birth of Cleantek

The pandemic was a shock. Sales dried up overnight, yet salaries and fixed costs continued. That's when the idea struck: we could repurpose our production line to manufacture sanitisers and disinfectants, which were in

Memories from Star Night, the annual function at Cleantek

massive demand. In just six months, we achieved sales of ₹3 crores, a lifeline that helped us weather the storm.

Following the COVID-19 pandemic, we expanded our hygiene line under a new brand, Cleantek. However, despite our efforts, the retail division proved to be a challenging terrain.

After five long years, I made one of the toughest career decisions, to shut down the majority of the retail division and focus solely on the real estate project segment, which was profitable and stable. The cumulative loss from the retail business ran into several crores—a heavy price, but also a profound teacher.

Today, our focus remains firmly on expanding the real estate project division, which continues to grow steadily.

Nationwide Startup Awards 2022 Distribution Ceremony

Entry into the Defence Sector

Last year, I embarked on a new venture in the defence sector. We received our first developmental order from a Defence PSU to design and manufacture an advanced navigation system for paratroopers. After months of rigorous work, development was successfully completed, and the product is now undergoing testing and trials. If all goes well, it will mark a significant step toward indigenous innovation, a proud contribution to the 'Make in India' vision.

Financial Metrics: A Key Focus Area

In recent years, I have taken a more hands-on role in managing the company's finances, including overseeing banking operations and ensuring financial discipline across all divisions.

Among all financial parameters, the one I value most is cash flow. Effective cash flow management ensures not only stability but also the agility to seize new opportunities as they arise. Beyond cash flow, I closely monitor key financial ratios such as Return on Equity (ROE), Return on Capital Employed (ROCE), Debt Service Coverage Ratio (DSCR), and the current and quick ratios, all of which provide valuable insights into the company's financial efficiency and resilience.

I maintain a detailed financial dashboard in Excel, tracking performance over the past several years, with all relevant ratios that potential investors or financial institutions typically review. My ongoing effort is to improve these indicators year after year, ensuring steady, sustainable growth and a stronger financial foundation for the future.

The Family Business Structure

Although ours is fundamentally a family-managed enterprise, it has evolved over time into a well-structured and professionally run group. My father's long-time business partner, Mr Manick Tater, manages the operations of the distribution division for the Panorama brand. His son, Piyush, has now taken over the reins of the mobile distribution vertical, bringing new energy and digital insight to the business.

My younger brother, Jay, was previously involved in overseeing the online sales of Panorama Consumer Electronics and Audio Systems, playing a key role in expanding the brand's presence in the e-commerce space.

My wife, Priyanka, manages both online and offline marketing initiatives for the chemical division. With her creative and strategic mindset, she continues to build strong brand visibility for our products.

As for my daughter, she is currently in Class XII at Mayo College Girls' School. For now, she is deeply focused on her artistic journey and is not yet inclined to join the family business, although she understands that one day she will inevitably be part of its legacy.

To help her and the next generation appreciate what this journey represents, I am creating a Legacy Document. It will capture the vision, values, struggles, and success stories that have shaped our business over the decades. It will serve as a reminder of our roots and the responsibility that comes with carrying forward the family name. I believe that this story, of my journey and that of our family, will help her understand the struggles, sacrifices, and significance of our business, as well as how deeply it is woven into our family's identity.

Going Ahead: The Road Ahead

As I look to the future, my vision is anchored around two enduring goals: profitability and value creation.

I am currently in discussions with a large technology company about a potential collaboration to set up a manufacturing facility dedicated to producing aspherical and glass-based lenses for both CCTV and mobile cameras. It's an ambitious plan that would require an investment of nearly ₹100 crores, but it aligns perfectly with my commitment to innovation and indigenous manufacturing.

Over the next three years, my goal is to scale our revenues to ₹500 crores, with improved EBITDA margins and stronger financial efficiency across divisions. Simultaneously, I plan to strategically expand our defence business, developing a portfolio of high-value products designed to meet the evolving needs of the sector.

And finally, one of my most personal ambitions, to revive our forty-five-year-old brand, Panorama. I intend to bring it back, modernised, reimagined, and relevant once again.

The journey ahead is not just about scaling businesses; it's about honouring a legacy, embracing innovation, and building a future that balances tradition and transformation.

Commitment to Community: A Social Impact

Beyond business growth, our group has always believed that true success is measured by the positive impact we create in people's lives. Over the years, we have undertaken several Corporate Social Responsibility (CSR) initiatives aimed at giving back to the community that has supported us throughout our journey. We regularly organise free health-check camps in underserved areas, ensuring that basic medical care reaches those who need it most. During the harsh winter months, our teams conduct blanket distribution drives for the underprivileged, bringing warmth and comfort to hundreds of families. Education, too, remains close to our hearts; we have sponsored the schooling of deserving students, helping them pursue their dreams and build a better future. In addition, our group has been proud to support local sportsmen and athletes, providing both financial aid and mentorship to help them excel. My wife, Priyanka, has been actively participating in organising such activities and insists that we start the 'Panorama Foundation' to extend our social services in a much more meaningful and organised way, not only for humans but also for animals.

Free Health Camp at Haripota, South 24 Parganas

Supporting & celebrating the caddies at a Golf Tournament with Mr Leander Paes

Mantra for the Budding Entrepreneurs

I feel that there is no shortcut to success. In my opinion, true achievement is built on relentless effort, hard work, focus, and the ability to learn from failure. To me, success isn't one big moment; it's a thousand decisions done right, one after another.

They say health is wealth, and I've come to believe that deeply. Golf became that balance for me. What began as a casual interest over a decade ago has slowly evolved into a passion that has endured for more than twelve years now. Every time I step onto the greens, it feels like hitting the refresh button, a space where work pressures fade, and focus takes over. I've realised that no matter how demanding your professional life gets, you must actively pursue a sport or some form of physical activity. It's not just about fitness, it's about finding rhythm, clarity, and the balance that keeps both the mind and body in sync.

—xxx—

Glossy Color and Paints Pvt Ltd is a paint manufacturing company based in Delhi, NCR, producing a range of paints and specialised coatings for walls, floors, wood, and metals, including both solvent-based and water-based divisions. Popular brands include 1001, Elite, Infinity, Autoking, Weathergold, Weatherite, Homecare, Shehnai and Rakshak.

The in-house R&D team focuses on maintaining consistent quality while staying up-to-date with industry trends and regulations. State-of-the-art testing machines, advanced systems, computers, spectrometers and accelerated weathering equipment are used to develop new products and standardise formulations. Every batch of finished products is individually tested and approved by our in-house laboratory before being released to the market.

Ashna Sachdev is a sixth-generation entrepreneur, born and raised in Delhi. She holds a Master's in International Management from King's College, London, where she was introduced to the concepts of sustainability and ESG, which would later shape her professional focus. After returning to India, Ashna joined her family business as a trainee and in 2024. As of 2025, Ashna is spearheading her company's environmental sustainability programme, with an aim to significantly reduce the firm's carbon footprint by making it leaner.

4

A Legacy in Every Bucket: The Story of Glossy Paints

ASHNA SACHDEV

Our family's story is not archived in dusty ledgers or forgotten corners of history, but lives on through the vibrant hues of the paints we produce and the enduring resilience passed down through generations. It is a story that began in the late nineteenth century in Lahore, during the era of Undivided India, where my ancestors made a bold shift from being traditional *halwais* to stepping into the world of trade and enterprise. This pivotal transformation was led by two visionary brothers, Sant Ram Sachdev and Nikka Mal Sachdev, who together founded *Sant Ram Nikka Mal*, a modest shop that dealt in paints and allied materials.

What began as a small venture rooted in trust, hard work, and integrity steadily grew into a respected name across the region. Their remarkable foresight and entrepreneurial spirit laid a strong foundation for a business that has endured the tests of time, colonial rule, Partition, modernisation, COVID-19 pandemic and economic upheavals.

By the early twentieth century, the family had firmly established their brand name across the Indian subcontinent. With two prominent shops in the bustling cities of Lahore and Karachi, they catered to a diverse clientele, earning a reputation for quality and trust. Over more than a century and a half, the business has evolved, but the core values of the founders have remained unchanged. Today, our legacy lives not just in the products we sell, but in the trust we continue to build, the relationships we cherish, and the colour we bring to people's lives.

One of the most fascinating reminders of this rich heritage comes from a current customer based in Agra. He proudly holds a bill dating back to the year 1911, a rare and valuable piece of our history. It reflects a time when personal relationships and handwritten transactions formed the core of business practices.

The business took a significant leap forward in 1921 with the establishment of a dedicated paint manufacturing facility in Lahore, marking a shift from trading to full-scale production. This expansion was formalised under the name *Anglo-Dutch Paints Colour and Varnish Works Private Limited,* a name that reflected both international aspiration and technical ambition. This strategiç decision proved to be a defining moment in the company's history, enabling it to scale its operations, meet growing demand, and establish a stronger national presence.

At the heart of this growth was the launch of our flagship brand, *1001*, which quickly gained popularity for its consistent quality and reliability. The brand was first trademarked in Lahore; however, with a keen eye on the uncertain geopolitical climate leading up to Partition, the family wisely applied for trademark registration in Delhi in 1946, ensuring continuity of the brand in post-independence India.

(NOT FOR LEGAL USE)

As on Date : 12/08/2024
Status : Registered View TM Application | View Additional Representation Sheet
Alert : Renewal of trademark is due. Renewal request in prescribed form is to be filed by the applicant.

TM Application No.	124357
Class	2
Date of Application	19/08/1946
Appropriate Office	DELHI
State	STATE NOT SPECIFIED
Country	India
Filing Mode	Branch Office
TM Applied For	NO 1001
TM Category	TRADE MARK
Trade Mark Type	COLOUR
User Detail	Proposed to be used
Certificate Detail	Certificate No. 0 Dated :
Valid upto/ Renewed upto	19/08/2024
Proprietor name	(1) ANGLO DUTCH PAINT COLOUR & VARNISH WORKS LTD Single Firm
Proprietor Address	MOHINDDINPUR (DIST: MEERUT)
Email Id	
Agent name	PURI & PURI (ADVOCATES)[2717]
Agent Address	4969/5, IST FLOOR, SIRKIWALAN, (NEAR HAUZ QAZI POLICE STATION) HAUZ QAZI, DELHI-6
Goods & Service Details	[CLASS : 2] PAINT, COLOURS (OTHER THAN THOSE FOR TOILET OR LAUNDRY PURPOSES), VARNISH (OTHER THAN INSULATING VARNISH).
Publication Details	Published in Journal No. : 106-0 Dated : 01/06/1952

Trademark Certificate for the brand 1001 showing the date of application, 19 August 1946, at Delhi by Anglo-Dutch Paints Colour and Varnish Works Private Limited. Now the 1001 brand is owned by Glossy Color and Paints P Ltd as per the Memorandum of Family Settlement, dated 02 September 1993

Even today, the brand *1001* remains a cornerstone of the business. Its most iconic product, the *Superior White 1001 Zinc Stiff Paint*, remains a bestseller, a testament to the enduring quality and trust the brand has built over generations.

The original registered design of Superior White 1001 Zinc Stiff Paint is still in use today by Glossy Color and Paints P Limited

Partition and Resilience

The actual test of our family's fortitude came in 1947, during one of the most tumultuous periods in the history of the Indian subcontinent, the Partition of India. Amidst rising tensions and widespread uncertainty, my great-grandfather, Sadanand Sachdev, proved to be remarkably forward-thinking. Sensing the winds of change, he had already shipped a vital triple roller mill, a machine for manufacturing zinc stiff paint, from Lahore to Delhi. What made this move even more extraordinary was that he had sent it without a specific delivery address. For months, it lay unclaimed in the transporter's godown, gathering dust and waiting for its purpose.

When the announcement of Partition was made, chaos swept through Punjab. My family, like millions of others, was uprooted overnight. Forced to abandon their home on Davis Road in Lahore, they left behind their possessions, memories, and the life they had built, carrying with them little more than grit, resilience, and determination. Eventually arriving in Delhi with barely any resources, they refused to be defeated by circumstances. With a passion that burned like paint and conflagration in their veins, they saw an opportunity for rebirth. The dormant triple roller mill was retrieved, and a new chapter began. Anglo-Dutch Paints was re-launched, and a new manufacturing facility was established in Meerut, bringing the dream back to life. As per the records of the Registrar of Companies at Delhi, Anglo-Dutch

Paints Colour and Varnish Works Private Limited was incorporated on 20 December 1948.

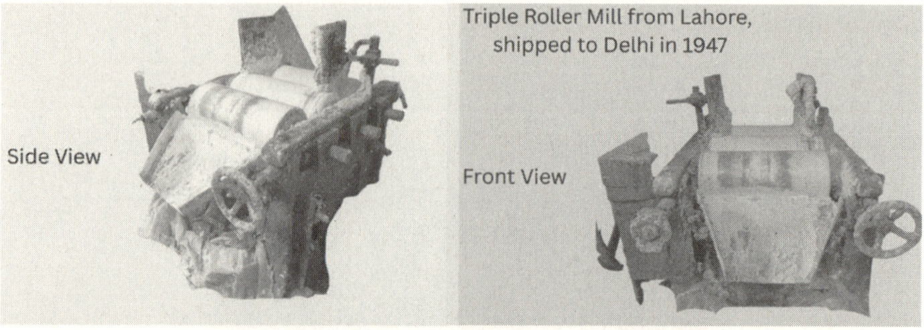

The more than hundred-year-old triple roller mill, originally sent from Lahore before Partition to Delhi, is still in use today to make Superior White 1001 Zinc Stiff Paint at Glossy Color and Paints P Ltd

Tragedy struck soon after when Sadanand Sachdev passed away, leaving behind his wife, Rajkumari Sachdev, and their three young children. She stepped into the void with remarkable courage and resilience. She took charge of both the grieving family and the fledgling business, despite having little

A photo from the early 2000s of the shop in Chandni Chowk, Old Delhi, originally opened in 1948 after the family moved to Delhi from Lahore during the Partition

experience and living in a profoundly patriarchal society. She revived the business under the name *Sant Ram Nikka Mal*, operating out of Fatehpuri, Chandni Chowk in Old Delhi. Under her stewardship, the company began to grow once again, founded on values of honesty, fairness, integrity, and respect for all stakeholders. She never allowed gender to become a barrier. She saw her role not just as a necessity but as a calling. Her fortitude and leadership not only kept the family afloat but also laid the foundation for a legacy of resilience and enterprise that continues to inspire the strong women in our lineage who follow in her footsteps.

Growth and Reinvention

Over time, the family business evolved to meet the changing needs of the market and the growing aspirations of each generation. In the 1950s, as Delhi began to emerge as an industrial hub, the decision was made to sell the Meerut plant and establish a new manufacturing facility in West Delhi. Operating under the same banner, *Anglo-Dutch Paints Colour and Varnish Works Pvt. Ltd.*, this new facility marked a significant step in consolidating operations closer to the capital. Remarkably, this plant in West Delhi has remained the linchpin of our manufacturing operations for over seven decades, consistently producing high-quality paints that are used nationwide.

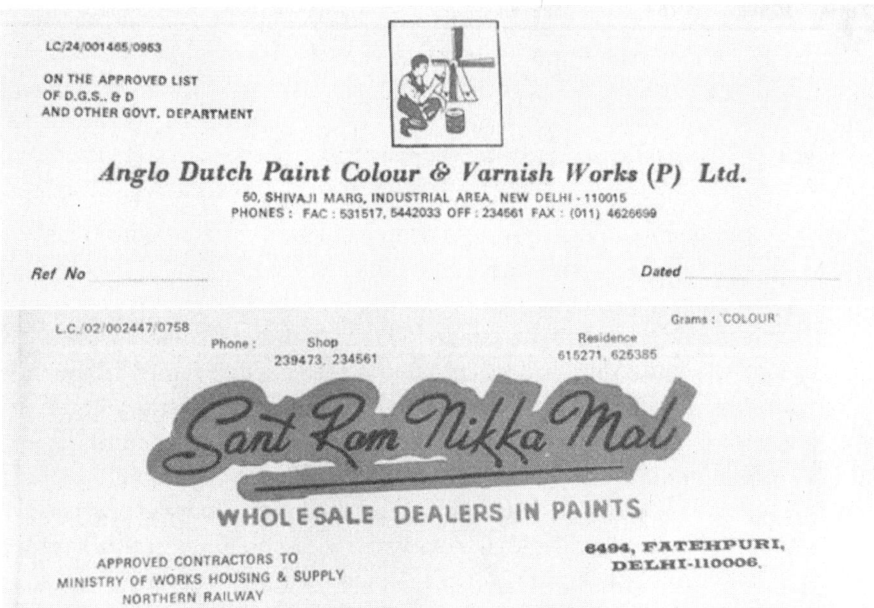

LC/24/001465/0953

ON THE APPROVED LIST
OF D.G.S., & D
AND OTHER GOVT. DEPARTMENT

Anglo Dutch Paint Colour & Varnish Works (P) Ltd.

50, SHIVAJI MARG, INDUSTRIAL AREA, NEW DELHI - 110015
PHONES : FAC : 531517, 5442033 OFF : 234561 FAX : (011) 4626699

Ref No .... Dated ....

L.C./02/002447/0758

Grams : 'COLOUR'

Phone : Shop 239473, 234561 Residence 615271, 625385

Sant Ram Nikka Mal

WHOLESALE DEALERS IN PAINTS

APPROVED CONTRACTORS TO
MINISTRY OF WORKS HOUSING & SUPPLY
NORTHERN RAILWAY

6494, FATEHPURI,
DELHI-110006.

A picture of the original letterheads from the 1950s. The phone numbers mentioned on the letterheads are still in use today, with slight modifications made by MTNL over the years

In the early 1990s, amid the transformative economic reforms of Liberalisation, Privatisation, and Globalisation, and following a family settlement to finalise the division of assets, my grandfather, Man Mohan Sachdev, and my father, Rajesh Sachdev, took bold steps to revitalise the business.

Recognising shifting consumer preferences and rising competition, they launched the Glossy Paints line, a clear signal of the brand's ability to adapt, reinvent, and remain relevant in a rapidly evolving market. The new line aligned perfectly with the aspirations of a modernising India and quickly gained traction for its superior finishes and durability.

Over the past thirty-five years, the business has continued to scale, with new manufacturing facilities established in Greater Noida, Uttar Pradesh, under the name Glossy Paints India Pvt. Ltd. These additional plants were constructed to meet the growing demand and ensure timely delivery across North India and beyond. The company came to be known for its 1001 Acrylic Washable Distemper, as it provided value for money with extra coverage compared to the competitors' products in the Indian market.

The iconic bucket of our flagship product – 1001 Acrylic Washable Distemper WT

The consistent growth of the 'Glossy' brand is a direct result of unwavering quality and the trust that customers have placed in our family's legacy. A poignant reminder of that legacy still stands today: the more than hundred-year-old triple roller mill, initially sent from Lahore before Partition, is still in operational use and serves not just as a functional machine but also as a powerful symbol of endurance, foresight, and the long road we've travelled.

In 2004, to align with global standards, Glossy Paints entered into a strategic technical collaboration with Resene Paints, operating in New Zealand and Australia. This pivotal partnership enabled a vital exchange of expertise, granting access to advanced paint formulations and international manufacturing practices. As a result, the company significantly enhanced its technological capabilities and expanded its product lines.

Furthermore, building upon the sustained success of our original retail store at Chandni Chowk, Delhi-06, the family expanded its retail footprint in 2005 by opening a second outlet in Kotla, New Delhi. This new store was strategically positioned to serve the expanding markets of South Delhi and Gurgaon, ensuring that the brand remains accessible, visible, and relevant to the next generation of customers. My grandmother, the Late Kusum Sachdev, and my mother, Shweta Sachdev, were the ones who made this shop a success.

Early in my career, I didn't fully appreciate the significance of BIS and ISO certifications, but I have come to understand their vital role in building consumer confidence and company goodwill. Our company has long held ISO 9001 for Quality Management and ISO 14001 for Environmental Management. In 2023, our sustained efforts to enhance our safety standards paid off when we successfully achieved the ISO 45001 certification for Occupational Health and Safety Management Systems.

For over thirty years, Glossy Color and Paints P Ltd has also consistently held the following two certifications from the Bureau of Indian Standards that showcase quality, safety standards, and regulatory compliance:

1. Ready Mixed Paint, Brushing, Bituminous, Black, Lead-Free, Acid, Alkali, and Heat Resisting – ISI Marked to IS 158 (Under Licence No. CM/L-8131661)
2. Ready Mixed Paint for Road Marking, Specification Grade I - ISI Marked to IS 164 (Under Licence No. CM/L-8137774)

Very few paint companies in India hold these certifications; as a result, we get a competitive advantage in the market. Both of the above products are sold under the 1001 brand umbrella.

Two products manufactured by Glossy Color and Paints P Ltd are ISI marked, which are sold under the 1001 brand (Left: IS 158, Right: IS 164)

Keeping in mind the principles of incremental innovation, we have introduced the following products: 1001 Special Paint for Speaker Cases, 1001 Fluorescent Coatings, 1001 Glow-in-the-Dark Paint, 1001 Premium Acrylic

Interior Wall Paint, and 1001 Chlorinated Rubber-based Anti-Slip Paint. Moreover, we believe in continuous improvement, so we manufacture many products that comply with both the RoHS and REACH environmental and safety directives.

Keeping in mind the principles of radical innovation, we have developed numerous new products over the past few years, including Infinity Automotive Refinishes, Infinity Wood Coatings, Weathergold Heat Reflective Paint for Roofs, and Weathergold Elastomeric Primers. The newly introduced 1001 Fire Retardant Coating ST and Rakshak Fire Retardant Coating WT can withstand fire for up to two hours, which is a significant breakthrough.

Our focus on continuous improvement and responsible innovation is a leading factor in our success in the Indian market; moreover, all these efforts lead to a sustained competitive advantage in the long run.

Joining the Family Business

Fresh out of my master's degree in 2020, the first COVID-19 lockdown scuttled my plans to find a job outside the family fold. Still, it presented an unexpected opportunity: joining the family business. The natural course of action became working from home, coordinating deliveries with vendors, customers, and staff.

My grandfather, at the *young* age of eighty-one, became my mentor. He even adapted to new technologies, such as learning Zoom and Webex, so that he could continue his meetings. His motto, 'work must go on, no matter what,' was a powerful lesson. He was a beacon of dedication and business acumen. His sudden demise in May 2021 was not only a personal loss for us but also for several associated with the Indian paint industry. His legacy is something I am determined to uphold.

With time, more responsibility came my way. Based on my early experiences, I have made a list of essentials for anyone thinking of joining a family business:

- Get at least one degree in commerce and management, such as a BCom or an MBA, to build a strong base in financial accounting and corporate finance, as well as to understand basic business terminology.
- Have a therapist on speed dial. Living and working with family can be tough because work never really stops. There are no fixed hours, and clocking out does not exist. Separating office and home is almost impossible.
- Spend time alone to introspect to figure out your own strengths and weaknesses. *'Finding yourself'* in today's fast-paced world is not easy.
- Work or intern in other companies and bring back ideas that you can implement in your own company.
- Have friends who also work in family-owned businesses. You can discuss problems, brainstorm ideas, and exchange thoughts with them.

- Bring your sense of humour to work every day. It helps to release the pressure.

From Humble Beginnings to Innovation

When I joined the family business at the age of twenty-two, I was filled with a mixture of excitement, responsibility, and uncertainty. Though I had grown up around conversations of paint formulations, product lines, and customer satisfaction, stepping into the business myself was an entirely different experience. The journey ahead felt intimidating, almost like standing at the base of a mountain with no visible summit in sight.

That first year was an intense period of learning, as I absorbed the technical aspects of manufacturing, understood customer behaviour, and navigated the daily challenges of running a legacy business. But all the hard work culminated in one moment that I will never forget: my first successful sale. I had been involved in developing a new product from scratch, closely monitoring every phase from formulation to packaging. When a client placed their first order and then began ordering weekly, it felt like I had just scaled Mount Everest. That defining success cemented my commitment to the company and made me feel like I had truly earned my place.

Then came the COVID-19 pandemic, and with it, an unprecedented period of global disruption. It would have been easy to wait for conditions to improve. But I saw in this crisis a unique opportunity. The post-pandemic world had become increasingly VUCA — volatile, uncertain, complex, and ambiguous — but it also saw a surprising new trend: a surge in outdoor activity. After months of being confined indoors, people were eager to move, play, and reconnect with others. Sports such as tennis, badminton, and pickleball have begun to gain momentum across all age groups.

That's when I identified a significant gap in the market. Our Sports Court Flooring Division, a once-promising vertical that had been sidelined for years, had untapped potential. Drawing on my lifelong passion for sports, I took on the job of leading the Sports Floor Coatings Division, turning a 'question mark' into a 'star' performer. It became more than just a project; it was a personal mission.

I knew I was starting from the ground up, both literally and metaphorically. I had to understand what goes into building a professional-grade court, layer by layer. First comes the Concrete Primer, which fills in cracks and smooths the surface, ensuring a safe playing area. Next is the Acrylic Black Resurfacer, designed to provide a consistent base for the remaining coats. Then comes the Cushion Coat, which helps to reduce stress on the players' ankles, knees, hips, and back. Finally, Acrylic-Based Top Coats are applied in vibrant colours, blue, red, green, and orange, depending on the sport or the client's preference. These top coats are then lined with white markings to define the boundaries and zones of the court. Interestingly, this layering system is used for various sports, including tennis, volleyball, basketball, netball, badminton, padel, and pickleball. These sports flooring products are sold under the 1001 and Elite brands.

We were not new to this field. In fact, over twenty years ago, we had been one of the first companies in India to manufacture sports court floor coatings that met international standards. Yet, somehow, this vertical had become a forgotten chapter. Reviving it wasn't just about revenue; it was about reclaiming a part of our legacy and giving it a new life.

It wasn't easy. There were countless late nights, extended site visits, tough negotiations, and moments of self-doubt. But I was fortunate to have the unyielding support of my family and colleagues, who believed in the vision. Slowly, orders started flowing in. We partnered with schools, community centres, sports academies, and residential societies. We weren't just selling paint, we were creating spaces where children could play, athletes could train, and communities could come together.

Today, I can proudly say that our Sports Floor Coatings Division is one of the fastest-growing arms of our business. Our courts have helped foster young talent, encouraged active lifestyles, and brought joy to countless people. We are reaching far corners of the country and touching various lives in small but meaningful ways by making high-quality sports court floorings accessible to all.

Looking back, what once felt like an intimidating path now feels like a mission fulfilled. And in many ways, this journey has just begun.

The Hard-Earned Lessons of a Family Business

I am the sixth generation in this business, and therein lies the beauty. The company has been carried forward with the same values that the founders envisioned, and that is why we remain standing today, despite intense competition from larger players.

My journey has also taught me that success is a team effort. Hiring the right people, those who share your values and drive, is the most crucial task. Looking back, I am glad I joined the Family Business Programme at IIM Calcutta. I have made life-long friends here and met people from across the country. I learnt about other cultures and how others are faring in their own family-run companies. I found solace in knowing we all face similar challenges, and I am not alone. Moreover, I made vendors and customers alike, which was the cherry on top.

With nearly six years of experience in the paint industry, I've seen how my academic journey and encouragement to think differently have paid off. Watching my hard work come to fruition has deepened my passion for my work.

After being immersed full-time for so long in my family's business, I've realised that running a company is not just about profits. It is a constant journey of growth and adaptation. It means finding harmony between work and home, navigating change in a fast-paced world, and building a foundation of integrity and respect. In addition to this, I've learned that a company's journey is a reflection of its family's fortitude. It is a path with many unique challenges but also deep rewards.

These are the lessons I've gathered along the way, lessons that go beyond balance sheets and business plans, and touch the very core of what it means to lead, learn, and grow.

1. Family and work are invariably interlinked. Even the non-working members affect both office and home life. Balancing work, home, and personal life is never easy, but it is essential to leading a fulfilling life.
2. Bringing about change even in your own company is hard. Terms like 'Change Management' and 'Organisational Transformation' sound fancy, but reflect the complexities of managing a business in real life.
3. Remember to take data-driven decisions with a calm mind.
4. Processes must be fair. Rules, policies, and systems should be applied uniformly to everyone.
5. Never stop asking questions. Be curious at every step. Make Google/ AI your ultimate best friend and keep learning.
6. *Prepare, prepare, prepare.* Prepare for every meeting, whether crucial or seemingly inconsequential. You never know which chance encounter could lead you down the path to success.
7. Stay grounded and don't fly too high. I genuinely believe in '*nazar*'. Keep your life private, and don't broadcast either success or failure.
8. Use the digital world wisely. Social media and the internet can help you establish new connections, whether with vendors or customers. However, digital marketing should be handled by a professional who has the time and experience to target the right audience using the most effective media.
9. Always be polite. Care for others and spare their feelings when nothing significant is at stake. Empathy always brings good '*karma*.'
10. Look after your mental health. Take breaks when life feels heavy. It is okay to fall down. No matter how many times. What matters most is that you are able to get yourself together over time and muster the courage to start again.
11. Keep a hobby. Play a sport, bake, paint, or read, anything that gives you 'me-time'. It helps you navigate the emotional rollercoasters that are an inevitable part of life.
12. Respect commitments. Honour your promises and be mindful of your own time and of others'.

Social Connections, Introspection and Giving Back

I consciously choose to live a life away from the spotlight, guided by principles of minimalism and introspection. Rather than seeking validation through external status symbols or material excess, I place greater value on meaningful experiences, the pursuit of knowledge, and purposeful work. This approach to life reflects a desire for authenticity and depth in both my personal and professional spheres. While it may not align with more conventional definitions of success today, it provides a strong foundation for long-term fulfilment and ethical decision-making.

Finding like-minded individuals at the *ripe* age of twenty-eight, particularly those who share an 'old soul' sensibility, can be challenging in a fast-paced, performance-driven world. However, I am fortunate to have cultivated a small circle of long-standing friendships that have withstood the test of time. These long-standing friendships, which date back over two decades, are rooted in mutual respect, emotional depth, and shared values.

I also recognise the profound influence of one's social environment on personal and professional growth. The people we interact with regularly shape our perspectives, choices, and ambitions. In my case, I have been fortunate to receive encouragement and wisdom from a few well-meaning relatives and older family friends. Many of whom belong to an earlier generation and bring with them a wealth of life experience, offering insights and support at times when I face uncertainty or obstacles. Their guidance is often shared in good faith, rooted in a genuine desire to see me succeed. This blend of solitude and selective social connection enables me to stay down-to-earth while remaining open to constructive feedback and communal learning.

As an avid reader, sports enthusiast, and staunch advocate for gender equality, I bring an energetic and empathetic approach to the world of business. Education and commerce, when guided by ethical principles and social consciousness, can serve as a powerful engine for progress and inclusive development. For me, business is not merely a vehicle for profit, but a means to contribute meaningfully to society and to help build a more equitable world.

I was actively involved with the Women's Studies Centre, the National Service Scheme, and Enactus during my college years. I observed firsthand the ripple effect of one person breaking the cycle of intergenerational poverty for her whole family. In line with this philosophy, our organisation collaborates with various NGOs to support underprivileged children and youth. We provide funding to initiatives that offer structured training programmes aimed at equipping participants with essential skills for full-time employment. Additionally, we contribute to educational advancement by funding the schooling of children from marginalised backgrounds, recognising that access to education is a fundamental step towards breaking vicious cycles of poverty and social exclusion.

We strive to create opportunities that extend beyond the boardroom and into the broader community. In doing so, we aim to demonstrate that sustainable business success is most meaningful when it uplifts others and contributes to the common good.

Looking Ahead: A Vision for the Future

Working in a family-run enterprise is a unique experience. It requires a 'jack-of-all-trades' mindset, because you often find yourself involved in every part of the business, from HR and operations to finance, marketing, and strategy. But this does not mean one person must do it all. The real key to success is sharing responsibilities among family members and professionals, so that everyone contributes their own unique skills.

Three years ago, we listed our products on Amazon and Flipkart within India as a pilot project to test the online space, using our existing human capital and infrastructure. It was not easy, as e-commerce comes with its own challenges. Yet, in 2025, the numbers have surpassed our expectations, and now additional infrastructure is required to fulfil orders received online.

We are currently building a separate e-commerce vertical to expand further in this space. We are moving towards omnichannel retail and have added the 'ship from store' model to reduce lead times. The next phase of our digital roadmap involves leveraging quick commerce platforms, such as Zepto and Blinkit, to further expand our market reach.

Looking ahead, our long-term goal is to develop our own robust e-commerce platform, which will expand our digital presence and make our products accessible to customers worldwide. Furthermore, we will continue to invest in our sports coatings division, exploring new markets such as synthetic running tracks and super-specialised industrial floorings.

As we look to the future, our vision is clear. We are not just selling paint; we are offering solutions. In the coming years, we plan to double our manufacturing capacity while using automation and sustainable practices to lower our environmental footprint.

Our ancestors shaped the past fifteen decades through rain, storm or hail; now it is our responsibility to ensure it remains a going concern for the foreseeable future and beyond. My role, and that of my siblings, is clearly divided into departments, allowing us to conquer the world together. With our family's legacy as our guide, the future is painted in bright and vibrant colours.

—xxx—

Kiran Group, was established in 1983 and now operates across diverse sectors, including steel, coke, food processing, recycling, and shipbreaking. Our group of companies includes Shree Electromelts Limited – Steel, Coke, and Oxygen, Khusbhoo India Pvt. Ltd. – Ship Recycling, Shree Food Processors – Cashew Processing, Green Tara Recyclers LLP – Ship Recycling, and Kiran Ship Breaking – Ship Recycling.

Saurabh Jain, who now leads the group, is an entrepreneur who believes in learning through experience, innovating with intent, and enduring through challenges. His journey in business has been shaped not just by market dynamics but also by personal discipline, much of which he owes to his passion for tennis and long-distance cycling, which have taught him focus, consistency, and the ability to stay calm under pressure.

5

From Steel to Cashews

SAURABH JAIN

Our business journey began in 1983, when we relocated from Punjab to Gujarat due to the unsafe conditions in Punjab, which were exacerbated by terrorist activities, particularly for us as a financially stable entity. At first, my Tauji moved to Gujarat; then, one by one, the other brothers followed suit, and we moved in 1992. There, we set up our first re-rolling mill, which expanded gradually over the years before being shut down in 2017.

Our Induction furnace establish in 1996 and expanded in 2008 and modified in 2020

In 1994, guided by the vision of my father, Shri Vipan Jain, and Tauji Shri Ram Kishan Jain (both families have been together from that day onwards), we entered the ship recycling industry. This was later expanded in 2008 under my supervision and again in 2023 under Mr Vishal Jain. Soon after, in 1996, we diversified into the HMS recycling industry. This segment complemented ship recycling well, as the finished products from one became raw material for induction furnaces, and the furnace output in turn supported our rolling mill. In 2008, we established an oxygen-refilling facility that supports our iron industry and also supplies medical care.

Our Induction furnace establish in 1996 and expanded in 2008 and modified in 2020

Our Ship Re-cycling facility at Gujarat establish in 1994 and expanded in 2008 and 2023

Oxygen Re-filling facility establish in 2008

In 2004, we made two crucial moves. First, we ventured into sponge iron manufacturing, though we exited in 2007. In the same year, 2004, we entered the low-ash metallurgical Coke production sector, where we introduced major modifications over time and are now in the process of doubling our capacity. This business became a milestone in our journey, as it marked the beginning of my independent business career and also gave us the strength to expand into other areas of the iron and steel industry, helping us manage downturns more effectively.

This venture also marked the beginning of my independent entrepreneurial journey, as I took on a more active role in the family business. Under my supervision, the LAMC (COKE OVEN BATTERY) operations expanded our wings within the iron and steel ecosystem, enabling us to reduce downside risks by spreading across multiple industry segments. Initially, we encountered financial issues due to losses resulting from a slowdown in LAMC and Sponge Iron, which I had faced during the early stages of my business era. It took three years to understand the new business, and by the end of 2007, we had covered all the losses through good governance and an understanding of LAMC, as well as the sale of sponge iron.

Most recently, in 2022, we stepped beyond our core iron and steel sector into raw cashew processing. The idea was first suggested by Shri Vipan Jain and his elder brother, Shri Bal Kishan Aggarwal, and was later further developed by Shri Vipan Jain and me. This move reflects the same legacy that has guided us throughout, expanding thoughtfully into new segments while remaining rooted in our family vision.

Finding My Footing

From very early on, I was clear that I would join our family business. It was not a forced choice, but rather something that came naturally from our family culture and sense of responsibility.

After years of watching the business grow and diversify under the vision of my father, Tauji (father's elder brother), and other family members, I gradually found my own footing within it. For me, the turning point came

Left to Right: me (Saurabh Jain), my Tauji Shri Ram Kishan Jain, my father Shri Vipan Jain, my brother Mr Vishal Jain. United at all times

around 2010-11, when I truly began to feel comfortable and confident in handling responsibilities. It was during this period that I realised I was not just a part of the family legacy but could also bring something new to the table. That was the moment I felt I was truly 'in business', when things started falling into place, and I could see opportunities to innovate and contribute to the next phase of our growth. Since then, I have never even thought of giving up on pursuing our family business.

I was not formally trained or educated in any specific area before stepping into the business. Instead, my learning came gradually, through day-to-day experiences and by observing how things were handled around me. The foundation was built under the constant guidance of my elders, who not only supported me but also shared their practical wisdom and instincts developed over decades. Every discussion, every decision, and even the mistakes along the way became part of my education. In our family, we often say and believe that business runs in our blood. This belief gave me the confidence to step in without hesitation and the courage to take on responsibilities that, at first, felt much bigger than me. Over time, I realised that while formal training can be valuable, the lessons learned within a family business through exposure, observation, and guidance are often also very profound and practical.

From Struggle to Strength

I was born with a stammer, and this affected my self-confidence in multiple ways as a child. During those early years, my family supported me in every possible way. Over time, I underwent speech therapy at various locations, but a major turning point occurred in 2003-04, when I met Dr Ruchi Shah of Krish Speech and Hearing Clinic in Ahmedabad. Her guidance helped me significantly improve my speech. Later, in 2021, with personal business coaching under Mr Manish Puri in Delhi, I realised that my stammer often came from low confidence. Here, I learned several things, and that learning also improved my fluency, while gaining the confidence to express my thoughts freely. With his help, I worked on myself and learned how to manage these situations, which enabled me to express myself more clearly and confidently in business. Today, I have largely overcome this obstacle, and I am pleased to say that it no longer affects me as it used to.

Sports and endurance activities also played a significant role in my personal development. In 2012, my weight was 120 kgs, which was, of course, very high. Between 2012 and 2015, I played tennis. I initially lost matches at crucial points because I could not manage my anxiety. Over time, I learned how to stay calm under pressure, a lesson that has been invaluable when translated to business. In 2015, I took up cycling and started participating in Audax events, completing back-to-back rides of 200 km, 300 km, 400 km,

Right: Me during the 200 km cycling on 14 August 2016
Left: Me during the 600 km cycling on 29 September 2018

We continuously travel and conduct R&D on new technologies for our industry whenever we get the opportunity. We custom-develop and adapt such technologies in-house to reduce the costs. By visiting other units in the same industry, we learn and implement similar practices in our workspace

and even 600 km in 2017, and repeated the feat in 2018. The journey was very tough, as I sustained numerous injuries, but day by day, the injuries are reducing as my fitness levels rise.

Additionally, this type of sport requires a great deal of dedication, and you must persevere alone on the journey. It is also heartbreaking to see others enjoying life, spending time with family and friends, while you are still training to achieve your goals. In my mind, I am clear that I need to pursue my goals, which are things I have previously struggled with.

One of my most rewarding moments as an entrepreneur came from our venture into the Metallurgical Coke industry. This was a completely different line from our core business, and it challenged me to think in new ways. I developed a concept that allows us to minimise the cost of production while enhancing the quality of the final product. Bringing this idea into reality gave us a double advantage: higher quality and better pricing power. For many years, from 2010 to the present day, this business has been the most valuable in our portfolio. It was a proper validation of my ability to innovate and create impact beyond the traditional family business model. To make it fruitful for so many years, we have travelled extensively and conducted R&D in the factory.

One of my achievements that I hold close is from January 2023, when I undertook the Chadar Expedition in Leh, where the temperature ranged from -20 degrees to -30 degrees. We had to stay in tents with no nearby support in case of a medical emergency. Preparing for it was as much a mental journey as a physical one. My parents initially did not want me to go, but I calmly told them to at least let me prepare, and that I would only go with their permission. After seeing the months of effort I had put in, they finally agreed. Reaching the frozen waterfall at the peak was an emotional moment for me—a victory over my fears, anxieties, and limitations. For example, our group was about 150 meters from a frozen waterfall, but there was no ice nearby. To reach it, we had to climb a steep 40-60 degree slope and descend, which felt dangerous—one mistake could be costly. Doubts crossed my mind about whether I could get down safely, and I'm sure my friends felt the same. Still, I was determined to complete the trek and return safely. With the help of my friends and guide, I finished the hike without incident. The frozen river shifts shape every time, meaning each type of ice requires a different walking technique, which we learned on site. That experience, combined with business achievements, gave me true fulfilment and reminded me that entrepreneurship is as much about growth, resilience, and confidence as it is about success.

The memories and lessons from the 2019 event stayed with me. When I later planned to go on the Chadar Trek, I made sure not to repeat the same mistakes. This time, I took the effort to understand my own body and its needs. I purchased clothing and accessories that suited my personal comfort level. I also spoke to experienced trekkers as well as local people in Leh.

Their practical insights helped me prepare myself in a much better and more informed way, ensuring that I was both physically and mentally ready for the trek.

Left: On completing the Chadar expedition.
Right: Climbing this high mountain and coming down again.

Social Service

From time to time, we participate in social service both through volunteering and financial support. These experiences provide deep learning, and such learning stays with you for a lifetime.

Let me share one of my personal experiences from the year 2021, during the peak of the COVID-19 outbreak in India. As I mentioned earlier, we have an oxygen refilling facility. During that time, the entire country was struggling with a severe oxygen shortage. Hospitals were overwhelmed, and families were desperately searching for oxygen cylinders to save their loved ones.

In our city, we were the first to open our home and factory, providing oxygen 24/7 free of cost. From the very first day, I received complete support from my family. After about a month, our staff members also joined in wholeheartedly. There was no difference between day and night, only the responsibility to help.

One incident from that period taught me a very hard and unforgettable lesson about what true responsibility means. On an extremely hot afternoon, around 12:30 p.m., a man in his early 50s came to our home to collect an oxygen cylinder. After verifying the required documents, we issued the cylinder to him. Around 2:00 pm, he returned with the cylinder in the same scorching heat. I noticed that the cylinder was still full. Out of curiosity, I asked him why he was returning it unused. He replied, "I had taken this cylinder for my wife. But by the time I reached home, she had passed away."

I was shocked. I could not speak for several minutes. He placed the cylinder down gently and walked away silently. That moment stayed with me. In the deepest moment of his grief, that man still had the conscience and humanity to return the cylinder so that it could save someone else. That day, I came to understand the deeper meaning of responsibility, humanity, and duty. And I continue to try to carry that sense of responsibility in everything I do.

Handling Uncertainty

Following the 2008 recession and the recovery from losses that exceeded our assets, I have always carried a sense of caution in my mind. The fear of falling into such a trap again shaped the way I approached business decisions. Since then, whenever commodity prices are unusually high, we consciously minimise our exposure to avoid getting caught in future downturns. When commodity prices are low, we increase our exposure. At low prices, the chances of decreasing prices are less, while stable or rising prices are more likely. For many years, we even chose not to expand into new businesses, instead focusing on building a cash-rich company.

On a personal level, I have also learned that handling uncertainty and failure requires both mental strength and healthy outlets for emotional release. Exercise has played a vital role in this regard for me. Whether it was tennis, cycling, or other physical activities, these practices have helped me release stress, clear my mind, and maintain balance during difficult times.

In 2011, another challenge came in the form of a legal battle. A government department filed a wrongful case against us, which not only caused heavy financial loss but also brought years of mental and emotional stress. It took over a decade of fighting, but in 2024, we finally won the case. The biggest lesson we took away from this episode was to remain practical and cautious in dealing with government authorities, even when their demands appear unreasonable, even if you are 100 per cent right, and even if the facts support it. That experience shaped the way we always pay full attention and treatment to compliance and government relations.

Then, in 2019, we began setting up a new industry from the ground up. However, due to opposition from a few local individuals, the installation was halted, and immediately thereafter, the lockdown of 2020 brought everything to a standstill. Financially and emotionally, this was one of the hardest moments for our family. Yet, when conditions normalised in 2021, we realised in hindsight that this setback had been a hidden blessing. Because that project did not move forward, we were able to expand instead into ship recycling and raw cashew processing, both of which became strong verticals for us.

Overcoming Operational Hurdles

One of the biggest operational challenges we faced in recent years was setting up a proper HR department. At that time, all salaries were manually handled by the supervisors. I suggested implementing biometric identification for all employees. Initially, there was strong resistance from the elders in the family, who were not convinced of the need for it. I stayed calm and suggested that we try it on a trial basis to see the benefits for ourselves. Over time, the positive impact became evident: less time is spent on dispensing salaries, labour and staff come on time, attendance is easy to handle, etc.

Another major challenge arose when we began operating the Metallurgical Coke and Cashew businesses independently. Both of these were in losses during the initial phase. I faced discouragement from some of my elders in the family, who suggested closing the ventures. However, instead of reacting, I chose to remain calm and let time and persistence show the results.

A third challenge came specifically with the cashew plant. Unlike our core businesses, where we had continuously operated through Foreign Letters of Credit to safeguard funds, in cashews, we had to make 100% advance payments, which carried a high counterparty risk. To manage this, I personally spent several months in different countries, meeting local people, checking supplier authenticity, and building trust through personal relationships. These experiences taught me that patience, calmness, and a willingness to adapt are key to overcoming operational hurdles.

Our Competitive Edge

In managing competition and market pressures, our approach has always been rooted in strong customer relationships. We make it a point to understand the market closely and make decisions quickly, something for which my elders gave me complete trust and freedom. At the same time, we focus heavily on keeping our costs lower than those of our competitors and of a much higher quality than theirs, whether through accessing low-interest funds or maintaining lean operations.

Another important part of our strategy is carefully studying our competitors' strengths. By doing so, we ensure that we always keep an extra edge, whether in terms of pricing, cost efficiency, supply quantity, sales terms, or other critical factors that help us stay competitive in the market. We understand our strengths and weaknesses, and we make decisions based on our own strengths, not those of our competitors.

Priorities in Finance

When it comes to managing the company's finances, my top priority has always been margins. In the early part of my business career, we faced significant losses, and that experience led me to prioritise profitability as my primary focus. Along with this, maintaining positive cash flow has always been non-negotiable. In fact, one of the main reasons we were able to emerge from the 2008 recession was that we maintained positive cash flows, even during the toughest periods. That discipline has stayed with me, as I see cash flow as the lifeline of any business.

Sales growth, on the other hand, was never at the top of my priority list. Growth occurred over time, but it wasn't until 2024 that I truly realised how important it is. For example, in one of our industries, the last quantity was expanded in 2008. While it remained profitable for many years, new companies entered the market between 2012 and 2014 with extensive production facilities, which reduced their production costs. After 2020, our business in that sector began to incur a loss. Although we modified our technology in 2020, it was not enough to stay competitive, and catching up with our competitors would have required an investment nearly ten times our existing capacity. That taking a call on expansion is very important, and it reinforced for us that sales growth and timely expansion are just as critical as margins and cash flow.

At the same time, we never ignored brand building. As a B2B business, our reputation has always depended on two key factors: quality and service. We ensure that our finished products meet the highest standards, and whenever necessary, we go the extra mile to support our customers. By staying consistent on these fronts, we have built a brand that customers trust, which in turn strengthens our business even in competitive markets.

Balancing Short and Long Term

Balancing short-term financial goals with long-term investments has always been about discipline and preparedness. For us, maintaining a positive cash flow is our top priority at all times. This gives us the flexibility to grab opportunities whenever they arise, especially in industries like ours where sudden requirements for large capital are common. Alongside this, we always keep in mind the Total Addressable Market (TAM), ensuring that any long-term expansion is aligned with real demand rather than just ambition.

Another important factor is learning from our past experiences. Since our business requires a substantial initial capital expenditure, we continually assess our capabilities before committing to any new investment. This careful approach enables us to maintain short-term stability while still laying the groundwork for the future. In this way, positive cash flow becomes the bridge between immediate financial health and long-term growth.

Lessons from Early Mistakes

Like many entrepreneurs, I made several mistakes in my early years, each of which taught me lessons that have stayed with me. Initially, I had the habit of doing everything myself because I could complete tasks more efficiently than my team. It was only during my two years of business coaching with Mr Manish Puri in 2022 that I realised the importance of delegation. Even if a team member takes longer, it is essential to let them handle responsibilities so they can develop their capabilities and confidence. This way, the business does not depend on me alone and can run smoothly even in my absence.

Another mistake was not speaking the local language with the people around me. This created an unintended gap, limiting my connection with them. Over time, I began interacting more in their language, which helped me build empathy and stronger relationships. I also regret not investing enough in continuous learning. While I had completed a few short-term courses during college that proved very useful, from 2012 to 2021, I neglected structured learning. Looking back, I feel that if I had kept updating my knowledge, my understanding and decision-making would have been sharper.

On the organisational front, we should have developed a biometric attendance system for the HR department much earlier. It would have brought more structure and support to the business during its growth phase. I also learned an important personal lesson about confidence. Being under-confident often meant delaying or avoiding decisions, which cost us opportunities. I discovered that it is better to be slightly overconfident and take action rather than get stuck with no decision at all. Finally, one hard lesson came from giving too much responsibility and power to a single person at the factory. In the long run, this led to misuse of power and forced us to part ways with employees, something that could have been avoided with better checks and balances.

How I Measure Success

For me, success goes far beyond just profit. The first and most important value is integrity in every decision and every relationship. I ensure honesty and fairness remain at the core. Success also means strengthening the legacy we have inherited. As our family business, we have received this legacy as both a gift and a responsibility, and I feel it is my duty to strengthen it with every passing year.

Another measure of success for me is our ability to expand into entirely new verticals. Over the years, we have diversified from iron and steel into Metallurgical Coke and then into agro commodities, including raw cashew processing, rice, and others. These ventures are rare, require immense hard work, and are not easy to sustain. But they provide resilience. This diversification has also given us a network across very different industries, which is an achievement in itself.

On a personal level, I also define success by the balance I have maintained between my business pursuits and my sports activities. My achievements in cycling, tennis, and expeditions while simultaneously handling the responsibilities of the business are a source of great pride. They remind me that success is not only about financial or business outcomes, but also about personal growth, discipline, and the ability to live a whole and meaningful life.

Balancing Work, Passion, and Family

Running a business has had a profound impact on my personal life and relationships. I enjoy working a lot, and because of that, I often find it difficult to give proper quality time to my family and friends. The constant pressure of targets and responsibilities keeps me occupied, and at times, this has affected my relationships. While I know they understand my commitments, I also realise that the balance has not always been easy to maintain.

Between 2015 and 2021, I was also deeply involved in cycling. During those years, I rode between 6,000 and 10,000 kilometres annually and participated in several Audax events, completing back-to-back rides and also undertaking the Chadar trek.

In 2017, I appointed a cycling coach, Mr Samir, to improve my cycling, based on a friend's suggestion. Initially, I believed that a coach would not make much difference in my cycling performance. However, I still decided to give it a try. After 3-4 months of training, I started noticing a clear improvement in my cycling skills, stamina, and overall fitness. I even lost a few inches from my waist. Along with physical training, I also developed healthy food habits and incorporated them into my daily routine. Overall, the coaching supported me in many aspects of my life.

After 2-3 years, if professional sports coaching could bring such positive and diverse changes into my life, then business coaching could also help me grow personally and professionally.

In 2019, I participated in the 1,200 km Paris-Brest-Paris international cycling event, held in France. As it was my first international event, I gathered suggestions from fellow participants on food, clothing, weather, and other preparations.

However, I had to quit the event at a very early stage because the weather, especially the cold conditions at night, was extremely challenging. I did not have the appropriate clothing and accessories for those conditions. After the event, I reflected on the reasons for my failure:

1. My tolerance for cold is lower than average, although I can handle hot climates better than most people. Therefore, blindly following clothing suggestions from other riders did not suit my personal needs.
2. I did not take proper guidance from experienced participants or professionals.
3. I did not speak to enough people before the event, which is why I missed gathering the necessary information.

I re-registered in another tournament, in which I completed 400 km in 24 hours and 26 minutes, gross timing. These self-supported rides taught me the importance of persistence; that you must keep going even when you are completely exhausted. This mindset translated directly into my personal and professional life. My cycling friends supported me greatly, and I learned many valuable life lessons from them.

When Views Differ

As a family-run business, one of the biggest challenges we face is the high level of expectations from within our own family. Unlike in non-family businesses, where performance is measured mainly by market results, here there is always an additional layer of pressure to prove ourselves to our own people constantly. This creates a sense of responsibility that is much deeper and often heavier. Additionally, elders in the family usually prefer to retain control over many aspects of the business, which can sometimes limit the younger generation's autonomy in making decisions independently.

The real difficulty arises when our views differ from those of our elders. Even when we believe strongly that our approach is correct, we still have to respect their opinion and, many times, follow their way. In such situations, patience is crucial. During tense times, I listen to and understand my elders' views first, and then I merge my ideas with theirs before replying. This has transformed debate into communication/discussion, yielding fruitful results.

My Support System

When things get emotionally challenging, I find strength in a few trusted sources. Sports have always been my first outlet, whether it is cycling, tennis, or other activities. It gives me both energy and perspective to face challenges more calmly.

I also lean on my family and close friends during tough times. Their support, understanding, and honest conversations remind me that I am not alone in this journey. At times, I also practise meditation, which helps me slow down, regain focus, and handle pressure with more balance.

Managing Family Expectations

In the early years, it was challenging to meet the expectations of my family elders. Their standards were high, and the pressure to prove myself was always present. For a long time, I felt I was falling short, no matter how hard I worked. It was only after 2016 that I truly felt I had begun to meet those expectations.

What made the difference was my willingness to keep learning and growing. Personalised coaching provided me with new perspectives, and meeting people in the broader business community helped me understand different ways of thinking. Slowly, I also began making independent decisions, which helped build both trust and respect within the family.

Preparing for the Future

Looking ahead, I see both challenges and opportunities that will shape the future of our business. For expansion, the first step is to identify and address the existing operational gaps. Only by strengthening the foundation can our growth be sustainable and fruitful. We already have a two- to three-year strategy in place to close these gaps, which will give us the confidence to scale further.

Succession is another essential part of the future. My wife, Sakshi Jain, joined the business in 2022, where she oversees HR and other key areas of the company. My son, Sarthak Jain (16), and daughter, Aaradhya Jain (13), will both eventually join the business. Preparing them, guiding them, and building systems that allow them to contribute meaningfully will be a big responsibility in the years to come.

Vacation photos with family.
Left to Right: Father, Mummy, Daughter, Wife, Son and Me

On the technology front, learning and adopting AI will be critical. We plan to implement ERP systems across our businesses and explore how AI can be applied wherever possible to improve efficiency and decision-making. Market changes will also require us to stay agile. We are preparing by expanding our present commodities while also researching opportunities in new ones. At the same time, our guiding principle remains simple: 'Control the controllable things.'

Growth and Diversification Ahead

My long-term vision for the business is to create a stronger, more diversified, and professionally managed group that can sustain growth across industries. I plan to increase raw cashew processing capacity twofold in two years and fivefold over the next decade. Also, double the Coke Oven Battery capacity within one to two years. Alongside this, I aim to introduce two or three additional agro commodities to our portfolio, ensuring our group continues to balance different industries and remains resilient even when one sector faces a downturn.

Our metallurgical coke business is another pillar of growth. Here, too, the objective is to double production capacity, reinforcing our competitiveness and securing a stronger foothold in the industry.

Expansion is underway as we focus on turnover.
Left: New Machinery. Right: Old Machinery

Another major priority is professionalising operations. I plan to implement a proper ERP system across all our businesses, starting with two or three segments on a trial basis, and then rolling it out completely. This will bring more transparency, efficiency, and data-driven decision-making into our organisation.

At a personal level, I see myself stepping back from routine paperwork and day-to-day tasks. Over the next decade, I aim to appoint more capable

With my wife Sakshi, my advisor and inspiration

individuals to handle operations, allowing me to focus solely on major decisions related to sales, purchases, and research and development. By building strong teams and systems, we can carry forward our legacy, diversify wisely, and position the business for long-term success.

Advice I Wish I Had

Respect your elders first. Don't argue or try to prove a point in the heat of the moment. Instead, research your idea thoroughly. Know the market, the risks, and the numbers. Then present it to them calmly. Ask for permission to implement it step by step, so surprises are minimised and everyone stays comfortable with the pace of change. Remember, our elders carry decades of hard-earned experience and have built the foundation on which we stand today. Approach them with humility, back your idea with solid preparation, and let careful, phased execution do the convincing.

I believe that profit or loss is the by-product of the daily activities we perform throughout the year.

—xxx—

CIPL

PATH LIGHTERS TO THE NATION

Current Infraprojects Limited (CIPL) was established in 2013 and has been operating in the EPC contracting sector for over a decade. Devvrath Singh is a first-generation business founder and owner who established the company under the guidance of his father and mother, with the vision of delivering quality and value-driven engineering services to India's infrastructure sector.

Over time, they have diversified into multiple areas, including electrical, solar, water works, and civil works. Today, they execute projects across more than fifteen states in India. A recent milestone in their journey was their listing on the NSE Emerge platform in September 2025.

This is a glimpse into his journey as a business founder and owner, where his personal growth and the growth of CIPL have been closely intertwined.

6

Wires, Watts, and Willpower

Devvrath Singh

I am a first-generation entrepreneur, and I established Current Infraprojects Limited (CIPL) under the mentorship and guidance of my father and mother. I am an engineer by profession, and I completed my Bachelor's degree in Chemical Engineering at The University of Queensland, Australia.

My company and I have been actively following and participating in India's growth story by executing projects in the infrastructure sector. I have a keen interest in the Renewable energy sector, and this has led to a recent pivot in CIPL's approach towards Renewable energy projects, especially in Solar Energy.

Apart from running the business, I am an avid sports lover and a travel enthusiast. I play Lawn Tennis and Cricket regularly to stay physically fit, and I frequently travel to different countries around the world to unwind and relax.

The Genesis of Current Infraprojects

After completing my graduation in 2015 from the University of Queensland, Australia, I returned to India at a time when the country was at a crossroads. A new government had just taken charge, and its key area of focus was infrastructure.

I sensed a massive opportunity to contribute to India's growth story by working in this sector. However, with a degree in Chemical Engineering, naturally, I felt that my expertise did not align with civil or electrical infrastructure.

At this juncture, my father encouraged me to take the leap. Being an electrical engineer himself, his assurance of guidance and back-end support gave me the confidence to begin. With his motivation, I founded Current Infraprojects Private Limited and took the first step in my entrepreneurial journey.

Expanding Horizons

I founded this company under my father's guidance in 2015. The major factor influencing this decision was the immense opportunity for growth in India's infrastructure sector.

Since 2015, the Indian government has placed strong emphasis on infrastructure development, particularly on new highways, expressways, and railway projects, including dedicated freight corridors. This created a huge opportunity for qualified engineers and professionals to contribute their expertise.

In the early years, we began with projects related to highways, such as street lighting, toll plaza lighting, and the shifting of 11 KV and 33 KV electric utilities. Over time, we expanded into civil infrastructure projects, including the construction of toll plaza buildings, MEP consultancy, interior works (for clients such as Reliance Smart), and water utility projects, including drinking water and sewage projects for the PHED department.

A major milestone for us in the last four to five years has been our entry into the renewable energy sector, particularly solar (both on-grid and off-grid). This shift has not only given our company a renewed boost but has also allowed us to diversify our portfolio. Today, we are proud to be associated with prestigious government organisations, including the Border Security Force (BSF), NHPC, Indian Railways, and THDC.

The Turning Point

The moment I truly felt that I was '*in business*' was when I decided to lead the Solar EPC division of our company.

As a chemical engineer, I had a strong interest in solar technology as it demanded technical knowledge of solar cells, modules, and batteries, areas I was naturally drawn to. Around the same time, India committed to ambitious net-zero targets (Removals balance human-caused emissions) under the Paris Climate Agreement, as emphasised by our honourable prime minister, Shri Narendra Modi ji. I realised that solar energy would be central to replacing conventional sources with renewables, and I wanted to be part of that transformation.

With this vision in mind, I began actively searching for solar EPC projects. After consistent effort, we secured our first project in 2019, a 1.9 MWp solar installation and commissioning at the Dasna-Meerut Expressway (NE-4). That project became a turning point. Building on this initial experience, we were soon able to undertake projects directly with the Government of India.

From there, our solar journey accelerated. We executed several large-scale projects for prestigious organisations and PSUs such as the Border Security

Force (BSF), THDC, NHPC, and Indian Railways. This strengthened our portfolio significantly and gave me the conviction that we had truly arrived as a serious player in the sector.

Milestone Moment: 1.9 MWp Solar Power Plant installed by CIPL at Dasna Meerut Expressway

Learning by Doing

While my formal education, a B.Tech., provided me with a strong technical foundation, I was not formally trained in management before entering the business.

The turning point came when I moved beyond hesitation and committed myself fully to participating in the development of Infraprojects. My education gave me the confidence to understand technology-driven opportunities, but it was the experience of securing and executing our early projects, especially in the solar EPC sector, that showed me that my ideas had momentum. From that stage onward, I knew I was on a committed path and could shape both my own journey and the company's future.

The BSF Solar Project

The most rewarding moment of my entrepreneurial journey so far has been the successful completion of one of the most challenging projects of my career, setting up twenty-two solar plants with a total capacity of 550 kWp for the Border Security Force (BSF) along the India-Bangladesh border.

I was fully committed to the execution of this project, which made its successful handover to the BSF. It was also a milestone because it was the first project we executed directly for the Government of India rather than through a private client.

The location itself presented unique challenges. It was located in a remote area, difficult to access, and situated in Tripura along the border. Completing it with value engineering, high-quality standards, and within the timeline was no small feat. This achievement not only gave me immense personal satisfaction but also helped me earn the respect and recognition in the industry. To date, it remains the standout moment of my career.

Managing Across States

In recent years, the biggest challenge my business has faced has been managing operations across multiple states. As a pan-India company currently active in about thirteen states, we have to deal with the logistical demands of deploying manpower, moving machinery, and transporting materials to remote corners of the country.

However, a newer and equally significant challenge has been navigating taxation and statutory compliance in different states. Each state has its own set of rules, licenses, and compliance requirements in addition to the central government regulations. Ensuring that every state-specific requirement is met demands a high level of proactiveness. Meeting these compliances has become one of our most complex operational challenges.

Strategies to Stay Ahead in Cut-Throat Competition

In the EPC sector, many players operate with a similar portfolio of services, including solar works, electrical works, and civil works. This creates cut-throat competition, and since tenders are typically awarded to the L1 bidder (lowest bidder), massive bidding wars break out whenever government tenders are published.

To stay ahead of the competition and keep our business sustainable, we constantly work on diversifying our portfolio and exploring new avenues where we can bid. Emerging sectors such as large-scale solar parks, battery energy storage systems (BESS), and green hydrogen are still in their early stages, and we actively seek to participate in these projects. This helps us manage competition more effectively while maintaining healthy operating margins.

We also undertake projects across various states in India. Also, we have built a team to work on tough states where large-scale infrastructure work is traditionally considered challenging, e.g., some areas of the north-eastern states, and Jammu & Kashmir, due to difficult terrain conditions. This strategy reduces competition during bidding, allowing us to secure projects with comparatively higher margins.

The COVID Setback

The lowest point in our business journey came during the COVID-19 pandemic in 2020 and 2021. With the entire country under lockdown, our projects came to a standstill. At the same time, client payments were delayed or withheld due to widespread uncertainty. This created a dual blow: we could not generate new revenue, and even our pending receivables were blocked.

To make matters worse, the banks did not extend any relaxation on the EMIs of our business loans. For the first time in our company's history, we were forced to make the painful decision of laying off some employees. We also had to ration the limited funds we received during that period, which meant reducing employee salaries by 50% for three months.

These were complicated steps, taken with a heavy heart, and they remain the lowest point in our journey so far. However, once the lockdown was lifted, we bounced back and regained momentum, proving to ourselves that resilience and tough choices can carry us through even the darkest phases.

Learning from Failure

I see uncertainty and failure as natural parts of life and business. I have always believed that failures teach us more than success can ever teach us. Once you learn how to bounce back, you gain the confidence to face any situation with greater ease.

In my business, there have been many instances of rejection, for instance, losing a project at the final stage of negotiations. In such moments, I remind myself to look ahead, telling myself that the next deal will be even bigger than the one we lost. This mindset keeps me motivated and prevents setbacks from becoming roadblocks.

Uncertainty and risk are also constant in the EPC business. Every day brings new technological advancements that challenge established ways of working, while competition continues to intensify with the entry of new players into the market. Instead of fearing this uncertainty, I see it as something that keeps me on my toes.

I firmly believe that change is the only constant, and the ability to adapt, manage risks, and embrace uncertainty is what makes both individuals and companies stronger.

Understanding and Targeting Financials

For me, the most important priority is to increase the company's revenue year after year while also maintaining healthy margins. These two parameters are set as targets at the beginning of every financial year, and all our energy and focus are directed toward achieving them.

The long-term sustainability and growth of a business depend largely on its order book and profit margins. To strengthen both, I always try to secure high-value projects concentrated in a single location or state. This allows us to use our fixed resources and assets optimally, thereby generating stronger margins and ensuring financial stability.

Tracking What Matters

To monitor the health of my business, I focus primarily on two key metrics: project cash flow and return on investment (ROI).

With thirty to thirty-five projects typically running across India at any given time, I closely monitor the inflow and outflow of funds for each project. This helps me identify early signs of stress and intervene with timely guidance before a project reaches a critical point.

I also pay close attention to ROI whenever a project requires fresh investment from the company. For instance, when we recently bid for RESCO solar projects under the Government of India's KUSUM Scheme, we conducted a twenty-five-year ROI analysis beforehand. This allowed us to determine the appropriate bid rate to ensure the investment would generate optimal returns.

Investing Beyond the Present

Balancing short-term and long-term goals is critical, and with the support of my top management team, I maintain a clear vision on this front. While we chase short-term targets of revenue growth and healthy margins, I always ensure that while we pursue short-term targets of revenue and profit margins, we remain committed to investing the profits earned back into the company

Asset creation has a dual benefit: it allows profits to flow back into the business and creates new avenues for diversification. For example, over time, we have invested in developing two assets: a farmhouse in the hospitality sector (under CIPL) and an EV charging station (under the name of a new start-up company, Thinkers Doers Private Limited), both in the rapidly emerging clean-energy space.

These investments have not only generated secondary sources of income but also expanded our portfolio with a long-term outlook. By reinvesting profits from these ventures back into the company, we continue to explore new business sectors, hedge risks, and position ourselves for future growth.

Strategy and Resilience: A Costly Lesson

In the early years of the business, we made several mistakes, but one stands out clearly. We focused too heavily on securing projects from private companies. Looking back, after four to five years in the business, we should have shifted our focus toward government projects, which hold far greater value in the eyes of banks and investors.

Our over-reliance on private projects created a significant challenge in managing cash flows, as private companies rarely release payments in a single lump sum. This weakness became painfully clear during the COVID-19 pandemic, when delayed payments from private clients left us struggling to cover fixed expenses and forced us to reduce our workforce.

That experience was a turning point. Since 2021, we have consciously diversified into government projects, which provide more security and stability for our revenue streams. It was a tough lesson, but one that reshaped our approach to risk and client diversification.

Beyond Profits

For me, success lies not just in profits but in the business model and culture we have built over the last decade. I take pride in never backing down from challenges and in embedding the same value of resilience into the company's DNA.

Having travelled widely across India and abroad, I have always believed that restricting one's work to just the local region is like clipping a bird's wings. From the very beginning, I instilled the belief that our company could take on any challenge and execute projects anywhere in the world, not just within India.

I have personally led this initiative, taking charge of projects that were far away or particularly difficult. One such milestone was in 2022, when, under my leadership, we successfully completed a 550 kW solar project for the BSF at the India–Bangladesh border. That achievement opened new doors for us in the renewable energy sector, and over the last four years, we crossed the remarkable milestone of ₹100 crores in turnover.

For me, the greatest success is not the number itself but the conviction within our team that we can execute any project in the EPC sector, anywhere in the world.

Going Global

My long-term vision is to take the company global. Having studied abroad and being a travel enthusiast, I have experienced the world from different perspectives, and I have always dreamt of building a company that works on projects across the globe.

Another key milestone I am working toward is moving the company to the main board of the Indian stock markets within the next four to five years. We are steadily progressing toward this goal by consistently taking on projects across India and focusing on strengthening both our topline and bottom line. At the same time, we are actively pursuing international opportunities to establish a global footprint. My vision is that within the next ten years, we will evolve into a truly multinational company with a presence in multiple countries.

The Emotional Landscape: Blurring Boundaries

Being part of a family-owned business means that almost every member of my family is involved in some way. My father is the managing director, my mother is the chairperson, and my wife heads the HR department.

While this close involvement strengthens our shared commitment, it also blurs the line between personal and professional life. Many times, conversations at home drift toward business matters, leaving little room for the kind of mental break that is often needed to recharge. At times, this lack of separation does lead to fatigue and mental exhaustion.

For me, every day feels like a day filled with opportunities. Since we operate across multiple fields, solar, civil, electrical, and on a pan-India scale, no two days are ever the same. Each day brings new excitement and the possibility of fresh projects, whether in a new region of India or even abroad.

This constant sense of opportunity drives my energy and keeps me motivated. Rather than being weighed down by anxiety or pressure, I choose to see each day as a chance to build something new.

Guidance vs. Interference

One unique challenge we face as a family-run business is the tendency to get too involved in the finer details of projects. At times, we step in to influence decisions or even take over tasks ourselves, believing we can do them better than the employees to whom we had delegated the work.

This can sometimes create resentment among employees, as there is a very fine line between supervising a project and providing guidance when required, versus interfering in day-to-day activities.

Maintaining this balance, offering guidance without crossing into interference, is a challenge specific to family-run businesses. In non-family businesses, this situation is far less likely to arise.

Wisdom I Rely On

Whenever things get difficult in business, I turn to my father for advice. He has been my guide and mentor throughout my twelve years in the business. With nearly twice my experience, his perspective often helps me see challenges more clearly and make better decisions. I deeply value his wisdom and steady presence whenever I find myself in a sticky situation.

Legacy, Family & Identity: Forged Under Pressure

As our company has grown, the expectations from my family, especially my father and mother, have also increased many times over. This is only natural, given that our turnover has risen from just a few lakhs in 2014–15 to ₹100 crores in 2024–25. Still, these growing expectations do add weight to my shoulders.

I choose to see this weight not as a burden, but as a privilege. As the saying goes, 'diamonds are forged under pressure,' and I believe the same applies here. The expectations from my family push me to improve myself every day and inspire me to take the company to greater heights.

My Business, My Identity

Yes, my identity is deeply tied to my business. I started it almost immediately after graduating from college, so it has been the central part of my professional journey ever since. In many ways, it is the only thing I have known after completing my studies.

Far from being uncomfortable with this, I take pride in it. As a chemical engineering graduate, I could never have imagined the path ahead, but today I feel immense pride and a sense of accomplishment in having built a company that operates across numerous diverse sectors. Looking back on the last twelve years, the journey itself has become a defining part of who I am.

Preparing for Tomorrow

A major milestone for our company has been our recent listing on the NSE Emerge platform of India's stock exchanges. This step will greatly support our scaling plans by providing access to new funds. But with great power comes great responsibility. Being a listed company brings its own challenges,

Listing of CIPL on NSE Emerge Platform on September 3, 2025 [Left to Right: Mr Satyavrat Singh (brother), Mrs Sujata Gangwar (mother), Mrs Sneha Singh (wife), Mr Devvrath Singh & Mr Sunil Singh Gangwar (father) with Ms Kashvi Singh in his arms]

from increased compliance requirements to heightened expectations from investors.

Looking ahead, the biggest challenge will be maintaining sustainable growth while consistently delivering on profit commitments, particularly in a world marked by global uncertainty and rapid technological shifts, such as artificial intelligence (AI).

To prepare for this future, we are diversifying our portfolio, increasing the ticket size of our projects, and steadily shifting towards government projects, which provide more stability than private contracts. At the same time, we are actively exploring how to integrate AI into our operations. A recent step in this direction has been the adoption of AI-based tender searching tools, which help us identify opportunities more efficiently.

Follow Your Gut

The single most important advice I would give to a new entrepreneur is this: never doubt your instincts. Trust your gut when making big decisions.

Looking back on my own journey over the past twelve years, I do have some lingering regrets about times when I chose to follow others' advice instead of my own intuition. Those decisions still leave me with 'what if' questions.

It is far better to make a wrong decision based on your own instincts than to live with the regret of not having trusted yourself. At least then, you know you gave your best judgment and stayed true to yourself.

—xxx—

Founded in 1882, G. Rajam Chetty and Sons Jewellers has been a part of my family's identity for over 143 years. While the legacy has provided a strong foundation, the journey has been about stepping into responsibility, navigating change, and finding my place within this long-standing institution.

G. Prasanth is a chartered accountant and fifth-generation entrepreneur from Kanchipuram, Tamil Nadu. After gaining professional experience at a Big Four Audit firm, he chose to return to his family business to lead its next phase of growth, blending traditional values with modern strategy and carving out his own leadership path.

Titled 'The Golden Chair: My Journey through Legacy and Leadership', this chapter explores how he balanced inheritance and identity, navigated generational dynamics, and led strategic transformation, all while honouring a century-old legacy.

7

The Golden Chair

PRASANTH UDAYAKUMAR

My journey as an entrepreneur began the day I was born into a family of jewellers with a proud legacy. Our business, G. Rajam Chetty and Sons Jewellers, was founded in 1882 by my great-great-grandfather, Mr Rajam Chettiyar. By the time I arrived, the company was already 111 years old, a number that felt as symbolic as the heritage itself. Today, that legacy stands at 143 years.

Though established long ago, the business grew to its current stature under the strong leadership of my father, Mr G. Udayakumar, and my mother, Mrs G. Varalakshmi, with the guidance of my grandfather, Mr G. Nagasundaram. We are based in the small but culturally rich temple town of Kanchipuram, Tamil Nadu, famous for its silk sarees and ancient temples.

The front elevation of the original showroom on Raja Street, Kanchipuram, situated adjacent to the historic CSI Mission Girls' School. A tiled roof, hand-painted signage, and a humble façade that became an icon

In the 1980s and 90s, women rarely played a visible role in family businesses in such towns. But my mother defied convention, running the business shoulder-to-shoulder with my father. I grew up watching our small, owner-driven shop with 3 to 5 employees gradually expand into a thriving enterprise with 70–80 direct employees and another 100–130 indirect staff. From a modest 750 sq. ft. showroom inside a house, we grew into a 3,500 sq. ft., two-storey flagship store.

As the only son in the family (my elder sister chose a life abroad), the mantle of carrying forward this heritage naturally fell on me. From childhood, I was struck by the deep trust and affection our customers had for us. In Kanchipuram, there has long been a sentiment that every marriage and every mangalsutra should be made by our family, considered auspicious by the townspeople. That unwavering faith shaped my belief that we were in the right line of work.

One of my earliest defining moments came while I was still in Grade 11. My mother was unwell, my father had to accompany her, and my sister was busy with her exams. That left me, along with my grandfather, to take care of the business during one of the busiest times of the year, the wedding season. For an entire week, I found myself at the heart of the showroom, attending to customers, managing payments to vendors, coordinating with employees, and handling day-to-day operations. What began as a family necessity turned into a personal revelation. I discovered a side of myself I hadn't seen before: energetic, decisive, and fully immersed in the rhythm of business. That week showed me I wasn't just the next heir waiting in line; I was already capable of being a livewire in the enterprise.

I believed that being born into a business makes you a *natural heir*, but at the same time, authentic leadership requires preparation. My father had once dreamed of becoming a chartered accountant, but could not pursue it. I decided to fulfil that dream. After completing my first year of undergraduate studies in Commerce at Ramakrishna Mission Vivekananda College, Chennai, I successfully cleared both my CA Foundation and CA Intermediate exams. This allowed me to shift into distance education for the remainder of my degree, freeing me to focus fully on chartered accountancy.

I joined a Big Four audit firm in 2017 as an Indirect Tax Associate, at the very moment when GST was being implemented in India. Between 2013 and 2019, my career exposed me to internal audits, statutory audits, tax audits, due diligence, and tax consultancy. This period provided me with the analytical grounding, discipline, and professional exposure that ultimately enabled me to return to my roots. By 2019, I felt ready.

Everything is Gold

One interesting aspect of being raised in a jeweller's family is that we tend to evaluate every major financial decision in terms of gold grams. It's almost second nature.

For example, when we bought our first Hyundai Accent in 2003 for around ₹8 lakhs, my father casually remarked, 'That's roughly 2 kilos of gold', since gold was about ₹4 lakh per kilo then. A decade later, in 2013, when we bought the Toyota Altis for ₹19 lakhs, that too was mentally pegged at around 2 kilos of gold. By 2019, when we purchased the Volvo XC60 for ₹75 lakhs, soaring gold prices meant it was equivalent to around 1.5 kilos.

This may sound quirky, but for us, gold is the ultimate reference point for value. Whether it's cars, property, or any big-ticket investment, the instinctive question is always: 'How many kilos of gold is this worth?' This way of thinking reflects how deeply the business mindset permeates our personal lives, shaping even day-to-day financial decisions.

Embracing Risk and Reform

When I stepped into the family business full-time in 2019, I quickly realised that the real test of an entrepreneur lies not in inheritance, but in facing

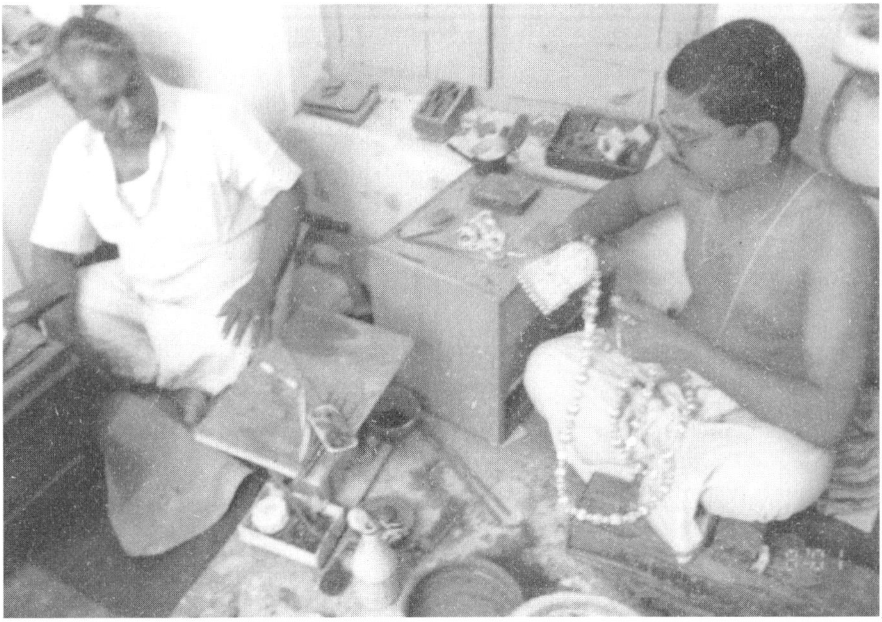

Artisans at work, the heart and hands behind every design. Their skill, patience, and silent pride keep tradition alive

challenges head-on. Some challenges were inherited, some were external, and some arose from within the family dynamic itself. Each of them shaped me in unique ways.

The jewellery industry often carries a poor reputation, perceived as a space where questionable practices thrive and unaccounted money is parked. To some extent, I agree with this perception. It is extremely difficult to stay clean in an ecosystem that is largely unorganised. For proper compliance, every part of the chain, suppliers, artisans, and customers, must align. If any one of these links is non-compliant, it compromises the entire system.

Educating this ecosystem and bringing them into a structured, compliant framework is one of the biggest operational challenges we face. While suppliers have gradually adapted, working with rural artisans and customers is an uphill task. To build a fully compliant ecosystem, there must be tangible incentives for compliance, something the current regulatory environment lacks. We actively engage with those who demonstrate an intent to comply, but changing mindsets across an entire rural ecosystem remains one of our most significant challenges.

The Lowest Point

One of the most challenging phases for our business came during 2010–11, when we underwent regulatory action by the Income Tax Department. While we had substantial grounds in our defence, specific documentation gaps worked against us, and the episode became a setback. It was a challenging period, but it also underscored an important lesson: the critical need for stronger compliance and systems.

Looking back, that experience was much like a bitter medicine, unpleasant at the time, but essential for our long-term health. It set us firmly on the right track. In the years that followed, we not only overcame the episode but also moved into a larger showroom, expanding our operations and growing many times over.

Facing Competition

Post 2013, while we were renovating our old showroom and operating from a temporary setup, several new players entered the Kanchipuram jewellery market. With flashy advertisements, celebrity inaugurations, and aggressive promotions, they briefly disrupted our business. For about two weeks, customer traffic dropped, but soon enough, our loyal base returned. This became a recurring pattern whenever a corporate chain came into town.

What sustained us was not glamour but substance. Our strength lies in reasonable pricing, lean operations, and transparency with customers. Unlike chain stores, we never spent heavily on advertising or celebrities.

This allowed us to operate at a lower price point with reasonable margins, focusing on volume and high stock turnover. Combined with our 143-year legacy and the deeply held local sentiment that mangalsutras must be bought from our store for auspiciousness, these factors consistently kept us ahead of competitors.

Operational & Family Business Challenges

After formally joining in 2019, one of the first issues I encountered was the inadequacy of our systems and controls. Perhaps this was the auditor in me, trained to spot weaknesses, but it was also true that our ERP system had grown outdated.

We had depended on the same vendor for over 20 years. My father had been visionary in 2003 when he first computerised our operations, but by 2019, the system was no longer sufficient. For me, the decision to upgrade to a modern ERP was straightforward; for my father, it was not. The old system represented both his boldness and two decades of trust. Convincing him required persistence, persuasion, and endless discussions.

I have always believed in the saying: '*What got you here will not take you there.*' Eventually, we made the switch, and in time, my father also came to see the benefits. Yet this episode revealed a larger truth about family-run businesses: logic and exposure alone cannot drive decisions. Every choice must be deliberated, discussed, and accepted collectively. The process can be painfully slow, and at times decisions remain unresolved, but when consensus is reached, it carries the strength of shared ownership.

Most Rewarding Moment & Handling Uncertainty

By 2023, what had felt like a 'big showroom' in 2015 was no longer enough for our growing customer base. We needed more space, and leasing was never an option I considered for our flagship. Ownership was non-negotiable.

That year, a rare opportunity arose: a large plot directly opposite our showroom came up for sale. It was the perfect chance to secure our future growth. But the timing was personally testing. My parents were abroad with my pregnant sister, my wife (also pregnant) was with her parents, and I was left managing both the household and the business. On top of it, I was inexperienced in real estate negotiations, which can be cutthroat.

My father had a rate in mind, but in the heat of negotiations with a difficult seller, I agreed to a price above market value. When my father heard the news, he was annoyed, and I was consumed by self-doubt. Yet time proved the decision right. Property values soared, and competitors began shifting to our street. Buying that plot allowed us to plan a larger showroom while blocking entry for rivals. My father, who initially questioned me, later acknowledged that under the circumstances, it had been the right call. That purchase has become one of the most rewarding moments of my journey.

What helped me cope with the uncertainty of that deal was a lesson from earlier in life: my CA Final exams. I had never really faced failure until then, and failing my first attempt, especially just months after my sister's wedding, was devastating. But I cleared it on the next try and qualified as a Chartered Accountant. That experience taught me that failure is only a comma, not a complete stop. Success may be delayed, but it is never denied if you persist. That mindset carried me through the land deal and continues to guide me whenever doubt or failure arises.

Jeweller's Accounting: An Underrated Discipline

Being a chartered accountant, I have always felt that jeweller's accounting is an underrated subject. It carries intricacies that are often overlooked in academic discussions, but in practice, it is far more complex than it appears.

In managing a jewellery company's finances, sales volume is the most important driver, with margins following next. This is because the base precious metal, gold or silver, makes up nearly 80–90% of the product's price. The remaining portion is the value addition, labour, wastage, and making charges, which are usually quoted as a percentage of the base metal.

Since gold and silver are highly volatile, margins are directly influenced by fluctuations in their rates. That is why the number of grams sold becomes the truest yardstick for performance. Sales growth measured in grams, not just rupee value, reflects both customer trust and business momentum.

Evolving Financing Philosophy

In our early years, we were not fond of relying on external money. We operated conservatively and only took our first bank loan in 2013–14 to fuel expansion, along with a cash credit facility to ease cash flow. Over time, however, we came to appreciate the cushion that bank finance can offer.

When deployed in a profit-generating business, debt is actually cheap money. It gave us both confidence and flexibility in decision-making. Our financing approach has since evolved from a purely internal capital structure to a balanced approach that leverages borrowed funds strategically.

Gold Saving Schemes, Strengthening Cash Flows

Another important step came in 2016, when I was preparing for my CA Final exams. That year, we introduced Gold Saving Schemes for our customers.

These schemes encouraged customers to invest monthly, fostering a disciplined saving habit while ensuring a positive cash flow for the business.

Customers were rewarded through discounts on value-added charges. Although such schemes were not new to the jewellery industry, for us, they represented a strategic shift, from merely serving customer demand to proactively engaging and retaining customers while strengthening the company's financial backbone.

Cash Flow and Stock Churn

Since gold and silver are precious metals subject to extreme price volatility, maintaining a healthy cash flow is critical. Unlike many other industries, dead stock risk is lower because jewellery can be melted, and the base metal value can be recovered.

Even with a 10–12 per cent conversion cost, this can usually be recouped in 12–18 months, assuming a conservative 9 per cent annual metal price growth. The real challenge is investing capital in moving stock, ensuring organic stock churn drives the business forward.

While bankers focus on PAT, NP ratio, and GP ratio, a jeweller's real concerns are stock churn and cash flow. With volatile metal prices and rising customer expectations for design variety, it's becoming increasingly difficult to operate solely with owned capital. Borrowed capital through bank finance is now essential, but it must be managed within sound financial metrics.

Financial Discipline and Strategic Decisions

When I joined the business, we were rated BB+. Over time, through greater emphasis on financial discipline and data-driven decision-making, we improved to BBB, with a BBB+ rating expected shortly.

We are also open to restructuring our business models and constitution to attract more capital to fuel growth. Balancing short-term liquidity with long-term strategic investments is a constant exercise. Short-term cash flow and margins keep the wheels turning every day, while long-term decisions, such as our ERP upgrade or strategic land purchases, secure future growth.

There are moments when we choose to endure short-term strain for structural gains, and these decisions have repeatedly proven to be turning points in our financial journey. Ultimately, financial management is a careful balance between sales, margins, and brand building, supported by strong cash flow and disciplined capital use. It is not merely about maximising quarterly profits, but about ensuring that our business remains strong, ethical, and sustainable for decades to come.

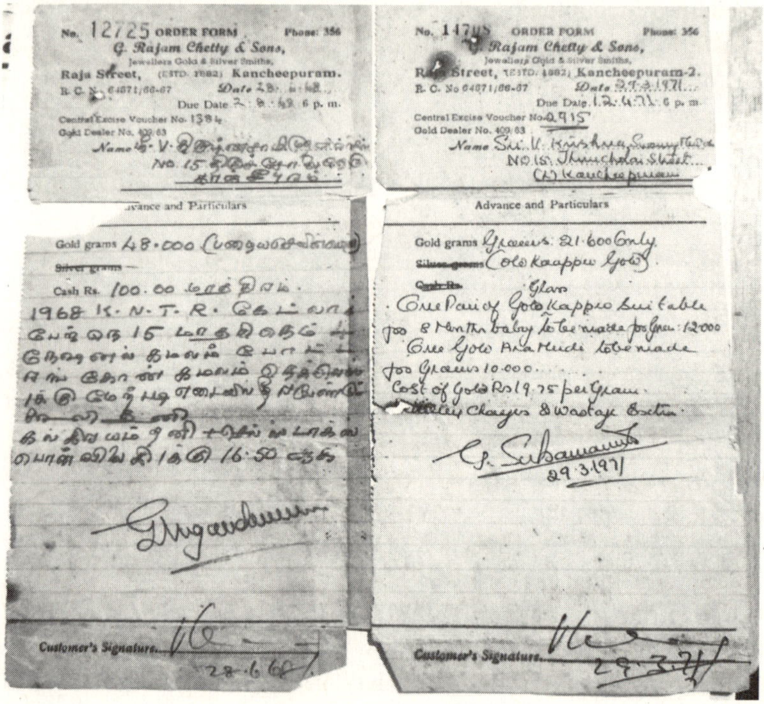

No. 12725 ORDER FORM Phone: 356
G. Rajam Chetty & Sons,
Jewellers Gold & Silver Smiths,
Raja Street, (ESTD. 1882) Kancheepuram.
R. C. No. 64871/66-67 Date 28. 6. 68.
Due Date 2. 8. 68. 6 p. m.
Central Excise Voucher No. 1384
Gold Dealer No. 409/63
Name [illegible]
No. 15 [illegible]
Advance and Particulars
Gold grams 48.000 [illegible]
Silver grams —
Cash Rs. 100.00 [illegible]
1968 K. N. T. R. [illegible]
[illegible]
Customer's Signature [illegible] 28.6.68

No. 14705 ORDER FORM Phone: 356
G. Rajam Chetty & Sons,
Jewellers Gold & Silver Smiths,
Raja Street, (ESTD. 1882) Kancheepuram-2.
R. C. No 64871/66-67 Date 29.3.1971
Due Date 12.4.71. 6 p. m.
Central Excise Voucher No. 2915
Gold Dealer No. 409/63
Name Sri V. Krishna Swamy [illegible]
No. 15 Thiruchalai Street
Kancheepuram
Advance and Particulars
Gold grams Grams: 21.600 Only
(Old Kappu Gold)
Glass
One Pair of Gold Kappu suitable for 8 Month baby to be made for Gram: 12.000
One Gold Arai Mudi to be made for Grams 10.000
Cost of Gold Rs 19.75 per Gram
[illegible] Charges & Wastage Extra
G. Subramaniam
29.3.1971
Customer's Signature [illegible] 29.3.71

Meticulous records, ethical trade. This 1967 and 1971 order voucher reflects the financial prudence and compliance-first mindset that has guided our family business for generations

Strategy and Resilience: Early Mistakes & Lessons

We have certainly made mistakes in the past and continue to make them to this day. One of the biggest lessons I've learned is that entering into commercial relationships based purely on emotions, without adequate analysis, can lead to poor business decisions.

I still remember a decision I regret: spending more than twice our planned budget on a television advertising campaign. Just because we had the capacity to pay didn't mean we should have committed to expensive artists and a large-scale production. At the time, we were motivated by what other jewellers were doing, and as a 140-year-old business updating our branding, we wanted to make a strong statement.

In hindsight, we overspent unnecessarily. We continue to air the ad in theatres and local channels, but the same impact could have been achieved within a far more reasonable budget. This decision was also preceded by several debates with my father. Eventually, he supported me, but we both trusted people who had promised to stay within a specific budget, a promise that was broken.

A still from our television commercial – a big bet on brand-building. We learned to pair ambition with prudence, ensuring impact without excess

The lesson for me was clear: commercial relationships should not be built solely on emotions, but on numbers, clarity, and the competencies of the parties involved. Elders possess wisdom that comes from experience. It can be debated, but it must never be ignored. This was a judgment error, and I now consciously strive to ensure that such lapses are minimised in future decisions.

Defining Success

Success is a deeply subjective concept. The first step toward achieving success and a sense of freedom is to let go of how others perceive us. It is essential to define and achieve success on our own terms, rather than through the lens of societal expectations.

That said, it's easier said than done. From childhood to adulthood, we are constantly exposed to pressures to measure, compare, and prove ourselves. This cycle never really stops. Even when we think we've risen above it, external opinions and comparisons have a way of creeping back in.

Success in business lies in creating a separate legal and functional entity that can exist even without us. I don't just mean a legal entity in the eyes of the law, but one that is recognised by everyone, including customers, employees, partners, and the community. The actual test of success is when a business can run indefinitely, regardless of who heads or runs it.

For me, success also lies in the positive impact we create on the people and community around us, whether it's the artisans who bring our designs to life, the employees who carry our values forward, or the customers who place their trust in us across generations. Even today, many customers fondly share stories about their interactions with my grandparents when they bought their jewellery from us. These interactions were deeply personal, each one had its own story and its own warmth.

We have always viewed our suppliers, customers, and artisans as an extended family, not merely through the lens of commercial transactions. Our constant endeavour is to maintain a win–win balance with all stakeholders, ensuring that trust and mutual respect remain at the heart of every relationship.

To achieve all this, it's essential to build a strong team that not only understands the vision but also shares and upholds the core values of the organisation. Equally important is establishing robust systems and processes that are self-regulating and capable of evolving with changing times.

On a personal level, success to me is not about earning tons of money at the cost of losing the simple joys of life. It's about having the freedom and time to pause and enjoy the little things, whether that's going on a vacation, meeting a friend, running a marathon, playing badminton, going to the gym, or simply maintaining a healthy lifestyle.

I recently heard a saying: '*Work-life balance is maintained only in two cases, one, if your wife insists on it, and two, if you don't like your work.*' I partly agree. I believe that these little moments we cherish in life are not separate from work. They are an integral part of living well. Life is work, and work is life.

Long-Term Vision

Looking ahead, I envision our business evolving into a professionally governed, institutionally strong, and technologically enabled organisation, one that carries forward our legacy while embracing change. Over the next decade, I see us:

- Expanding into a larger, purpose-built showroom that reflects both our heritage and modern aspirations.
- Strengthening our Innila silver line and exploring select adjacent verticals.
- Deepening the use of technology, from ERP systems to customer engagement platforms, to improve efficiency and personalisation at scale.
- Building a strong leadership team and governance framework that ensures smooth generational transitions and decision-making discipline.
- Continuing to be a trusted pillar in the Kanchipuram ecosystem, supporting artisans, employees, and customers alike.
- Building a dedicated financial corpus that can generate risk-free passive income, providing stability and supporting both business growth and family aspirations, regardless of operational fluctuations.

My vision is to build an organisation that thrives for decades to come, not merely because of who leads it, but because of the strength of its people, systems, and values.

The Emotional Landscape

The greatest challenge in a family business setup, at least in my case, is the lack of compartmentalisation between business and personal hours or spaces. I dislike discussing business at the dining table, yet that's often where most conversations happen. Boundaries blur easily when work and family are so deeply intertwined.

My father often says, 'One generation in a family has to struggle so that the rest can live happily.' I've always wondered whether that struggle is rooted in sacrifice or fuelled by passion and zest.

It is therefore essential for the previous generation to clearly communicate that the business is a product of their passion, not something that happened by chance. If this is not conveyed properly, the next generation may begin to see themselves merely as substitutes, waiting in line to inherit a burden rather than a dream. When that happens, the flow of passion breaks, often quietly and irreversibly.

What's critical here is not just communication, but the manner in which it is communicated, with honesty, openness, and inspiration, rather than pressure.

Impact on Personal Life and Relationships

In a family business, the lines between work and personal life often blur, and in my case, this has been one of the biggest emotional challenges. Business conversations often spill into personal spaces, such as the dining table, leaving little room for separation.

When communication is unclear or absent, both generations end up making assumptions that the other has never even considered. These gaps can unintentionally strain personal relationships and influence individual decisions in subtle but powerful ways. Over time, as mutual understanding deepens, these tensions tend to ease. However, this requires deliberate effort.

Tier-2 vs Urban Life: A Personal Shift

Moving from a bustling urban life in Chennai to a Tier-2 town like Kanchipuram brought both challenges and unexpected gifts. In Chennai, life was structured, fast-paced, and surrounded by peers who shared similar professional journeys. There was a certain anonymity and stimulation that came with corporate life.

Kanchipuram, on the other hand, offers deeper roots, people know you, legacy carries weight, and every interaction feels personal. While the social circles are smaller and business often overlaps with personal identity, there's also more time and mental space here. The slower pace has allowed me to pick up hobbies, reflect more deeply, and evolve as a person in ways that a frenetic urban lifestyle rarely permits. This shift has been both grounding and transformative.

A Normal Day: Excitement, Energy, and Emotional Drain

A typical day in the family business is a mix of excitement, challenge, and energy, but it can also be emotionally and mentally consuming. There's a unique thrill in running a legacy business; every day brings new situations, decisions, and interactions that keep me fully engaged.

However, having experienced the highly structured environment of a Big Four firm, I constantly feel the urge to bring structure and discipline into our unorganised way of functioning. Implementing systems, processes, and accountability measures has become a personal mission for me. But this is where emotional complexity kicks in.

When policies and procedures are enforced upon outsiders, it's usually straightforward: compliance is expected, and change is part of the job. But when you try to enforce structure on family members who have worked a certain way for decades, it's far more challenging. Some people are reluctant to leave their comfort zones, and their ability to change can be sticky, as the saying goes, 'Old habits die hard.'

To address this, we are now focusing on thoroughly discussing every process before finalising it. Once agreed, the aim is to fully commit to following it consistently. But getting to that point requires significant patience and emotional energy.

In a Big Four environment, there's a clear career roadmap: you join as an associate, work your way up systematically, and have a peer group for support and deliberation. In a family-owned business, you are often given the 'golden chair' right from the start, with no structured peer group to brainstorm with. It can be a lonely space, where decisions are critical and the stakes are significantly higher.

Living and working in a Tier-2 town brings a different emotional rhythm to each day. There's a certain calmness, shorter commutes, more familiarity, and the comfort of being deeply embedded in the community. At the same time, the lack of structured peer conversations and external professional push can make it feel like you're operating in a bubble.

This resistance to change, coupled with the weight of responsibility, can be emotionally draining. The very energy invested in building systems for the betterment of the organisation sometimes feels depleted by the friction it creates within the family. Yet, despite these moments, running the business remains a deeply rewarding and exciting experience. The blend of challenge, legacy, and impact makes each day meaningful, even when it's tiring.

The Healing Process

When I moved from Chennai, I deliberately joined several social organisations and networks to build meaningful connections outside of work. Through these platforms, I interact with college students, school students, and members from other chapters of social organisations, while jointly engaging in community activities.

This involvement provides me with an outside perspective, keeps me in touch with evolving trends, and serves as a healthy side hustle that breaks the monotony of routine business life. It offers a sense of belonging and balance that purely professional spaces can't provide.

I also make it a point to maintain an active lifestyle, going to the gym, attending learning conferences, and picking up new skills. These activities help me preserve my creative energy and maintain emotional equilibrium amidst the intensity of business operations.

Equally important, I'm blessed with two to three close friends who act as my sounding board. They listen to my point of view, offer honest criticism, and are unafraid to be blunt when I'm wrong. Their candid feedback keeps me grounded and helps me navigate decisions with greater clarity and efficiency.

Managing Generational Dynamics & Expectations

In any family business, there is always a particular set of expectations from the elder generation regarding how the company should be run. These expectations are often shaped by their own experiences and what worked for them in their time. However, from the perspective of the next generation, some of these expectations can feel unproductive or misaligned with current realities.

For example, my father firmly believes that every single customer should be personally known, and that engaging in small talk is a key differentiator in our B2C setup. He views this as a core USP that has helped establish deep trust over the decades. While I value this sentiment, I also find it highly time- and energy-consuming, especially as the business scales. I believe that there should certainly be a personal touch, but it should not remain purely transactional or dependent on the owner's physical presence.

As we grow, the connection between the customer and the owner will naturally evolve. If we don't consciously build a strong organisational culture that reflects these values, the business could falter when those personal connections fade. The challenge lies in honouring the essence of the old approach while redesigning its execution for scale.

While elders do recognise the need for this transition, their expectations often remain anchored in the past, which can sometimes be unrealistic for us to fully fulfil in today's context. Managing this delicate balance between respecting legacy and steering towards scalability is at the core of navigating generational dynamics in our business.

Identity and the Business

It is easy for outsiders to comment and demean my journey by saying that I have inherited wealth from the fourth generation and that my path to prosperity has been straightforward. I fully recognise that I am privileged by birth; I have, in many ways, *won the birth race*.

However, I have consciously chosen not to take the easy route. When my father suggested the more straightforward path of completing a B.Com. And directly joining the business, I instead took up the challenge of pursuing Chartered Accountancy, widely regarded as one of the most rigorous professional qualifications. I not only cleared it but also gained valuable work experience in a Big Four firm, equipping myself with the skills and exposure required to lead responsibly.

This journey has enabled me to develop my own self-image, one that is distinct yet complementary to that of the family business. The business's image has been shaped over generations by my predecessors, while my personal identity has been shaped by conscious choices, challenges, and the values I bring to the table. I ensure that my identity doesn't overshadow the business's legacy, but rather enhances and elevates it.

Looking ahead, any successor who chooses to return to the business must follow a similar path. They should build their own capacity and capability, put themselves through challenging experiences, and earn their leadership, rather than inherit it passively.

If Not This, Then What?

Had I not returned to the family business, I would have continued my career as a consultant, where I was already experiencing a reasonable degree of professional success. I had built a solid foundation in taxation and audit, and I could have grown steadily within that ecosystem, taking on increasingly challenging roles in the corporate world.

If I were to think beyond that trajectory, I would have seriously considered attempting the UPSC examinations and pursuing a career in the civil services. The idea of contributing to governance, policy, and systemic change has always appealed to me. If financial constraints were not a consideration, I would have gladly donned the role of a bureaucrat, serving the nation in a meaningful capacity.

In addition, I have always had a natural inclination toward teaching and mentoring students. Sharing knowledge brings me immense satisfaction, and I can easily envision myself as a guest lecturer or academic facilitator, combining my professional expertise with my passion for education.

Looking Ahead

As we look ahead, our vision is to scale the business strategically and sustainably, while preserving the essence that has brought us this far. One of the immediate opportunities we are working on is expanding our showroom to a larger space on the same street. This will enable us to separate our operations into a Front Office (customer-facing) and a Back Office (purchasing, finance, and accounts), allowing for more focused and efficient functioning across departments.

We are also working to integrate technology into every aspect of our workflow, including CRM systems, task management platforms, and data-driven dashboards. Enhancing already enabled technologies such as our e-commerce platform and mobile scheme application is a key focus area, allowing us to build deeper customer engagement and streamline internal processes. The introduction of a task management system will help bring structure, accountability, and transparency to our daily operations.

On the growth front, we aim to formulate a prototype branch model, which can then be replicated in multiple locations. The target is to establish 5 to 6 branches in key markets and achieve a 20% year-on-year growth in sales volume. While this target is ambitious, especially in a high-interest-rate environment, we see it as a necessary push to prepare the organisation for future value discovery and eventual public listing.

Parallel to this expansion, we are consciously working to build a passive income corpus. This will help segregate financial security from the ambitious strides of the business, ensuring that while the organisation pursues growth aggressively, the family's financial foundation remains stable and risk-free. This dual approach of prudent security-building and strategic expansion is central to our long-term vision.

An Honest Piece of Advice

Anyone can do business. But to do it with passion, while keeping one eye firmly on the future, is what separates the ordinary from the exceptional. Business is never a straight road; trial and error are part of the terrain, and missteps often become your best teachers.

Showroom inauguration, New doors, Old values

The real beauty of entrepreneurship lies in owning your decisions, both the wins and the failures. One of the most corrosive attitudes in business is when people claim credit for success but shift blame for failure. This mindset weakens both individuals and organisations and must be consciously avoided.

Instead, indulge in meaningful conversations, debate with clarity, and present your point of view fearlessly. Don't hide behind silence or indecision. If something isn't working, dare to pivot, adapt, or let go.

Business rewards resilience. Keep trying, not blindly, but with reflection, humility, and persistence.

Sitting on a golden chair is a privilege, but it is not a guarantee. Legacy may give you the seat, but leadership decides what you do with it. The real test of an entrepreneur is whether you can carry the weight of that chair, reshape it when needed, and build a future that honours the past without being trapped by it.

—xxx—

JI

JUPITER INFRAWORKS Pvt. Ltd.

BUILDING FOUNDATIONS SINCE 2009

Jupiter Infraworks Pvt Ltd traces its origins to MPRP Pvt Ltd, established in 1949 in Kolkata, capitalising on the post-independence industrial boom. What began as a manufacturing company of iron and steel components for the Indian Railways has evolved over the decades into a diversified business group with interests spanning infrastructure development, warehousing, and real estate.

Through subsequent ventures such as the Kona Trading Company and Resolute Infrastructure Pvt. Ltd., now known as Jupiter Infraworks Pvt. Ltd., the company has steadily transitioned from traditional manufacturing to modern infrastructure and property development. Each phase of our growth has been driven by a commitment to adaptability and long-term value creation, ensuring that the business remains relevant in an ever-changing industrial landscape.

Today, their operations continue to be based in Eastern India, with projects that contribute to regional connectivity, industrial capacity, and urban development. As the fourth generation to be part of this journey, Armaan Jaiswal's focus is on strengthening governance, fostering innovation, and building upon the foundation of trust and resilience that has defined their family business for over six decades.

8

Finding Opportunities in Adversity

ARMAAN JAISWAL

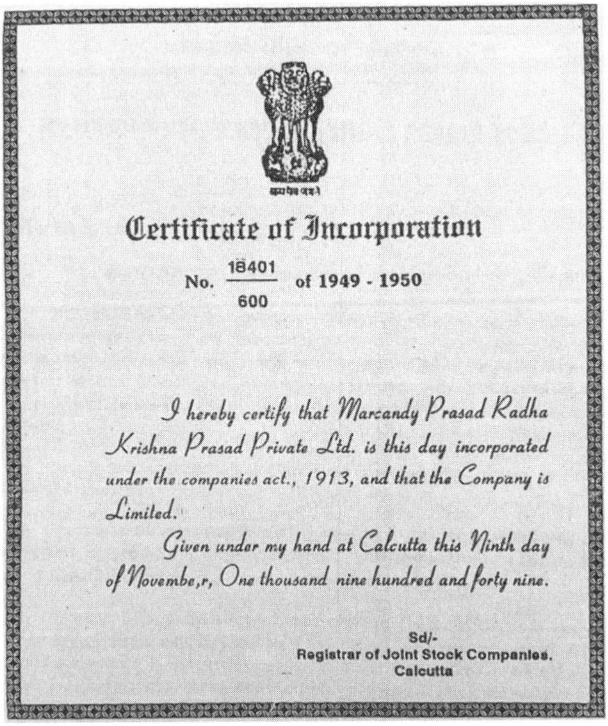

Certificate of Incorporation

No. 18401/600 of 1949 - 1950

I hereby certify that Marcandy Prasad Radha Krishna Prasad Private Ltd. is this day incorporated under the companies act., 1913, and that the Company is Limited.

Given under my hand at Calcutta this Ninth day of Novembe,r, One thousand nine hundred and forty nine.

Sd/-
Registrar of Joint Stock Companies.
Calcutta

Certificate of Incorporation of MPRP Pvt. Ltd

Our primary family business, MPRP Pvt. Ltd., was founded in 1949 to manufacture cast iron sleeper plates for the Indian Railways. By the 1970s, it had grown into one of the largest suppliers of CI sleeper plates in Eastern India, with an annual production of 55,000 tonnes. These were years of industrial growth, and our family took pride in contributing to the backbone of India's infrastructure. Yet, success also came with a lesson: markets evolve quickly, and unless businesses adapt, they risk decline. The industry's shift toward concrete sleeper plates, coupled with mismanagement following the untimely death of the founding directors and the absence of a succession plan, left the company vulnerable. Partition suits among family branches, many of which remain unresolved to this day, remind us that legacy alone cannot sustain a business without foresight and effective governance.

In 1989, my father stepped in as director during this turbulent phase at the tender age of 19. His journey was one of resilience and repair, navigating bitter succession battles while rebuilding trust inside and outside the firm. Under his leadership, the business regained momentum with the establishment of a forging and foundry unit, followed by the introduction of iron and steel trading. From him, I learned that leadership in a family business is not only about growth but also about healing divisions and steadying the ship when legacy feels fragile.

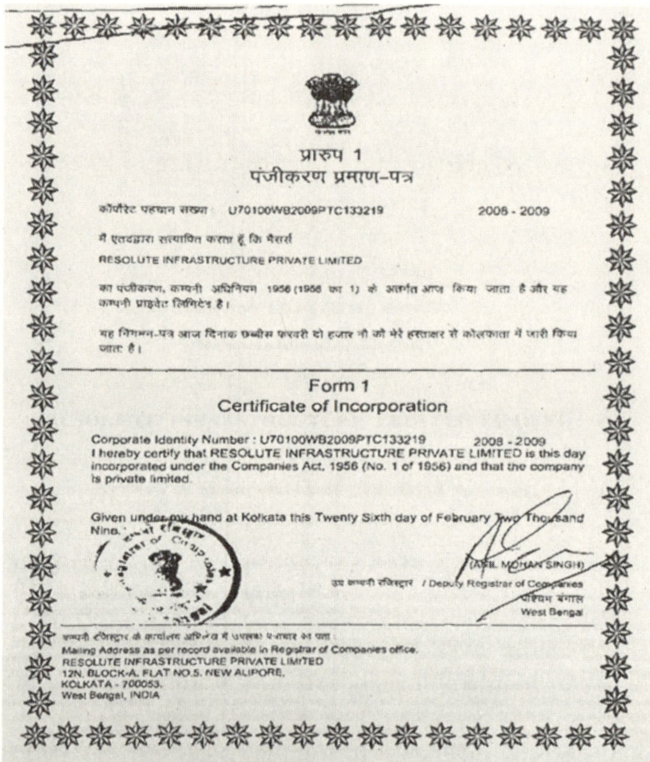

प्रारुप 1

पंजीकरण प्रमाण-पत्र

कॉर्पोरेट पहचान संख्या U70100WB2009PTC133219 2008 - 2009

RESOLUTE INFRASTRUCTURE PRIVATE LIMITED

Form 1

Certificate of Incorporation

Corporate Identity Number : U70100WB2009PTC133219 2008 - 2009

I hereby certify that RESOLUTE INFRASTRUCTURE PRIVATE LIMITED is this day incorporated under the Companies Act, 1956 (No. 1 of 1956) and that the company is private limited.

Given under my hand at Kolkata this Twenty Sixth day of February Two Thousand Nine.

(ANIL MOHAN SINGH)

/ Deputy Registrar of Companies

West Bengal

Mailing Address as per record available in Registrar of Companies office.

RESOLUTE INFRASTRUCTURE PRIVATE LIMITED

12N, BLOCK-A, FLAT NO.5, NEW ALIPORE,

KOLKATA - 700053.

West Bengal, INDIA

Certificate of Incorporation of Resolute Infrastructure Pvt. Ltd., now known as Jupiter Infraworks Pvt. Ltd

By 2009, it was clear that traditional manufacturing and trading in iron and steel had limited scope for expansion. The key lesson of that era was that diversification was not optional – it was essential for survival. With this conviction, our family launched Resolute Infrastructure Pvt. Ltd., entering the infrastructure and construction sector. Through our participation in the Pradhan Mantri Gram Sadak Yojana, we contributed to rural road construction, an experience that reinforced the importance of aligning business with national development goals. At the same time, we began developing small-scale residential and commercial properties, broadening our exposure and proving that adaptability could breathe new life into an old enterprise.

Since 2015, we have ventured into warehousing and industrial real estate, a step that reflected not just diversification but also anticipation of future demand. Developing one of the first gated commercial complexes in Howrah's manufacturing hub, spanning three acres with leased manufacturing and storage units, gave us a renewed sense of direction. This stage of our journey taught us that entrepreneurship in a family business is about building platforms for the next generation—spaces where they can innovate while still standing on the foundations laid before them. Alongside this, our ongoing residential and commercial projects reflect our conviction that steady, incremental growth supports both families and businesses.

Looking back, each generation of our business has been a teacher. The first generation showed us courage - the willingness to take risks and build from limited means. The second generation proved that goodwill from the past cannot excuse mistakes in the present. The third generation demonstrated resilience, finding opportunities even in the gravest adversities. As the fourth generation, I believe renewal comes through diversification and alignment with the nation's changing needs. And as I take on the mantle, I see my role as blending legacy with foresight: carrying the lessons of the past while preparing our business for the demands of the future.

Finding My Place in the Business

I cannot recall a single moment when I consciously decided to join the family business. Instead, it was a gradual realisation that came with age. Childhood dreams of becoming a superhero slowly gave way to more practical aspirations–doctor, lawyer, engineer, or police officer–and I, too, began to see my path clearly. From early on, I knew I would one day join the family enterprise and carry forward its legacy.

I began working actively in the business in 2023, shortly after graduating with my Bachelor's degree from St. Xavier's College, Kolkata. At first, I felt somewhat disillusioned, not because the business was underperforming, but because of its simplicity. I had imagined that a well-performing company would have more pomp and grandeur. Instead, my initial assignments felt tedious and monotonous, as they were designed to teach me the processes and help me familiarise myself with our workforce and stakeholders. All I wanted was to contribute more concretely and visibly to the business.

With time, however, the monotony faded as I began to understand the purpose behind these tasks. Since last year, I have been working more closely with my father on dynamic aspects of the business, such as future planning and ongoing litigation. This shift has been very motivating for me, as I now feel my skills are being better utilised for the benefit of the company.

What I value most is that, despite my youth and relative inexperience, my suggestions are not dismissed outright. They are heard, discussed, and considered seriously. I particularly appreciate this because my father and I have very different personalities and often hold contrasting views. Yet, we are able to set aside pride and weigh all options before deciding on what is best for the family and the business.

More recently, as I have had opportunities to share my vision for the future and seen those inputs positively received by family members, I have truly begun to feel that I am 'in business,' no longer just an observer, but an active contributor helping shape its direction.

The Delicate Art of Communication

One of the biggest challenges in family-run businesses, especially within the Indian cultural and household context, is communication. More specifically, it is about striking a balance between transparency and factual analysis, and sentiments and emotions. In other words, providing feedback, criticism, or opinions in a manner that is honest and transparent, yet respectful of the reverence owed not only to the older generation but also to long-serving employees who have worked closely with the family for decades.

In non-family businesses, structures and norms often require people to 'speak truth to power' without much hesitation. While diplomacy is part of every organisation, I feel it is far easier to maintain in non-personal environments where relationships are primarily professional. In family businesses, however, personal and professional ties are intertwined, which makes communication more delicate and layered.

That said, I count myself fortunate. Unlike in many family businesses where younger members hesitate to share their ideas because they feel their voices will not be heard, in my family, there is at least an open, two-way dialogue. I have seen bright younger generations in other families lose interest in management because they were sidelined. In my case, the challenge is far more desirable: I need to choose the right words at the right time to elicit the desired response.

A practice that has helped is the way major decisions in our family are seldom taken unilaterally. Even as a child, I recall essential conversations taking place at the dinner table. At that time, I could barely grasp the details, but the discussions left an impression. As I grew older, they began to make sense, and I found myself asking questions and engaging in discussions. These dinner table conversations became more than just recaps of what each family member had done; they evolved into a system of accountability and a way to foster empathy. Both working and non-working family members gained awareness of the company's challenges, as well as personal issues others might be facing, allowing everyone to plan and support each other more effectively.

To sum up, my challenge lies in striking a balance: as a member of the family business, I am expected to present my unbiased and honest opinions, but as part of the younger generation, I must also ensure that sentiments are respected and relationships are preserved.

The Role of Transparency in Turbulent Times

Given the nature of our business since my father took over, certainty and stability have become privileges we have only recently come to know. While we were always fortunate as a family to have our basic needs met, turbulence and risk became a regular part of life.

From my limited experience in life and business, I have learned that uncertainty and failure by themselves do not necessarily ruin morale. They are natural occurrences that everyone must face at some point. What truly hurts, in my opinion, is disappointment, especially when family members' expectations or ambitions cannot be realised due to a business setback they were unaware of. This disappointment often leads to bitterness and, at times, blame games within the family, where everyone feels equally aggrieved. Depending on the circumstances and who knew what in advance, the environment can quickly become strained.

One important lesson I have drawn from my parents is that transparency is essential in coping with such times. They had already lived through one downfall, largely caused by poor communication and reactions within the family. Since then, they made sure that whether family members were actively working in the business or not, everyone remained informed. I remember many evenings when my parents would sit my brother and me down after dinner and update us on what was happening in the business. At first, I didn't fully grasp why they did this. Later, I understood that it wasn't only to spark our interest in the business but also to prepare us for the immediate future and help us manage our expectations. This practice meant that even during turbulent times, disappointment was rare, and when it did occur, we were more empathetic toward what our parents were going through.

I firmly believe that in a family business, working members must sometimes put aside pride and openly share the business reality with everyone at home. While this may be uncomfortable initially, it fosters empathy, trust, and resilience. Cementing family bonds through transparency and mutual understanding, in my view, is the only way to survive and thrive in the face of uncertainty and failure.

Turning the Tide: Revival

Growing up, I often heard stories from relatives and family friends about how our business was once among the most prominent in the region, a great success story of its time, well-connected, and widely respected. In my mind, I came to think of that period as the 'glory days' of our family business. I became deeply interested in understanding both the growth and the decline that followed. I also consider myself fortunate to have witnessed firsthand how my father invested the better part of his life in reviving the business and keeping it alive.

Unlike many new ventures that grow from '0 to 1', our journey was closer to '-9 to 0', given the dire circumstances under which my father took over. Since then, we have grown steadily, with both progress and setbacks along the way—natural for any business. A turning point came in 2017 when our company finally became debt-free, and a long-standing partition suit was finally settled in our favour. From that moment, our true '0 to 1' journey began, built on three stable sources of income: a well-functioning warehousing and real estate business, alongside investments in new ventures.

Our 10-Year Vision: From 1 to 100

Looking ahead, I see the next 10 years as our '1 to 100' phase. With both my brother and me supporting my father, the business now has the strength and

Aerial snapshot of one of our pipelined projects in development

capacity to enter new markets and extend its presence beyond West Bengal. Within the next two years, we will establish a new warehousing complex in Odisha and launch small-scale residential and commercial projects under our own brand, Jupiter Infraworks.

Further, we are developing plans to enter the education sector, specifically in tier-2 cities, where we see strong potential for impact and growth.

My long-term vision is not only to scale the business but also to build an organisation that is sustainable, diversified, and respected—one that honours the legacy of our past while creating new opportunities for future generations.

The Emotional Landscape: The Ripple Effects on Relationships

In all honesty, my first year of working in the family business was a huge jolt to my social life. Unlike my friends and college batchmates who joined large conglomerates, where they found peers their own age to interact and bond with, I entered a very different environment, which at first felt suffocating. Although there were people my age in the organisation, a professional boundary always existed, and rightly so.

Another challenge was that I couldn't relate to the workplace issues and experiences my friends talked about, and they couldn't relate to mine. Gradually, as priorities shifted and schedules diverged, the gap between us widened.

What many people don't realise about working in a family business is how deeply intertwined your professional and personal lives become. Because we are so closely connected to decision-making, action plans, and outcomes, the work rarely leaves our minds, even after office hours have ended. And since we return home to family members who are also involved in the same business, whether on the same projects or different ones, maintaining a healthy work-life balance becomes even more difficult.

From Monotony to Motivation

When I first started, my days often felt weighed down by lethargy because of the monotonous nature of the work I was assigned. However, since mid-2024, as I have become more involved in the business's dynamic aspects, each day now carries a sense of excitement coupled with determination.

What helps me maintain a stable mindset through all this is, quite honestly, sticking to a disciplined personal schedule. Another key factor has been building a network of peers who are in the same situation. In this regard, the Family Business Management course at IIM Calcutta has been invaluable. Having people who can truly understand and relate to the challenges I face, and who share their own insights and experiences, has made a tremendous difference in keeping me motivated and grounded.

Building Trust Across Generations

At this stage, we have managed expectations and generational dynamics primarily through transparency. Being a smaller family unit makes open communication come more naturally. Still, we consciously ensure it extends to all facets, whether discussing plans and contingencies, clarifying expectations among one another, or examining whether those expectations are justified and feasible to fulfil.

We also maintain an open attitude toward mistakes. Accountability is shared, and the focus is always on solving the problem rather than assigning blame. This collective approach not only reduces conflict but also strengthens trust, making it easier to navigate both the emotional and practical balancing act that comes with a family business.

Is My Identity Tied to My Business?

Yes and no. A gradual awareness of our business profoundly shaped my childhood – what it was, where it was, and where it needed to go. A fundamental part of my character developed with the intention of reclaiming the status our family business once enjoyed. Since our identities are often shaped by the people and environment in which we grow up, it is only natural that mine became intertwined with the business.

For better or worse, the lines between family and business have always been blurred. That does not mean we are constantly working or that we don't spend time as a family. It simply means that we view work less as a conventional job and more as a shared responsibility, something akin to a family obligation. In that sense, it would be impossible for my identity not to be tied to the business.

At the same time, I do have parts of my life that remain separate from each other. Although such instances have become fewer since I started working, I still maintain friendships and circles where my identity is not linked to the business but to the bonds, experiences, and memories I share with those people.

Looking Ahead: Anticipating Challenges

Looking ahead, as we scale our business both vertically and horizontally, I anticipate challenges in finding the right talent to manage the new portfolios that will emerge. While we already have an organisational structure in place with clearly defined job roles and minimum qualifications, effective delegation and division of labour should not be an immediate hurdle. The real challenge lies in entering unfamiliar markets and identifying individuals who not only fit these roles but also uphold the company's integrity and long-term interests. This is an area we have already started preparing for.

Before formally entering any new market, we are making deliberate efforts to build networks and gain industry insights. By attending events organised by both private and government associations, we are better equipped to understand the ground realities and challenges. At the same time, these platforms give us opportunities to scout for talent and explore partnerships that could prove mutually beneficial.

The Balance Every Entrepreneur Needs: My Advice

I believe that, as entrepreneurs, whether in family-owned ventures or independent ones, it is very easy to get distracted from the accurate picture. With the constant inflow of information through various media, we often lose sight of who we really are and why we do what we do. It becomes tempting to measure our achievements through someone else's perspective instead of our own.

My advice would be to deliberately create moments in your schedule where you cut out the noise, retrace your steps, and remind yourself of your motivations and goals. Equally important is surrounding yourself with people you can be completely raw with, people who ground you, remind you of who you are, and help bring you back to the right place when you drift.

I also strongly believe in maintaining boundaries between the different facets of life, including career, relationships, and health. While it is easier said than done, segregation prevents one area from overwhelming the others. For example, just because you are going through a stressful period at work does not mean you should let it spill over into your relationships; similarly, strained relationships should not cause you to neglect your health. Protecting these boundaries enables you to remain balanced and resilient, regardless of the challenges that entrepreneurship presents.

—xxx—

FROM OUR FARM

-SINCE 1949-

Patanwala®

NOURISHING FAMILIES

MILK | DAIRY | SWEETS

Patanwala has been part of the dairy industry since 1949. Mr Taj Mohammed Patel, a first-generation entrepreneur, came from Patan, Gujarat, to Mumbai in 1935 and started the dairy business with just seven buffaloes. Over time, it has grown into an enterprise with over 2,000 animals, home to one of Asia's fully automated buffalo farms, a modern manufacturing unit, and one of the largest suppliers of farm-fresh milk catering to well-known brands.

It has been a journey of pride, progress, challenges, and resilience, and above all, of being together as a family business. Currently, Mr Junaid Patel, representing the fourth generation, is actively involved in the business along with his family, working hard to learn from the experience, business legacy, and earlier mistakes, and to take the family business to new heights.

This is not just a story of success, but of persistence, learning, and constant evolution, both personal and professional. It is about finding the right balance between tradition and transformation, and about building something that will continue to grow stronger for generations to come.

9

Milk from One Family to Many Families and Beyond

Junaid Patel

Our family business story began in 1935, when my great-grandfather (the first generation) moved from Patan, a city in northern Gujarat, to Mumbai. He started with a job at a farm and, after a few years, ventured into business with a few animals. His first attempt failed, forcing him to return to employment. But with the support of the farm owner, who gave him seven buffaloes, he tried again. This time, the business grew steadily, animal by animal, in the heart of Mumbai. In 1949, when the government established the Aarey Milk Colony to centralise dairy farming, our family relocated there, and we have remained there ever since.

My grandfather, after completing his MBA at Boston University, returned to India and entered the business as a second-generation participant. This was a daring step at a time when few people who studied abroad were willing to

My grandfather, Mohammed T. Patel (2nd generation), in Boston, USA, where he did his MBA in the 1960s

return to India. Despite the challenges at the time, he committed himself fully to the family business. Through his education, persistence, and hard work, he helped stabilise operations, expand the farms, and slowly increase our animal capacity.

Thereafter, the third generation, my father and uncles, joined the business. This occurred during a period of family and business separation, when my grandfather's brothers branched off into separate entities. That was a difficult and uncertain phase, which tested us on many fronts. The family structure, which has been the main support system, was now split. However, my grandfather's grit and vision gave us the strength to rebuild. My father and uncles brought fresh energy and modern ideas. They scaled the business significantly, introducing systematic processes and automation in farming, as well as manufacturing dairy products. This laid the foundation of the goodwill our brand enjoys today.

Seeds of Inspiration

I'm a fourth-generation member of our family business, and I officially joined after completing my twelfth grade. Before that, during vacations, I worked at our traditional stores, learning the basics of operations. Once I joined formally, I started from the ground up, working at the farm level, learning about animals, and understanding the daily processes. My routine began at 5 or 6 a.m. at the farms, followed by college. Later, I transitioned to factory operations, B2B sales, and eventually established my own retail chain.

My interest in business started in childhood. During school breaks, I would often join my father at farms and offices where my grandfather, uncles, and father worked together. I would observe their discussions and meetings quietly, which sparked my interest in business. Watching people come to consult my grandfather and engage in serious conversations left a deep impression on me. Growing up in an environment surrounded by business discussions and the respect my elders earned, I was inspired to follow the same path and contribute to our family business.

In 2020, the lockdown during the COVID-19 outbreak marked a turning point for us, forcing us to rethink our business model. That's when we launched 'Patanwala', as a B2C dairy retail brand. Since then, my role has evolved to leading the B2C side, overseeing operations and strategy.

I believe that any family business that survives into the third or fourth generation is built on strong principles, values, and a shared vision. For us, this has been our guiding force for decades. It is now my responsibility to uphold these values and pass them on to future generations. A family business legacy is a rare privilege, and we must honour and preserve it.

From Rookie to Responsibility

When you first step into a family business, it's a grind. You have to learn a lot, stay patient, and observe everything closely. It is not easy to find your voice at the table or become a true support to the management. No matter how impressive your degrees are, in the beginning, you're still just a rookie, and your opinions may not carry much weight.

In those early years, you often question yourself: *Is this really going to work? Am I cut out for this?* But over time, responsibilities start growing bit by bit, and you slowly become 'test-proven'. In a family business, everyone and everything will test you. And once you survive that phase, things begin to shift. You start to feel: *This is my role, this is my responsibility, and it's on me to deliver.*

For me, that turning point came a few years into our retail journey, after we had opened multiple stores. I realised that if I was assigned something, I had to complete it. If something wasn't working, it was on me to figure out why and fix it.

That was when accountability set in. Excuses weren't an option, and I pushed myself to take ownership of outcomes, regardless of self-doubt. Slowly, this built strength and trust. My opinions began to carry more weight, I was involved in bigger decisions, and I became a reliable force for the management.

That was when I could finally say to myself: *Yes, now I'm truly in business.*

Early Lessons, Later Learning

Although I wasn't formally trained in a specific area before stepping into the business, I was introduced to the business environment from an early age. As a child, I often accompanied my father to the farms and offices, and through casual discussions with my grandfather, father, and uncle, I gained an early sense of how the business functioned. I had the privilege of observing both the second and third generations build the business, which naturally shaped my understanding. It was also thanks to the mentoring of my father and uncles, who supported me and encouraged me to keep pushing ahead. Without them, it would have been difficult. That's the beauty of a joint family – we are one.

Later, I studied Business Management and enrolled in the Family Business Management programme at IIM Calcutta. Since it was an online course, it suited me well, as I was already deeply involved in the business and couldn't commit to a full-time programme. The course helped me gain new perspectives and apply structured frameworks to my real-world experiences.

In the meantime, I also invested time in reading business books, attending seminars, and engaging in online learning, especially during the lockdown. Although it was a tough time, these activities made it somewhat busy and enriching.

When B2B Collapsed, B2C was Born

One of the biggest operational challenges we faced was during the lockdown. Since most of our business was B2B, our major customers, like sweet manufacturers, ice cream makers, and other bulk buyers, had all shut down. This left us with large volumes of fresh milk every single day that we couldn't dispose. Our only option was to convert the milk into products with longer shelf life, such as butter and skimmed milk powder. But this came with added conversion and storage costs, and eventually these products had to be sold in the commodity market at a significant loss. Considering the scale of our daily production, these recurring losses, along with the capital tied up in unsold stock, felt like a nightmare.

This crisis unexpectedly became a pivotal moment in our business, reshaping everything. It forced us to re-evaluate our business model and rethink how to make the business more resilient. That's when we decided to launch our own B2C dairy retail brand. The idea was simple: If we are increasing our production capacity, we must also build our own consumption capacity. By creating a direct-to-consumer channel and retail presence, we ensured that our production had a steady outlet. More importantly, we have built a safeguard that enables us to better sustain ourselves in times of disruption.

Our First Retail Store

Our factory in Goregaon, a prime road-facing property in Mumbai, had always held the potential to become a store. The front space was even designed like one, but for years it remained shut. Many people encouraged us to open it, but we never fully focused on it. However, deep down, we always wanted to build our own retail stores and brand, something that truly represented who we are.

In 2021, we opened our first factory outlet in light of the COVID-19 business disruptions. We started small, with a limited product range, and weren't completely confident about how it would turn out. But the response exceeded all expectations. Customers loved the products and the branding. That gave us the confidence to believe in the concept and scale it further.

In less than two years, we grew from a single outlet to eight, then ten stores across Mumbai. Today, we operate fourteen stores in Mumbai. Although we have temporarily paused expansion due to capacity constraints, we have acquired a new property that will increase our production capacity by five to seven times. This will support the next phase of growth.

Our retail segment alone now employs around 80–100 people and serves nearly 2,000 guests daily. Across the organisation, we employ approximately

450 people and generate an annual revenue of ₹150–200 crore. What began as an uncertain step during a crisis has now become one of our strongest growth drivers and the foundation of a retail brand we are proud to build.

Our first retail store opened in 2021 – a bold step and a turning point for us

Trust That Stands Us Apart

The dairy industry is highly competitive, with both small local players and large national brands. For us, as a family-owned business, our biggest strength lies in the reputation, consistency, and trust we've built with customers over generations.

All our products come directly from our own farms, ensuring farm-fresh milk of the highest quality, something neither small participants nor large corporates can fully replicate. This farm-to-customer model is what sets us apart from others.

We focus on maintaining strict quality standards and driving continuous improvement throughout the entire value chain. Our prices may be slightly higher, but our customers, especially those who value quality, understand that the finest end products can only come from the best raw materials. That is where our advantage lies.

Milking parlour at our farm with buffaloes on both sides. They are washed and sanitised before milking. We follow an untouched milking process, transferring milk directly from clusters to coolers and chilling it to 4°C to preserve freshness and quality

Unique Realities of Family Businesses

Family-run businesses operate differently from non-family businesses because they involve not just professional roles but also personal relationships. In our firm, we follow a majority-voting system for decision-making. If two out of three members agree, the decision moves forward. Once it is made, everyone stands by it, regardless of whether they initially agreed or not. This ensures unity and eliminates blame or friction later.

Another key to smooth functioning is assigning each family member a dedicated responsibility or department. This way, everyone contributes individually while supporting the larger organisation. It also prevents interference in each other's roles, which can otherwise lead to conflict. Importantly, responsibilities should be assigned based on competence and capacity, rather than relationships.

Communication can also be tricky. At times, it can be difficult to give clear instructions to a family member, fearing that it may hurt their feelings. In the office, we maintain a professional attitude; outside, we are family. This distinction helps us to be clear, respectful, and work effectively.

Bouncing Back Stronger

Uncertainty and failures are a natural part of business and life. What truly matters is how quickly you can bounce back and focus on getting the game going again. The only way to win is to keep playing, not to stop when things get uncertain or when failures appear.

Whenever I face setbacks, I focus on what's right in front of me and get to work. As you continue to move forward, clarity returns, and the brighter side begins to emerge again. That is what keeps me going.

I don't believe in overthinking or procrastinating just because something didn't work out. What helps is pausing to reflect, then starting again with renewed strength. Progress comes when you choose to bounce back stronger every single time.

Margins, Growth, and Brand

I believe it is important to maintain a balance between margins, sales growth, and brand building. Margins are critical because they keep the business healthy and sustainable in the long run. Sales growth matters just as much, as it opens doors to new opportunities and markets. Brand building, meanwhile, goes beyond numbers and connects directly with our family's legacy. The stronger the brand we create, the greater the legacy we leave behind, and that in turn fuels growth and reputation.

Building Credibility Before Building Systems

One of the biggest mistakes I made early on was being too soft on people when it came to getting things done and ensuring accountability. Over time, I realised that as a responsible member of a family business, strong accountability and reporting systems are non-negotiable.

Initially, I overlooked this. As a result, the business objectives remained unfulfilled, and departmental goals were inconsistent, with low employee motivation. I learned the hard way that accountability should be a priority for any business leader.

In a family business, this challenge is even greater. When you're new, you don't always have authority or control. Many people in the organisation are older, more experienced, and have been with the company and the family for years. Getting them to report or be accountable isn't easy.

The only way to earn that authority is to first prove yourself – to the family and to the team – by showing that you can solve problems, think strategically, and, above all, be accountable yourself. That's how credibility and trust are built. Once that credibility comes, it becomes possible to put systems in place.

Our fully automated buffalo farm, spread across 15 acres of land, was established in 2007, with machinery imported from Europe

Success: Growth, Legacy, and Contribution

As a leader in the dairy industry, particularly in farm-fresh milk, I see success in helping the broader dairy farming community thrive. It is our responsibility to guide farmers, help them modernise their practices, and become more efficient and profitable. The quality of our products also thrives when the community thrives. While I aim to continually expand our family's portfolio, I understand that success is a long game.

Overall, I view success as a balance of growth, legacy, and contribution – creating a business that is often stronger than what we started with, while ensuring that our values, our name, and our purpose grow even stronger over time.

Finding Balance Between 'Family' and 'Business'

Running a business inevitably impacts personal life and relationships. It is essential for the family to understand and support the leader's vision. Only then can the leader have a significant impact on both the business and the family.

Many people see spending less time with family as a sacrifice, but I think it's about making that time count. The quality of time spent together must be the key. Neglecting it can eventually lead to breakdowns in both business and personal relationships.

As a young person entering the family business, I had to give up things my peers enjoyed – late nights, frequent parties, or endless outings with friends. At first, these felt like restrictions, but I came to see them as conscious choices that came with a sense of responsibility.

The key lies in structuring both life and business. Without systems, everything feels like a compromise, leading to frustration. However, with the right structure, you can manage time, energy, and focus in a way that supports business progress while also nurturing personal relationships and overall well-being.

Carrying the Legacy Daily

A normal day for me feels like a responsibility. There's always a thought running quietly in the background: *Am I doing enough for the legacy I carry?* It's not a burden, but a constant reminder of the purpose I'm working for. Alongside this responsibility is the belief that I'm building something meaningful that will last for generations.

Naturally, there are days when fatigue sets in, especially when progress feels slower than expected. Frustration also arises when I can see potential for faster growth, but certain decisions are beyond my control.

What recharges me most are the moments when the family comes together. Laughter, open discussions, or simply seeing everyone happy fills me with energy and a sense of satisfaction. These moments remind me why I do what I do.

But I've noticed something about myself: my comebacks are always stronger. After every low phase, I return with higher energy and sharper focus, almost as if I've undergone a reset. I believe this resilience stems from the positive environment around me and the deep motivation I derive from my purpose and family.

My Ways of Handling Stress

When things get really difficult, I tend to withdraw a little and manage them on my own. I don't usually open up much, though at times I share a bit with my partner. I have always been someone who prefers to handle situations independently, and that approach has stayed with me.

During such phases, I usually take a short break - a day or two away from everything. Changing the environment helps me breathe, reflect, and regain clarity in my thought process. Sometimes, I also share my thoughts with mentors or a select few close family members who understand my mindset well.

I've also realised that physical activity plays a big role in keeping me balanced. Whether it's working out, playing football, or engaging in any sport, it keeps me energised and motivated.

Leadership Philosophy and the Future Ahead

One of the biggest challenges ahead is to professionalise the business for long-term sustainability and scale. Incorporating technology is essential. As the third generation transitions out, succession will mean bringing in a professional attitude to ensure a sustainable and more successful business in the future.

To avoid stagnation, we must continually evolve our strengths and explore new opportunities. As part of the fourth generation, I'm also focused on developing leadership, people management, and strategic thinking, while grooming both family members and employees to grow together.

Our growth so far has been steady but slow due to limited systemisation and professionalisation. I believe the way forward is to establish clear processes and data-driven systems that enable faster, more accurate decision-making and better alignment with our goals.

Bringing in professionals and giving them the right environment to perform is key. For our generation, implementing these systems is vital for long-term success. Growth becomes meaningful when individual aspirations align with business objectives, and nurturing both is central to my leadership approach.

Looking ahead, I envision Patanwala becoming a recognized retail brand in the dairy space while expanding beyond Mumbai into Pune, Nashik, and Surat. We aim to integrate dairy tech and sustainability into our operations to enhance efficiency and reduce waste. The journey of professionalising and structuring the business has already begun, marking a clear shift toward a scalable, data-driven, and sustainable future.

Advice for the Next Generation

If I had to offer some honest advice to a new generation already in the business or planning to join soon, it would be this: things are going to be very challenging, and everything you have will be tested. That's why the first step is to leave your ego behind; ego creates barriers, slows down progress, and prevents collaboration. In a family business, success cannot be about 'me' or 'you,' but about 'us.'

Always keep an open mind. When people give feedback or raise complaints, don't take it personally – instead, see it as guidance and an opportunity to improve. The faster you accept this, the less time you'll waste.

Patience is essential. Young entrepreneurs often desire quick results, but business rarely works that way. Success requires consistency and persistence. It's also important to view the business holistically, avoiding a narrow focus on a single department, product, or process; always keep the bigger picture in mind.

Furthermore, having a clear vision and a mentor can make all the difference. Knowing what you want to achieve helps create the path toward it. Without a vision and guidance, the journey can feel endless and aimless. Writing down your vision allows you to realign yourself whenever you feel lost.

Lastly, don't chase perfection. It's a myth. Waiting for everything to be flawless before starting is unnecessary – being 60–80% ready is often enough. You can always improve and adapt as you go. Remember, progress matters far more than perfection.

—xxx—

10

Inheritance of Passion

SUKRUTHI SANJAY

The story of our business began in 1932, when my great-grandfather, Late Shri H.N. Lingappa Setty, laid the foundation for what would become one of the most enduring and respected bicycle establishments in Mysore. With remarkable foresight, he recognised the growing fascination with bicycles, introduced under the British influence and swiftly embraced by both the working class and the elite. Acting on this vision, he opened the first-ever bicycle showroom in the Kingdom of Mysore.

The location of this establishment gave it a significance beyond commerce. Standing proudly in front of two of the city's greatest landmarks, the Mysore Palace and the Silver Jubilee Clock Tower, inaugurated by Motilal Nehru, the

GOVERNMENT OF MYSORE.

"STORESTC", 20478 — Office of the Secretary, Stores Purchase Committee, Bangalore, dated 31st Decr. 1942 6th Jan. 43

OFFICIAL MEMORANDUM.

The name of Messrs. Sharada Cycle Stores, Lansdown Buildi[illegible] Mysore. is included in the list of approved firms for the supply of stores to Mysore Government Departments under the headings "Bicycles and Accessories".

By Order,

Secretary,
Stores Purchase Committee.

1943, Pre-Independence Era: Official memorandum from the Government of Mysore recognising our establishment as the first ever showroom in the Bicycles & Accessories segment of the Kingdom

showroom soon became a landmark in its own right. As the only showroom of its kind in the Kingdom, people from across the region flocked here to purchase bicycles that symbolised progress and freedom.

Over time, the store has become deeply woven into the city's identity. Families have returned generation after generation, sharing stories of how their parents and grandparents had bought their first bicycles from us. This continuity has created an emotional bond that has extended beyond mere transactions. Just as generational value lives within our family and business, it has also lived within the families who have trusted us through the decades.

A Royal Connection

My great-grandfather's pioneering spirit was honoured in a historic way when he was invited to teach Sri Jayachamarajendra Wadiyar, the last ruling king of Mysore, how to ride a bicycle. For this contribution, he received formal recognition and honours from the kingdom's government, an extraordinary moment that forever tied our family's story to Mysore's history.

Middle: My Great-Grandfather (Founder) Late Shri H.N. Lingappa Setty honoured by the Mysore Kingdom for teaching the art of Cycling to Sri Jayachamarajendra Wadiyar, the last ruling King of Mysore.

The Second Generation: Carrying the Torch

As the years passed, the responsibility of nurturing the enterprise fell upon the second generation. My grandfather, Late Shri Premkumar, along with

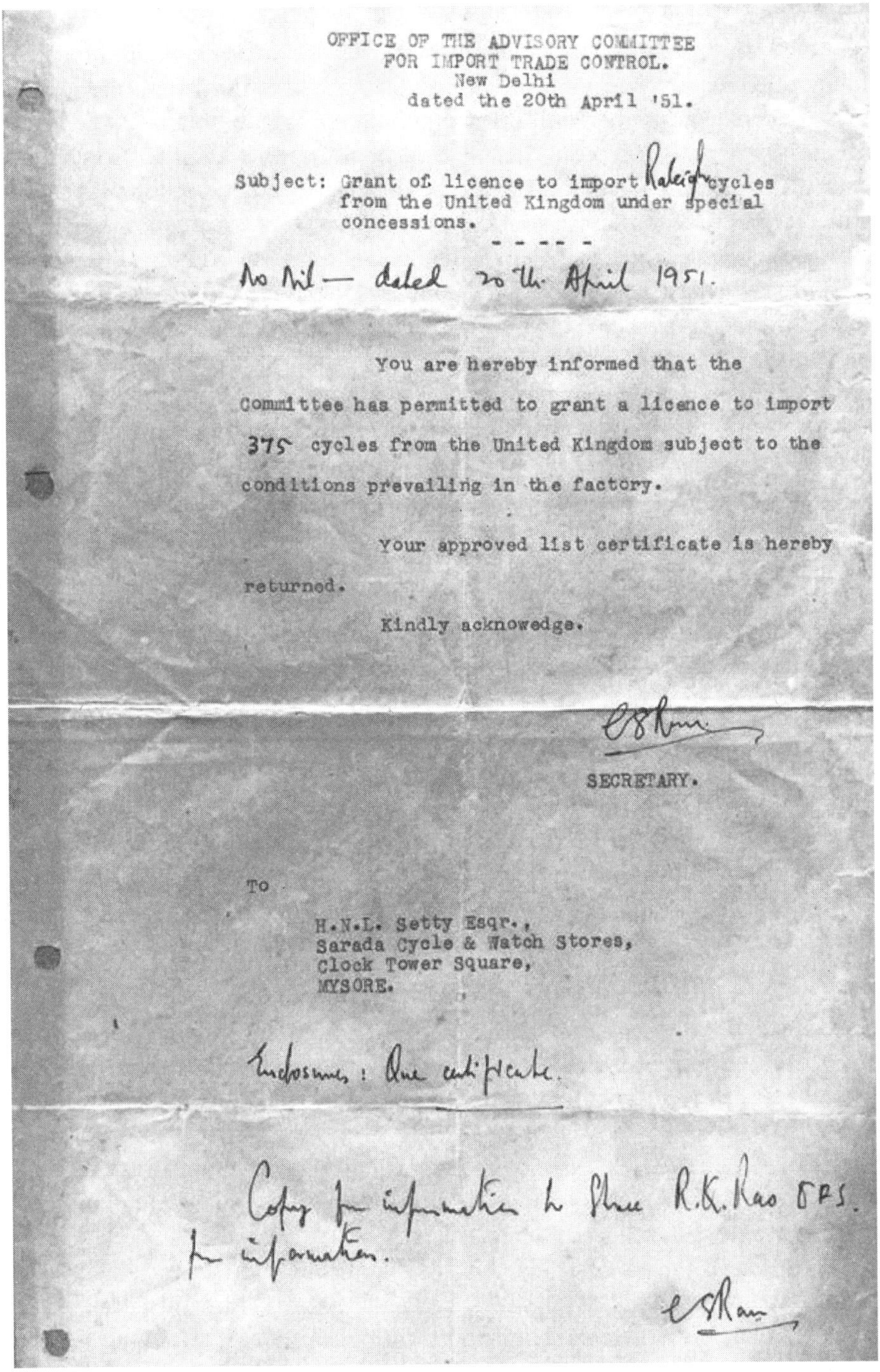

OFFICE OF THE ADVISORY COMMITTEE
FOR IMPORT TRADE CONTROL.
New Delhi
dated the 20th April '51.

Subject: Grant of licence to import Raleigh cycles from the United Kingdom under special concessions.

- - - - -

No Nil — dated 20th April 1951.

You are hereby informed that the Committee has permitted to grant a licence to import 375 cycles from the United Kingdom subject to the conditions prevailing in the factory.

Your approved list certificate is hereby returned.

Kindly acknowedge.

SECRETARY.

To

H.N.L. Setty Esqr.,
Sarada Cycle & Watch Stores,
Clock Tower Square,
MYSORE.

Enclosures: One certificate.

Copy for information to Shree R.K. Rao OPS.
for information.

1951 – Importer License from the Government of India to import Raleigh Cycles from the United Kingdom his brothers, carried the legacy forward with dedication. While his brothers eventually pursued other ventures, my grandfather's foresight was unmatched. In the mid-1970s, when many doubted the future of cycling, he stood firm in his belief that India's vast and diverse population would always create space for cycles, whether as a means of transport or a lifestyle choice. His conviction kept the business rooted during uncertain times and prepared it for growth when new opportunities arose.

The challenges he faced were immense, ranging from financial struggles, the burden of managing operations alone and the uncertainties of a changing market. Yet his resilience never faltered. With quiet strength, he transformed hardships into stepping stones and made the toughest battles look effortless, always carrying a smile that inspired those around him. His unshakable spirit not only kept the business alive but also laid a strong foundation for the next generation. He became the greatest pillar of support to my great-grandfather, ensuring that the business was well-positioned for growth.

By the mid-19th century, under my grandfather's stewardship, the business had grown into a name synonymous with trust across the state. We were the sole importers of bicycles from Birmingham until the 1970s, introducing some of the finest models from the United Kingdom to Indian customers.

Our showroom proudly held exclusive dealerships for iconic brands such as Sun Raleigh, Hero, BSA Hercules, Dunlop, Humber and Ridge. We were also the first to introduce imported accessories to Karnataka, setting new standards for the cycling industry. Such leadership did not go unnoticed: our family was invited to historic occasions such as the foundation stone ceremonies of TI Cycles (Murugappa Group – Tube Investments of India) and Raleigh, honours that reflected the respect and influence our enterprise commanded within the cycling fraternity.

The Third Generation: A New Era

The torch was then passed to the third generation, led by my father, Mr P. Sanjay, whose vision propelled the business into a new era of expansion. In 2008, he spearheaded the opening of what was then the largest cycle showroom in South India, a bold move that redefined both scale and customer experience in the industry. By 2012, he once again broke new ground, making us one of the earliest retailers to branch into multiple stores and setting benchmarks for organised cycle retail.

However, his most defining move was yet to come. At a time when most dealers were still struggling to expand within their own cities, my father dared to look beyond Mysore and set his sights on Bangalore. Many questioned the decision, warning of the risks, but he stood unwavering in his conviction. He not only established a strong presence in a competitive market but also developed his own systems and processes, enabling the business to run efficiently across multiple cities. Those Standard Operating Processes (SOPs), born out of his courage and foresight, continue to guide us today, binding every store in unison and standing as proof that true vision is about seeing possibility where others see only risk.

Our tradition of 'firsts' continued on. In 2020, we unveiled an 8,000 square-foot flagship showroom, once again the largest in South India. This milestone reaffirmed our position as the destination where every leading cycling brand entering India aspired to be showcased.

These years marked not just growth, but also transformation, as the business adopted modern retail practices while remaining firmly rooted in its traditional values. My father envisioned the stores not merely as points of sale, but as experiences, spaces where every customer felt personally connected to their purchase. Long before marketing experts began speaking of customer experience and personalisation, he was already living that philosophy.

Today, we are recognised not only as one of the biggest bicycle retailers in India but also as a living institution. What began as one man's foresight in 1932 has grown into a story of heritage carried through generations. Today, our legacy is not only a symbol of Mysore's history but also a pillar of India's cycling fraternity, standing tall as one of the greatest family business stories in the trade.

My father's vision was never limited to adding value for customers. He also built a workforce that has now become our extended family. They are as much a part of this establishment as we are, having poured their heart and soul into its growth, often with the same tireless dedication, never once glancing at the clock. Many of them joined even before my father's era and continue to stand by us today, working alongside me, as they once worked alongside him. Their loyalty and commitment have become the unseen strength behind our success, and they remain the true pillars of our institution.

Serving Icons of Industry and Society

Over the years, our clientele has grown to include some of the most distinguished names across various industries, including Infosys, Ideal Jawa Factory, Automotive Axle, Meenakshi Sundaram Textiles, and hospitality leaders such as Serai Resorts, Mahindra Resorts, Evolve Back Resorts, and Jungle Lodges. These enduring associations stand as a testament to the trust we have earned and the reputation we uphold as one of India's foremost bicycle retailers.

Apart from the esteemed clientele who have been part of our decades-long journey, our story is also deeply interwoven with the people of Mysore. One in every few families here has at some point in their lives, been our customer, making us not just a store, but a part of their family history too. For Mysoreans, there is hardly anyone who does not know where we are or what we stand for. Our name has become synonymous with the city itself, a presence as familiar as the landmarks that surround us.

Top: Our Founder, My great grandfather, Late Shri H.N. Lingappa Setty, First Generation; Left: My Grandfather Late Shri Premkumar, Second Generation; Right: My Father, Mr P. Sanjay, Third Generation

The Fourth Generation: My First Steps

My journey into the family business began during my college years, though at first, I did not fully grasp its importance. For me, it was just a part-time involvement, something that fit around my education. What I did not realise then was that this involvement was the first step towards inheriting not just a business, but a legacy. It was my parents who opened my eyes to this truth. They reminded me that very few people are given such an opportunity, and that it was not merely about running a venture, but about carrying forward a dream and a responsibility larger than myself.

In the beginning, I was unsure of my place in the business. Growing up in a city with conservative views, I had rarely seen women take leadership roles in business. This absence of role models made me question whether I truly belonged in that world. My parents, however, stood firm against such stereotypes. In a society where many still believed that women could not go far in business, they chose to bring their daughters into the fold. They defended that decision with pride, making it clear that gender would never limit one's potential. For my sister and me, this was more than an act of courage; it was a lifelong lesson in equality and conviction.

Encouraged by their faith, I began working in the business at the age of eighteen. What started as a tentative step soon became my greatest teacher, providing me with opportunities to make decisions and take on responsibilities early on. The lessons went beyond finance or operations. They taught me resilience, problem-solving and the confidence to lead with both values and accountability.

Turning Points

In 2020, we introduced the idea of concept stores, deciding that every future showroom would carry a distinct identity, so that anyone who saw it would instantly recognise it as ours. Though the concept was relatively new, we brought it to life quickly by transforming an old house into a modern showroom. Even today, that store continues to turn heads, standing out as a landmark in its own right. Its unique presence has also drawn attention from across the country, with new companies eager to associate themselves with it.

For many years, my role in the business was limited to managing one store. Though it gave me responsibility and independence, it also kept me away from the larger canvas of our enterprise. I was efficient with day-to-day operations, yet my exposure remained narrow. The real transformation occurred in 2022, when I began working closely under my father's guidance. For the first time, I stepped into the broader world of business, managing multiple stores, learning the intricacies of operations, and experiencing what it truly meant to be *in business.*

Under his mentorship, I was part of the decisions. Each responsibility pushed me to grow, teaching me how to remain steady under pressure and act with conviction even in uncertain times. In that process, I discovered that leadership is not about avoiding challenges but about facing them with courage and guiding others with clarity.

The greatest lesson has been resilience, learning to adapt quickly, balancing the demands of business with personal life, and recognising time management as vital as strategy. Today, the business is more than a livelihood; it is a living story that connects me to the vision and struggles of those before me. That foundation eventually led me to IIM Calcutta, where I honed my skills and prepared myself to carry our legacy into the future, not just managing a company, but ensuring the next chapter is stronger than the last.

In 2025, with the changing times, we diversified further, expanding our presence with new stores, entering the EV scooter market, and strengthening our toddlers' range, a segment we see immense potential in. These form

Left: My Younger Sister, Surachitha S– Fourth Generation;
Middle: My Father, P Sanjay – Third Generation;
Right: Myself, Sukruthi Sanjay – Fourth Generation

our short-term goals, but our long-term vision reaches further. We aim to establish a strong online presence that leverages the credibility we have earned over generations, providing doorstep service and meeting the rapidly growing demand for online purchases. We also envision Sharada Cycles evolving into a company supported by multiple investors, backing our ideas and fueling future growth. Above all, we look forward to our centenary in 2032, a hundred years of legacy, resilience and impact. It will be more than a celebration, it will be our chance to leave a lasting mark on the city, just as our founder did a century ago.

Building Trust Across Generations

Like most family-run businesses, the transition between generations is a delicate process. Such legacies are carefully guarded, and stepping into that space is never easy. It is like entering a house lovingly built brick by brick; you cannot simply walk in and take over - you must prove that you will embrace it, protect it, and strengthen its foundations.

For me, this transition meant gradually earning my father's trust. Not his affection, he always gave that generously, nor his encouragement, which was constant. What I sought was his confidence that my sister and I could run the enterprise responsibly, without needing his involvement in every small decision. This did not happen overnight. There was no dramatic gesture of passing the torch. Instead, it was a slow process that unfolded through daily actions. Each decision became an opportunity to demonstrate that we saw the business not as an inheritance but as a responsibility we were prepared to carry forward.

What we experienced is not unique. This is the reality of many family businesses where the balance between respecting tradition and proving one's own capability is never simple. Yet, when that balance is achieved, trust becomes the strongest foundation on which to build the future.

The Need for Balance

The ripple effect of being in a family business extends far beyond the showroom floor or the balance sheet; it touches every corner of life. For me, one of the constant challenges has been finding balance between the demands of business and the time needed for myself, my hobbies, and my relationships. Running a family enterprise is deeply rewarding, but it often blurs the boundaries between the personal and the professional.

Over the years, we realised that to truly sustain and grow, the business could not rely solely on one individual. It had to be built on strong processes, capable teams and systems that could function smoothly even in our absence. This realisation pushed us to introduce better Standard Operating Procedures

(SOPs) and explore automation, creating space for us to pursue new ventures, nurture personal connections and view the bigger picture without feeling that stepping away meant neglect.

This shift also reshaped my approach to leadership. Delegation, once difficult, became central to growth. Trusting others with responsibility not only freed my time but also gave my team the confidence to lead, solve problems and grow with the company. Yet there are moments when the long hours and constant demands feel overwhelming. At such times, I have learned the importance of taking a step back. Sometimes that means retreating to nature to restore my clarity. At other times, meditation and spirituality ground me, reminding me that success is not only about profits or expansion but also about inner peace and the ability to endure.

In those quiet moments, I often think of the generations before me, their patience, sacrifice, and unshakable perseverance. They worked long hours, faced financial pressures and made countless sacrifices, often without complaint. Their quiet strength humbles me and reminds me that true success is not about avoiding challenges but about meeting them with dignity, courage, and responsibility.

Finding Passion in a 'Normal' Day

A normal day in a family business feels anything but ordinary. Every choice, whether seemingly small or undeniably pivotal, adds to a mountain of experiences. Far from routine, my days are driven by curiosity and excitement, because I never quite know what new challenge will unfold next. Every day in the business brings me into contact with different personalities, each interaction carrying its own lesson on how to navigate situations, not just in business, but in life itself. These daily encounters have become a source of constant learning, shaping perspectives that I know will influence every decision I make, both now and in the future.

Of course, there are also days filled with mistakes. Yet even those have become part of my education. Each misstep adds to the foundation of my learning, and with my father's patient guidance, I am steadily learning how to turn them into stepping stones. His ability to correct with grace while allowing me the space to grow has been one of the most valuable lessons I have learned.

What makes this experience truly fulfilling is the transformation of my relationship with the family enterprise. What once began as a responsibility has steadily grown into my passion. I no longer find myself watching the clock; the hours slip by almost unnoticed because they are purposeful and deeply engaging. I often think back to my childhood, watching my father burn the midnight oil. I would wonder why he worked so tirelessly, often long into the night. At the time, I couldn't understand his devotion. Today, standing in his shoes, I realise that once a business becomes your passion, it ceases to feel like work. It becomes a calling, one that no distraction and no obstacle can take away.

This journey is shaping me into a woman I never thought I would become. The lessons are countless, but the greatest of them all has been discovering the zeal to pursue something wholeheartedly. Our business has unlocked an ambitious side of me that, perhaps, had always been there, quietly waiting to come alive. That, to me, is what makes even a 'normal' day extraordinary.

The Weight of Expectations

Managing expectations in a family business has been and will always remain one of my greatest challenges. What began as a modest establishment decades ago has, over time, evolved into a legacy built by three generations of visionaries. There is an unspoken weight that comes with being part of a family enterprise. I am watched not only by my family but also by friends, peers and the larger community. My name is no longer just a name; it is an identity tied to our enterprise.

In such an environment, innovation, growth and continuity become expectations, benchmarks against which my role and contributions are constantly measured. Every decision I make carries implications not only for the business but also for the family reputation that surrounds it. Adding to these expectations is the unique challenge of being a woman in the business world. The balance between personal responsibilities and professional ambition often feels like walking a tightrope. There are moments when tradition pulls one way and the demand for change pushes the other.

During discussions about business, I have often been required to prove myself twice over, once as a business leader and again as a woman in leadership. Yet, these very challenges have strengthened me and taught me to be firm without losing compassion. This belief transforms responsibility into motivation. It reminds me that I am not walking this path alone but with the strength of generations behind me, guiding me as I navigate today's complexities and tomorrow's uncertainties.

Shaping the Future

How far I take our family legacy forward, only time will tell. However, one thing is certain. My commitment to honouring the past remains unshakable. For me, legacy is not about clinging to what was, nor is it about discarding tradition in pursuit of the new. It is about continuity with change, preserving the values that built the foundation while adapting to the realities of a changing world.

This is the story I live every day: one of Resilience, Responsibility, Renewal and most importantly *Passion*. And it is the story I hope to hand over, stronger, richer and more meaningful, to the next generation.

—xxx—

Heera Business Group is a diversified family enterprise with a strong presence across retail, construction, hospitality, pharmaceuticals, and consumer goods. They are driven by a commitment to excellence, ethics, and progress.

Mr Pranav Ravindra Chaudhari, since joining Heera Business Group as Director in 2018, has focused on bringing a modern and growth-driven approach while staying true to the values and vision that have built the legacy of the company.

At Heera, he oversees the alcobev (alcoholic beverage) division, managing the entire value chain from imports and distribution to retail and experiential formats. His goal has always been to strengthen operations and foster brand partnerships. Over time, they have evolved from being a traditional trading company into a forward-thinking organisation rooted in professionalism and innovation.

He believes that success is built through people, relationships, and clarity of purpose. His leadership philosophy is grounded in collaboration, creativity, and taking action, ensuring that every decision fosters growth and builds trust.

11

Lessons of a Young Heir

Pranav Chaudhari

What has always inspired me to become an entrepreneur is my family and the legacy they built. Business runs in my blood. My grandfather laid the first foundation stones of Heera Business Group with a vision to provide quality and reliability to customers while creating opportunities for the family and community. He believed in hard work, integrity, and the idea that business is not just about transactions, but about relationships and reputation. My father and uncles carried that torch forward, expanding into multiple industries, from alcobev (alcoholic beverage) distribution and retail to construction, sugar factory, hospitality, pharmaceuticals, and imports. Beyond diversification, each expansion focused on seizing opportunities with foresight and hard work.

Where our legacy began: Hotel Heera Palace

I pursued a Bachelor's in Business Administration (Entrepreneurship) from ISME, which gave me a strong academic foundation in entrepreneurship, strategy, and management. That formal education helped me understand business in theory, and global perspectives on how businesses are built and scaled.

I formally decided to join the family business in March 2018. Growing up, I had always been surrounded by business. It was the language of our home. The discussions at home shaped my mindset and gave me an early sense of responsibility. But the turning point came when I realised that the legacy my grandfather and father had built wasn't just an enterprise, it was a responsibility. I wanted to contribute to that story, not as an outsider, but as the next generation who could carry it forward.

By the time I joined the business, I had received both structured entrepreneurial education from ISME and the hands-on mentorship that comes only from being deeply involved in a family enterprise. That blend of formal and informal training shaped the way I approach decisions today, with both strategy and instinct.

By the time I stepped in, our liquor industry arm had already become a strong pillar. My inspiration came from seeing how each generation had added something unique and distinct. I felt it was my turn to build on that, to modernise, innovate, and take the business into new spaces, like premium imports, nascent hospitality concepts, or exploring international opportunities. My decision, although shaped by our family legacy, is guided by my ambition to evolve the business for the future.

The first load of sugarcane, the first prayer, the start of a sweet revolution

Sealing a Legacy, Scaling New Heights

The moment I truly felt I was 'in business' was about a year after I joined in 2018. Until then, I was learning and absorbing the workings of our group. The shift came when I took ownership of an import deal under Yash Wines Pvt Ltd, negotiating with international suppliers, aligning distribution, and ensuring the products reached our stores and bars. The first time I saw those bottles being poured at a bar, enjoyed by customers, it struck me that this was no longer just my grandfather's or father's business, it had become mine, too.

At the same time, I began to see the tangible impact of my decisions. Sales were growing, our distribution became more efficient, and our retail outlets began to reflect a new energy. That gave me the conviction that I could bring my own vision into the family legacy and make it work. It was then that I stopped seeing myself as someone 'joining' the business and started seeing myself as someone building it further. From that point on, I knew I was fully committed to this path.

Challenges of Liquor Distribution in India

The liquor industry in India is one of the most complex to operate in. Our biggest challenges are regulatory, with each state having its own licensing rules, taxation structures, and frequent policy shifts that slow down operations. Logistics is another hurdle. Managing distribution across districts means even minor delays or transport issues can disrupt the entire chain.

Financially, upfront excise payments combined with long retail credit cycles create pressure, while shifting consumer demand toward premium and international labels requires constant adaptation.

These challenges are demanding, but they've also made us more resilient, pushing us to build stronger compliance systems, modernise logistics, and diversify our portfolio to stay competitive.

Competing with Strategy and Consistency

Competition in the alcobev industry is intense, with both established domestic players and global brands fighting for consumer attention. We manage this pressure by focusing on three pillars: relationships, portfolio, and consistency.

First, our distribution strength is built on long-standing relationships with suppliers, retailers, and customers. These ties, developed over decades, give us resilience against market shifts. Furthermore, we continually adapt our portfolio—from mass-market staples to premium imports—to meet the evolving preferences of our consumers. This ensures we are relevant across segments, from retail to high-end hospitality. Finally, we believe in consistency. In an industry where delays or lapses can result in lost market share, our focus on reliable supply, compliance, and service gives us a competitive edge.

Competition will always exist, but our approach is to outlast it by being trusted, adaptive, and future-focused.

Managing Relationships with Professionalism

Being a family-run business comes with both advantages and unique challenges. One of the challenges is striking a balance between tradition and modern practices. We carry a strong legacy, and with it come expectations from within the family as well as from the outside. Decisions are not just financial. They are emotional because every choice reflects on the family's name and history.

Another challenge is governance. In non-family businesses, decisions often follow a strict corporate hierarchy, but in family businesses, leadership roles and responsibilities can overlap. Aligning the perspectives of different generations, from conservative risk-taking to modern growth ambitions, requires constant communication and trust.

At the same time, succession planning is critical. Ensuring continuity while giving the next generation room to innovate is not always easy.

These challenges make us sharper, because they push us to professionalise our systems while retaining the family values that built our business.

Rising Above Internal Roadblocks

The most formidable challenge I have faced so far was a severe cash flow crunch resulting from poor decisions made by the previous management. Funds were blocked, receivables were delayed, and instead of solving the problem collectively, egos within management made decision-making even slower. For me, as the younger generation stepping in, it was baffling to see how internal hurdles could sometimes be more challenging than external competition.

Navigating that phase required both patience and firmness. I focused on improving collections, tightening credit control, and streamlining expenses. More importantly, I aimed to change the culture, replacing ego-driven decisions with transparent discussions and data-driven choices. It wasn't easy, but slowly we rebuilt trust internally and confidence externally.

That period, although difficult, proved to be one of my most significant learning experiences. It taught me that for a leader in a family-run business, navigating emotions, aligning people, and turning setbacks into learnings are just as important as growth and strategy.

Betrayal into Breakthrough

Another low point in my journey came when someone very close to us, a relative and trusted manager who had handled a significant part of our distribution business, betrayed our trust. He embezzled funds and even attempted to start his own firm, trying to take away the very brands we had worked so hard to build relationships with. For a family-run business, the emotional blow was as heavy as the financial one.

However, that betrayal also served as a wake-up call. We tightened governance, brought more transparency into our operations, and rebuilt direct relationships with our supplier partners to ensure loyalty stayed with us. It forced us to professionalise systems that had earlier relied too heavily on trust alone.

In hindsight, what felt like a personal and professional setback actually strengthened the foundation of our business. It taught me that while trust is essential, controls and accountability are equally critical in sustaining a business.

Reflection and Resilience

For me, uncertainty and failure are part of the entrepreneurial journey, but that doesn't mean they don't take an emotional toll. When faced with setbacks, whether it's financial pressure, regulatory hurdles, or even betrayal, my first instinct is to pause and reflect, rather than reacting impulsively. I have learned that clarity emerges when you give yourself space to process, rather than letting stress dictate your decisions.

My coping mechanism has always been balance. I ground myself in fitness, travel, and spending time with close family, which helps me detach from immediate pressures. Spiritually, I remind myself that every failure is temporary and often a stepping stone to growth. Most importantly, I focus on learning. I ask: What is this failure teaching me? How can I adapt? That shift from self-blame to problem-solving keeps me steady.

Entrepreneurship comes with uncertainty every day, but I handle it by combining emotional resilience with a problem-solving mindset, accepting that not everything can be controlled, but everything can be learned from.

Financial Management

I believe that it is important to maintain a balance between sales growth, margins, and brand building. Sales growth is essential because it enables the business to expand and motivates its teams. Margins are crucial for sustainability because, without profitability, even growth loses meaning. And brand building is what ensures we remain relevant and competitive in the long run.

What matters most to me is the quality of growth. I don't just want numbers on paper. I want profitable growth that aligns with our brand identity and adds long-term value to the legacy my family has built. That's why I pay attention to all three factors, but I weigh decisions by asking: Will this strengthen our foundation in five or ten years?

In short, I see finances not just as numbers, but as a reflection of balance, between short-term results and long-term vision.

Measuring Business Health Beyond Just Numbers

In our business, I focus on a mix of liquidity, profitability, and efficiency metrics. Cash flow is the lifeline in liquor distribution, so I closely track working capital cycles and days sales outstanding (DSO), ensuring receivables don't stretch too long, as excise duties are always due upfront.

I also monitor gross margins and net profit margins to understand how well we're balancing volumes with profitability, especially in a high-tax, low-margin industry. Return on investment (ROI) and inventory turnover are equally critical, as holding too much stock can tie up cash in a regulated market.

From a long-term perspective, I closely monitor the debt-to-equity ratio to ensure we're not over-leveraged, and I also track EBITDA margins as a measure of operational efficiency.

These ratios together provide a clear picture, not just of growth on paper, but of the actual financial health and sustainability of the business.

Liquidity Today, Growth Tomorrow

In distribution and retail, short-term financial discipline is critical. Cash flow, receivables, and margins decide whether operations run smoothly, excise duties must be paid upfront, retailers often work on credit, and margins are already thin. If these aren't managed tightly, even a large business can face a crunch.

At the same time, I don't see the business only in terms of daily numbers. Long-term growth comes from building strong brand portfolios, investing in premium and international labels, and modernising our retail experience so that customers see us as more than just a shop, but as a trusted destination.

I balance the two by making short-term discipline the foundation for long-term ambition. Healthy cash flow allows me to confidently invest in expansion, new districts, new retail formats, and stronger brand relationships.

For me, short-term and long-term are not opposites, they are two sides of the same coin.

Early Mistakes, Lasting Lessons

When I first took charge of our liquor imports and distribution, I made the classic mistake of believing that spending more automatically meant building faster. I invested heavily in expensive software systems we didn't really need, overspent on tools and services that weren't aligned with our ground realities, and spread resources into projects we never completed. At the time, I thought I was modernising the business, but in fact, I was burning cash without a return.

The other mistake was not following through on specific initiatives. We would start with big plans, whether a marketing push, a technology adoption, or a new import line, but without structured follow-up, those investments would often sit there, half-done, draining capital and time. That lack of discipline taught me that money and energy are only as valuable as the execution behind them.

The lesson I will never forget is that efficiency, and not spending, is of utmost importance in business growth. Every rupee has to work as hard as we do. Now I evaluate investments with sharper discipline–if it doesn't solve a real problem or generate tangible value, we don't pursue it. That early failure gave me a lasting principle: focus, finish, and measure everything. No distractions, no vanity spending.

Defining Success – People at the Core

Success goes far beyond profit. Growing up in a joint family business, I saw firsthand that true wealth lies in values, relationships, and the ability to build something lasting together. My family's journey taught me that success also includes the growth of others alongside you.

I define success as a balance of four things:

1. Family Legacy – protecting and growing what my elders built, while shaping a new chapter that future generations can inherit with pride. Success is when my work honours my family's name and adds to it.
2. People First – the heart of any business is its people. If our employees are happy, loyal, and feel valued, then we have truly succeeded. The same applies to business partners. Long-term, respectful, and trustworthy relationships are more important than one-time wins.
3. Luxury & Lifestyle – I do believe success should be enjoyed. To me, it means creating a life where I can experience the best, whether that's travel, fine dining, or leisure, without losing balance or responsibility.

4. Impact & Growth – building businesses that stand the test of time, contribute to the economy, and create opportunities. That's the kind of growth that defines real success.

At the end of the day, if I can look around and see a thriving family legacy, happy employees, loyal business relationships, and a life well-lived, then I know I have succeeded.

On Considering Giving Up

Yes, there was a time I felt like quitting. At a young age, the responsibilities on me were heavy, and the financial mistakes and poor decisions I made only added to the pressure. When the business faced a crunch and even degrowth, I felt every wrong step would become a regret I'd carry for life.

However, what pulled me back was spirituality. It gave me hope and the strength to persevere. My parents also stood by me, strong enough to accept my mistakes and guide me, rather than blaming me. That support, combined with the lessons I learned, helped me come back stronger, more disciplined, and more determined never to repeat the same errors. Ultimately, those failures laid the groundwork for the leadership approach I employ today.

Long-Term Vision – Legacy, Growth, and a Global Footprint

It was upon me to contribute to our legacy that would carry forward for generations. Ten years from now, I envision our group as a strong, diversified player with a global footprint, not only in liquor but across the industries in which we are present—hospitality, retail, real estate, and beyond.

One of my biggest dreams is to create our own liquor brand, built on the decades of trust and experience we have in this industry. I want that brand to be a reflection of our legacy, our story, our values, and our expertise, captured in a bottle. More importantly, I want it to become a global product, proudly representing where we come from while standing shoulder to shoulder with international names.

But beyond liquor, the vision is to build Heera Business Group into a family-driven yet professionally run enterprise that grows across multiple sectors, creates jobs, nurtures loyal employees, and builds long-term partnerships. Our aim is not just expansion, but sustainable growth, so that when the next generation steps in, they inherit not only wealth but also a culture of discipline, innovation, and trust.

The way I plan to achieve this is by staying focused on three pillars:

1. Legacy & Values – making every decision in a way that honours the foundation laid by my family.
2. Innovation & Ownership – creating brands and experiences that reflect who we are, not just distributing someone else's products.
3. Global Mindset – thinking beyond markets, and building products and companies that can travel the world while staying rooted in our values.

Ten years from now, I don't just see a bigger business. I envision a more substantial legacy, a group that thrives across industries, employees who take pride in being part of our journey, and a global brand that tells our family's story with every bottle.

The Emotional Landscape

Running a business at a young age changed my personal life in ways I didn't expect. While most of my peers were still figuring out their careers, I was carrying the weight of a family legacy, handling financial pressures, and making decisions that affected hundreds of people. It gave me confidence and maturity, but it also meant sacrifices, less time for myself, friendships that drifted apart, and moments of burnout that few could truly understand.

Being part of a joint family business made family both my greatest strength and my most significant responsibility. Business discussions don't stop at the office. They continue at the dinner table, during holidays, and even in personal conversations. At times, it felt overwhelming, but it also reminded me of the values I grew up with: resilience, trust, and the importance of building something that lasts for generations. My parents, in particular, played a huge role. They accepted my mistakes, supported me through my failures, and gave me the courage to keep moving forward.

Entrepreneurship also reshaped my view of relationships. Some friendships faded because I couldn't always be present, but the ones that stayed became deeper and more meaningful. I learned to value loyalty and patience above all else, qualities that matter just as much in business as they do in personal life.

Ultimately, running a business has taught me that success is hollow if it comes at the expense of family and relationships. Balance is difficult, but essential. For me, real success means not just growing the business, but also ensuring that my family is proud, my employees are happy, and my personal relationships are nurtured alongside the legacy I'm building.

A Day Shaped by Challenges and Small Wins

A typical day for me is a mix of pressure and purpose. Carrying the weight of responsibility at a young age means every decision feels important, and that naturally brings anxiety. But that same pressure also fuels my drive, reminding me that what I'm doing has a real impact on my family's legacy, my employees, and our partners.

There are moments of excitement, too, especially when I'm building something new or seeing ideas come to life. That creative energy gives me the push to get through the grind. What drains me the most are inefficiencies, unfinished tasks or wasted efforts, because they steal time and energy without adding value.

What keeps me balanced is spirituality, discipline, and the small wins my team achieves every day. Emotionally, my days are a mix of stress and satisfaction, but I have learned to see both as necessary. The anxiety keeps me sharp, the excitement keeps me motivated, and the bigger vision keeps me moving forward.

Who I Turn To in Difficult Times

When things get emotionally challenging, I always turn to my parents first. They've been my strongest anchors, guiding me with patience and reminding me that mistakes are part of learning. Just being able to talk openly with them gives me clarity and the courage to carry on. Their acceptance of my failures has been one of the biggest reasons I have been able to bounce back stronger.

Spirituality is my second anchor. Meditation, prayers, and self-reflection help me steady my mind when anxiety takes over. It keeps me grounded and reminds me that challenges are temporary, but the discipline to face them must be permanent. Spirituality has given me the perspective that success and failure are both phases, not destinations.

And then, there's travel and scuba diving. Stepping away from the daily grind, exploring a new place, or being underwater surrounded by silence completely resets me. Travel gives me relaxation and inspiration, while scuba teaches me patience, focus, and calm under pressure. These experiences recharge me and remind me why balance is as important as ambition. In many ways, the ocean has become my escape and my teacher, keeping me centred when life on land gets too heavy.

Legacy, Family & Identity

Being part of a family business means I'm constantly balancing inheritance with innovation. On one side, there's the weight of expectations, the responsibility to protect what generations before me built. On the other hand, there's my own vision, the urge to modernise, to take risks, and to create something that reflects who I am as an entrepreneur.

Managing this balance is both emotionally and practically challenging. Emotionally, it means respecting the values my family instilled in me, trust, resilience, and integrity, while also having the courage to say, 'We need to do things differently.' Practically, it means open communication with family members, accepting that disagreements will happen, and always remembering that the larger goal is growth, not ego.

Inheritance doesn't just include the passing on of titles or assets, but also family values and mindset. I aim to honour the family legacy while building new brands and businesses that will stand the test of time for future generations. In that sense, I see myself as a bridge, connecting the past to the future, ensuring the legacy continues but evolves with time.'

Identity and Business – Intertwined, But Not Confined

Yes, my identity is deeply tied to my business. Growing up in a family where business was not just work, but a way of life, it naturally became an integral part of who I am. The successes and failures of the company often feel personal because it's my family's legacy, my responsibility, and my contribution to building something bigger than myself. My sense of purpose is very much connected to how the business grows and how I carry that legacy forward.

At the same time, I try not to let my entire self-worth depend on it. I have learned through mistakes and failures that if I only see myself through the lens of business performance, it becomes emotionally draining. That's where spirituality, travel, and passions like scuba diving give me balance. They remind me that I am more than my titles or numbers and that life outside the boardroom is equally essential.

I'm comfortable with my identity being connected to the business because it reflects the values I was raised with: responsibility, resilience, and vision. But I have also come to terms with the idea that my individuality extends beyond it. My business is my biggest platform for self-expression, but it's not the only thing that defines me. I see it as a part of my identity, not the whole of it.

If Not This, Then What?

If I weren't an entrepreneur in my current line of work, I think I would still have chosen to be an entrepreneur, but probably in another industry. I have always had the drive to create, take risks, and build something of my own, so even if it wasn't liquor, distribution, or hospitality, I know I wouldn't be satisfied with simply working for someone else. Entrepreneurship is a spirit.

That said, my personal passions would have pulled me toward something experiential and lifestyle-driven. I could easily see myself building a business around travel, scuba diving, or luxury experiences. The ocean, especially, gives me clarity and balance–it's an escape but also a source of learning. If not alcobev, I might have built a brand around that passion, maybe even creating luxury scuba ventures or curated travel experiences that blend adventure with comfort.

What I know for sure is that I would still be creating something tied to people, experiences, and legacy. Whether in liquor, hospitality, or another passion industry, my instinct has always been to build, not just consume. So yes, even if I weren't here, I'd still be an entrepreneur, just telling a different story.

Looking Ahead

As a family business, our biggest challenge and opportunity lies in professionalising while staying rooted in our values. In the past, we faced setbacks due to poor decisions, trusting the wrong people, and not always having the right systems in place. Those experiences were challenging, but they taught us where we need to be sharper: in governance, accountability, and surrounding ourselves with the right advisors and managers.

Looking ahead, I see opportunities in scaling across sectors, both domestically and globally. Whether in liquor, hospitality, real estate, or future ventures, the world is becoming increasingly competitive and rapidly changing. Technology, new consumer behaviour, and stricter regulations will test us, but they also open doors for innovation and global expansion.

The way forward, for me and my family, is to grow with discipline. That means putting the right professionals on board, consulting the right experts, and building a structure where decisions are not just emotional, but strategic and data-driven. While family will always be at the heart of our business, I also believe that someday, this group should run like a thoroughly professional enterprise, where systems are stronger than individuals, and where continuity is never dependent on just one person.

In short, the challenges of the past have prepared us for the future. We're no longer chasing growth mindlessly. We are focused on building sustainably, with the right people, the right culture, and a vision that ensures our legacy grows stronger with every generation.

One Piece of Honest Advice

I could offer one piece of advice to a new entrepreneur: it's okay to fail; it's better to fail early, not later. Don't be afraid to try new things, but make sure your foundation is stable first. Experiment when your core is strong, not when your house is shaking.

Control your impulses. You don't need to prove yourself to anyone by overspending or chasing vanity investments. Every rupee matters, and the money you save today will be the cushion that protects you tomorrow. I learned this the hard way, by burning cash on things that looked impressive but created no value.

And finally, learn to balance the Indian approach to business with the Western approach. Respect family, relationships, and values, but also adopt systems, governance, and professionalism. Ego has no place in business, adaptability does. If you can adapt to the culture around you, remain humble, and continue learning, then no setback will ever be the end of your journey.

—xxx—

From a teenage helper earning ₹300 a month to the founder of a thriving engineering enterprise, Sri Sai Siva Engineering Works Pvt. Ltd. was built on one man's relentless curiosity and hard work, Mr Subramanyam Raju.

Decades ago, a young boy from a small village in Andhra Pradesh moved to Hyderabad with his father, taking up jobs as a gardener and later as a helper in a small workshop. But instead of stopping there, he chose to learn. He spent nights observing machines, understanding their rhythm, and mastering every detail. That curiosity turned into craftsmanship, and soon, his one-machine workshop grew into a trusted name in the crusher spare parts industry.

What makes his story extraordinary is his self-taught brilliance, as he learned engineering by watching YouTube videos without knowing the language, guided only by his observations and determination. His persistence laid the foundation for a legacy of integrity, skill, and innovation.

Today, his son Pavan Raju, an AI and Robotics engineer, continues that legacy, modernising the business through systems, automation, and strategic vision. Together, their story is one of transformation, from a humble workshop to a modern powerhouse serving India's crusher industry.

12

Crushing Limits: How a Village Boy Built a Legacy in the Crushing Industry

Pavan Raju

Every legacy has a beginning, and ours began in a small corner of Hyderabad, with a young boy who arrived from his village carrying nothing but determination and an unshakable will to learn.

My father came to the city in his early teens with my grandfather, who worked as a watchman. He took up a job as a gardener at a farmhouse, earning barely enough to get by. Later, they moved closer to an industrial area, where he found work as a helper in a small workshop. His job was simple: clean the machines, assist the workers, and earn ₹300 a month. But what set him apart was his curiosity.

My Father (on the left) started his own machine and performed pooja during Dussera celebrations in 2004

While others finished their work and went home, he stayed behind watching the machinists closely. He observed how they handled the tools, how the parts came together, how raw metal transformed under precision and patience. Whenever the machines were idle, he practised, repeating every move he had seen.

That curiosity didn't go unnoticed. His employer, impressed by his dedication, encouraged him to buy a machine of his own and start something independently. That slight push changed his life forever. With borrowed money and boundless courage, he purchased his first lathe machine and established a small workshop. That was the beginning of Sri Sai Siva Engineering Works.

From that point on, it was pure perseverance. My father worked long hours sometimes through the night, slowly adding machinery and workers as he learned more. The small workshop eventually outgrew itself, and he relocated both our home and the machines to a new space. It was a modest setup that served as both house and factory. That's where our family's true family business story began.

Over time, he became a vendor for Puzzolana, manufacturing spares for their crushers. The work was steady, but my father's curiosity wouldn't let him settle. For almost a decade, he invested every rupee he earned into developing his own machines, corrugated box-making units, pellet-based bio stoves, rolling machines, bending machines, and slitting machines, each designed and built with his own hands.

Those 8-10 years were the most challenging phase of his life. Financially, nothing improved. Every penny went back into experimentation. Some machines reached 90 per cent completion before failing at the final stage. But even through those struggles, he never lost faith. 'If the machine doesn't work, that means I haven't understood it well enough yet,' he'd say. That kind of mindset became the DNA of our company.

We began focusing on the crusher spare parts business after relocating to this workshop in Jeedimetla in 2018, where we rented space and were fully dedicated to crusher spare parts and repairs

Eventually, he returned to his foundation, the world of crusher spares. In 2018, with all the knowledge he had gathered, he built a 400-ton hydraulic press from scratch, a machine that became a turning point for us. It allowed us to enter the crusher repair segment with a strong competitive edge. From that moment, our reputation for quality and on-time delivery spread quickly through word of mouth. Customers who came once stayed not because of fancy marketing, but because of trust built through consistent performance.

And though he is a man of few words, his actions have always spoken louder than anything else. From earning ₹300 a month to building a company with over 40 employees, 20+ machines, and 1,500 SKUs, his journey stands as a testament to what relentless learning, faith, and hard work can create.

I often say that my father is not just the founder of our business, he is the foundation of everything I am today. His hands built machines, but his vision built a future.

My Journey: From AI to Engineering

From as early as I can remember, I was fascinated by how things work: machines, systems, and technology. That curiosity naturally led me toward robotics, and my dream was to build a career in that field during my master's program. Tech, I took a bold step with a few classmates. We started an AI and robotics firm called Heu.ai. It was less about business and more about curiosity, a simple question: *Can we turn our ideas into something that makes a real impact?*

The years 2020-22 were an incredible learning curve, marked by numerous experiments, challenges, and small victories. But as I was busy building a future in robotics, I noticed something closer to home–my father's business was growing stronger than ever. He had a vision to take it to the next level and invited me to be part of that journey.

At first, I hesitated. Transitioning from the world of AI to heavy engineering felt like a leap. But my father has always been my role model, with his work ethic, discipline, and quiet determination. I realised that working alongside him wasn't just joining a business, it was a once-in-a-lifetime chance to learn, explore, and build something lasting.

When I finally joined Sri Sai Siva Engineering Works Pvt. Ltd. in 2022, I came with no expectations, only curiosity. Over time, I began to feel something more profound: that I didn't choose this industry; *it chose me.* Today, I see immense potential in it, and I believe I am here for a reason to build upon a legacy, modernise it with innovation, and make a mark that goes beyond just business.

Carrying Forward a Legacy: From Robots to Reality

I have always been the kind of person who loves learning, building, and understanding how things work. From a very young age, robotics became my world. I spent nearly eight to nine years immersed in it, learning programming languages, mastering CAD design for 3D modelling, and building hardware for functional robots, during my B.Sc. Tech, I earned several awards for my work in robotics, and later, during my M.Tech at Amity University, I even developed humanoid prototypes.

That journey introduced me to artificial intelligence, and I was instantly captivated by it. Along with two classmates, I co-founded Heu.ai in 2020, a startup focusing on AI and robotics solutions. We began taking up both domestic and international projects, and for two years, I poured everything into building it.

A Crossroad of Choices

Around 2021, another opportunity emerged. My father's company, Sri Sai Siva Engineering Works Pvt. Ltd., which he had built from the ground up, was entering a new phase of growth. He expressed his wish for me to join and help take it forward. That moment became a turning point in my life.

I stood at a crossroads: continue down the path of robotics that I had pursued for nearly a decade, or step into a completely different world—the heavy engineering industry—and carry forward a family legacy. It wasn't an easy choice. However, after considerable reflection, I realised something profound: my true passion wasn't confined to robotics. It was more about learning, growing, and creating an impact through whatever I do.

There were other considerations, too. My startup was still young, and running a business with classmates, people I had known only briefly, came with its own uncertainties. In contrast, my father's company had decades of credibility and a foundation built on trust and hard work. Most importantly, there was no one else to carry that legacy forward. It was either me or it would eventually fade.

Blending Tradition with Innovation

So, in 2022, I decided to join my father's business not as a successor, but as a learner. The company was founded with a simple goal: to deliver reliable engineering solutions and spare parts to the stone crusher industry. Over the years, it evolved from a small workshop into a full-fledged manufacturing and repair facility serving clients across multiple states.

Bhoomi Pooja for the Construction of our New Unit in 2022

Today, as we modernise our operations and expand our capabilities, I see immense potential in blending the traditional wisdom that my father built the company on with new-age innovation and technology. In hindsight, joining the family business meant not only continuing a legacy but also shaping it for the future.

Learning by Immersion

It's been about three years since I joined my father's business, and to be completely honest, I am still finding my place. Unlike a startup, where you build everything from scratch, stepping into an existing legacy business comes with its own unique set of challenges.

When I joined, I made it a point to explore every department, from manufacturing to repairs, operations to sales, to understand not just what we do, but also *how* we do it. My father, who built this company through sheer hard work and determination without any formal education, has been the backbone of every process. He is hands-on involved in every detail, every decision, and every bit of firefighting that keeps the business running smoothly.

Every day, I am learning to bridge two worlds: my father's experience-driven approach and my vision for a system-driven, scalable future. Somewhere in between, I am slowly carving out my own space one process, one system, and one lesson at a time.

Learning to Lead

I had no formal training related to our line of work when I joined the business. My background was in artificial intelligence and robotics, a world utterly different from heavy engineering and manufacturing. For a while, it felt as though everything I had learned earlier was of no direct use here.

But one thing I have always been good at is observation. As I spent more time on the shop floor and interacted with various teams, I began to notice deeper issues that affected our operations, including delays, communication gaps, a lack of standardised systems, and an overdependence on individual experience rather than structured processes. I didn't yet know how to fix them, but I could clearly see where the cracks were.

That curiosity led me to apply for the Family Business Management Program at IIM Calcutta, a decision that completely changed my perspective on business. The program provided me a new lens through which to view my company, enabling me to balance legacy with modern management practices.

Learning from professors who had mentored multiple generations of entrepreneurs, and interacting with peers who were running their own family businesses across India, gave me tremendous clarity. I realised I wasn't here merely to run my father's business; I was here to *transform* it.

That exposure provided me with a clear roadmap for where I could take Sri Sai Siva Engineering Works Pvt. Ltd. to introduce systems, structure, and scalability to a business built on decades of trust and hard work.

When Technology Met Tradition

One of the most rewarding moments in my journey came after I joined the Family Business Management Program at IIM Calcutta. That experience completely changed the way I viewed our company. I realised that building a legacy involves creating systems that can sustain growth even when you arenot around to manage every detail.

With that understanding, I began observing our operations more closely and soon discovered one of our biggest challenges was inventory management. Our business is a complex mix of manufacturing, service, and trading, yet we had never tracked inventory in a structured way. Every part movement, every material purchase, and every repair job depended heavily on people's memory and manual records.

When I explored commercial software options, none truly fit our workflow. That's when my background in AI and software development came back into play. Drawing on my earlier experience in technology, I began learning new tools and frameworks, determined to build something customised for our business.

After months of trial and refinement, I launched a custom-built inventory management system: simple, mobile-friendly, and powerful enough to track all part movements in real time. When we ran the pilot, it worked beautifully. For the first time, we could see clarity across departments, with no more guesswork and no missing items.

That moment watching my team actually use something I had built from scratch to solve a real problem felt like a genuine breakthrough. It gave me confidence that I could blend my tech background with my business journey to modernise our operations, one system at a time. That small win strengthened my belief that sometimes, transformation begins with a simple idea that works.

Earning Trust in a Competitive Market

The stone crusher spare parts industry is highly competitive, with constant pressure to deliver faster, cheaper, and better results. Yet over the years, we have built a strong reputation for a straightforward reason: we never compromise on quality or commitment.

Although our turnover may not yet match that of some of the larger players, the customers who come to us rarely leave our services. Our business has grown almost entirely through word of mouth, thanks to genuine recommendations from satisfied clients who trust us not only for our products but also for our reliability and integrity.

Our biggest strength lies in the speed and precision of our service. In this industry, machine downtime directly translates to financial loss. We have earned our customers' loyalty by ensuring their downtime is the lowest in the market, often delivering repairs and parts in less than half the time taken by competitors. That responsiveness has become our most significant differentiator.

We're now working to expand our portfolio to cover spare parts and repair services for multiple crusher brands. This diversification will enable us to reach a broader market and further strengthen our competitive edge. At the end of the day, we see competition as a reminder to continue improving, to innovate more quickly, and to never lose sight of what truly matters: trust, quality, and dependability.

Loneliness in Leadership

Every entrepreneur faces moments of uncertainty, but for me, the most challenging part of this journey hasn't been financial or operational; it's been emotional.

When I joined my father's business, I expected challenges, but I didn't anticipate the sense of isolation that sometimes comes with it. I spend nearly twelve hours a day at the factory, surrounded by hardworking people from very different backgrounds and age groups. My father remains deeply involved in day-to-day operations, and while that's admirable, it also means there's little space for discussion or creative exchange. There are days when I feel like I am trying to figure everything out on my own, with no one to really talk to or brainstorm with.

450 Ton Capacity Hydraulic Press developed by my father, which played a very crucial role in our early stages getting more and more customers from the crusher industry, hence paving our way into the industry.

The other major challenge has been to change itself. I have always loved learning new things and finding better ways to do them. When I began observing our business closely, I could see several areas where we could operate with greater efficiency and structure. But introducing change in a long-established, family-run company is never easy.

I am still learning to balance my ideas with my father's experience, blending tradition with innovation without clashing the two. It's an ongoing journey, but I believe that one day these small efforts will align into something much bigger: a modern, structured version of the legacy he built.

Balancing Cash Flow and Legacy: Building for the Long Term

For me, the most critical aspect of financial management is cash flow. In the crusher spare parts and service industry, maintaining consistent cash flow is one of the most challenging tasks. Most businesses operate on credit, and even a slight delay or uncertainty on the customer's side can hold back payments for months, sometimes even years.

Over time, I have realised that profitability doesn't just come from high margins, it comes from velocity. If we can maintain steady cash movement and faster inventory turnaround, even a modest margin can yield substantial profits. A well-managed cash flow keeps the business stable, reduces stress, and gives us the freedom to take on new opportunities without being dependent on credit cycles.

At the same time, being a family-run business, I believe brand building and legacy are equally important. A strong brand not only earns customer trust but also aligns the family around a shared long-term vision. It shifts focus from short-term emotional decisions to sustainable, generational thinking.

For me, managing finances isn't just about numbers; it's about balance. It's about maintaining liquidity for the present while building a brand that carries our family's name and values into the future.

Learning the Language of Numbers: Becoming Financially Fluent

Financial analysis wasn't always a strong area for us. Until I joined, the company was run as a proprietorship, and instinct rather than data primarily guided financial management. We never really tracked financial ratios or performance metrics in a structured way.

When the company transitioned into a Private Limited entity after I joined, I began to understand the importance of understanding what the numbers actually mean. Profit and sales alone don't tell the whole story. It's the underlying ratios that reveal a business's true financial health.

I have always been passionate about learning, and over time, I have gradually built my understanding of finance. I am now learning to interpret company data, including cash flow statements and key financial ratios, to make more informed decisions.

It's still a work in progress, but I believe financial literacy is one of the most potent skills any entrepreneur can develop because once you can read the numbers, you can truly understand the story your business is trying to tell.

Lessons from Growth

Every growing business has its share of mistakes, and for us, most of them stemmed from one root cause: the lack of systems and processes.

My father built this company entirely from scratch. He started with just one machine and a dream, handling everything from machining to delivery on his own. Through sheer hard work and persistence, he grew that single-machine setup into a full-fledged company with over 20 types of machinery, 40 employees, and a loyal customer base of more than 500 clients. From earning ₹5,000 a month in the early days to achieving an annual turnover of ₹12 crore, his journey has been nothing short of inspiring.

However, as the company grew, its complexity also increased. What once ran efficiently under the control of one person began facing challenges that demanded a more structured approach. There were no clear systems for communication, inventory, or department-level accountability. That realisation, that passion and experience alone were no longer enough was one of the biggest early lessons for us.

When I joined the business, aligning our perspectives wasn't easy. My father relied on intuition and experience; I focused on systems and data. There was friction not in intent, but in approach. Over time, with patience and mutual respect, we began finding balance, identifying areas where his experience and my structured methods could complement each other.

The biggest lesson I have learned through this process is that growth needs discipline. Building a sustainable company isn't about replacing the old ways, but about strengthening them with structure, systems, and a shared vision.

Holding on Through the Hard Days

Yes, there have been many moments when I have felt like giving up. Running a family business isn't always a romantic story of growth and legacy. There are days of loneliness, self-doubt, and quiet struggle.

I spend nearly 12 hours a day at the factory, surrounded by people much older than me and from entirely different backgrounds. The most challenging moments are when my ideas aren't welcomed. It's disheartening to feel like the work you are doing or the changes you are proposing don't fit or, worse, don't matter. In those moments, I have questioned whether I am in the right place or if I am truly capable of making a difference here.

But every time I have come close to giving up, something deep inside pulls me back. My father is my hero not just for what he has built, but for how he has built it: with decades of relentless hard work, long-term vision, and unwavering dedication. I can't let that go to waste.

Building the Future, Honouring the Vision

My father has always had a simple yet powerful vision to make our company a one-stop solution for all crusher needs. Whether it's spare parts, repairs, or technical support for crusher plants, he wanted customers to find everything they needed under one roof. That vision has guided us from the very beginning, and it continues to shape our direction today.

Currently, we primarily specialise in manufacturing and supplying spare parts for Puzzolana crushers. However, we're actively expanding our expertise to cover other major domestic and international brands. Our goal is to become what I like to call the 'D-Mart for crusher needs', a comprehensive hub where customers can find quality parts, quick repairs, and expert support, all in one place.

We have already taken significant steps in that direction. Last year, we established our second unit in Hyderabad, and both facilities are now operational and running successfully. Over the next five years, our focus will be on strengthening our infrastructure, investing in advanced machinery, acquiring land for expansion, and expanding our customer network across India.

Scaling for a Global Tomorrow

Currently, we supply over 1,500 SKUs of spare parts and accessories, and our target is to scale that to 5,000+ SKUs within the next five years. Once we

Our New Fully Operational Unit in 2024 was built entirely with hard-earned money without relying on any loans or finance options

achieve that milestone, our next phase will be export expansion, establishing our footprint in international markets and making Sri Sai Siva Engineering Works Pvt. Ltd. a recognised name globally.

Over the next decade, I envision our company as a self-reliant, technology-driven engineering powerhouse trusted not only for its high-quality products but also for its reliability, innovation, and exceptional service.

At its core, our long-term vision is to carry forward my father's dream while infusing it with modern systems, scalability, and global reach, building a legacy that stands strong for generations to come.

The People Who Keep Me Grounded

Entrepreneurship can often feel like a lonely road, but I have been blessed with a small circle of people who have been my constant source of strength and grounding.

At the top of that list are my mother, sister and wife. They have an incredible ability to understand my emotional state, even without me having to say much. Whenever I feel overwhelmed or drained, they help me regain perspective, guiding me to stay patient and calm, especially in moments when dealing with my father becomes challenging. Their quiet strength and unconditional support are what keep me centred.

Another pillar of inspiration in my life is my Vedanta guru, Preeti ji. Her teachings and personal guidance have helped me view life with more clarity, balance, and detachment. Whenever I feel mentally or emotionally stuck, her wisdom reminds me to rise above the situation and focus on what truly matters.

And then there are my dearest friends, Arun and Mahalaxmi, who have been by my side for over a decade. They've seen me through every high and low, encouraging me when I doubted myself, challenging me to grow, and reminding me that vulnerability is not weakness.

These people are my emotional anchors. I owe a large part of my resilience to them for standing by me, believing in me, and constantly pushing me to turn my weaknesses into strengths.

Bridging Two Generations

Managing a family business is both emotionally and practically challenging. My father built this company from nothing, and with that comes immense respect and responsibility. The biggest challenge lies in balancing his experience with my ideas, finding a middle ground between tradition and transformation.

It has taken patience and understanding to align our visions. Still, today I see it as a partnership between two generations–one that built the foundation and another that is preparing it for the future. Together, we're learning how legacy and innovation can not only coexist but also strengthen each other.

A Journey of Growth and Purpose

Yes, very much. Over time, this business has become a reflection of who I am and what I stand for. It's not just about machines or parts, it's about discipline, persistence, and purpose. Every process we refine, every challenge we overcome, adds a new layer to both the company's story and my own.

My personal growth and the company's growth are deeply intertwined, and I am comfortable with that because this journey gives meaning to my everyday effort. It connects me not only to the business but also to my family's legacy, reminding me that what we're building today will someday inspire the next generation to continue the story.

Reflections from the Journey: Grow Before You Prove

If I had to share some advice, it would be: *Don't rush to prove yourself; take time to understand yourself.*

Entrepreneurship isn't just about ideas, money, or opportunity. It's about endurance. There will be days when you feel lost, unheard, or disconnected from the very dream that once excited you. In those moments, remember growth doesn't always look like success. Sometimes, it looks like patience, self-doubt, and small steps forward.

I have learned that passion can start a journey, but purpose sustains it. Your ideas will evolve, your business will change, but your integrity and persistence must remain constant.

Also, keep the people, keep the purpose. Never forget the people who stand quietly beside you. Whether it's family, friends, or mentors, they are your invisible strength when things fall apart. There will be times when giving up feels easier. But if your work has meaning, if it carries a part of your heart and someone else's legacy, keep going. You might not see the results immediately, but every struggle is shaping you into the person your dream needs you to be.

—xxx—

REW ©

Ranjna Engineering Works

Ranjna Engineering Works is a family-owned business that designs and manufactures precision instruments for the cable and healthcare industries. The firm was founded in 1980 by Sh. Sharda Singh, who migrated from Gorakhpur to Delhi and started a modest workshop, more out of necessity than choice. From his earliest machines, reliability became our hallmark.

His son, Mr Sanjay Singh, carried this legacy forward with a focus on quality and relationships in a highly demanding sector. Over the decades, the enterprise has evolved from a small workshop into a manufacturer supplying critical testing equipment across India and to MENA markets. The enterprise caters to two exacting industries: cable and healthcare, where accuracy, consistency, and resilience are non-negotiable.

His grandson, Mr Shobhit Singh, joined the business after gaining managerial experience in the corporate sector. His approach has been hands-on, learning the production processes, understanding the rhythm of factory operations, and working closely with our teams on quality, design, and delivery.

Ranjna Engineering Works is a living story of survival, trust, and reinvention. It carries the aspirations of three generations, and now Shobhit holds the responsibility to continue that story into the future.

13

Third Generation, First Lessons @ Ranjna Engineering Works

SHOBHIT SINGH

Our story began in the 1980s with my grandfather, Sh. Sharda Singh, who became an entrepreneur out of necessity rather than choice. Born in a village near Gorakhpur as the eldest son in a large joint family, he lost his mother at a young age and took on the responsibility of raising his siblings while his father worked as a farmer.

The first workshop, built in the same home where the founder Sh Sharda Singh once lived with his five children

With little education, few resources, and no grand business plan, he moved to Delhi and found work in a comb factory, literally wrapping combs by hand. His only goal was to survive and create a stable income for his family. Initially, he set up a small manufacturing unit so that his younger brother could join him in Delhi. The brother never came. The scaffold became the building, and that modest unit grew into Ranjna Engineering Works.

His machines were built with limited means, but what he offered customers was priceless: reliability. He believed in keeping his word, no matter the cost, and that trust became the company's true capital.

He also discovered a gap in the market. Lab instruments and cable-testing machines were mostly imported, expensive, fragile, and slow to service. If a machine failed, customers had to wait weeks for overseas support. My grandfather's solution was simple, Indian, and practical: build it here, build it tough, and make it serviceable.

He converted a rented house into a workshop, factory and family under the same roof, and prototyped machines that matched imported quality at local prices. That mantra, '*export quality, Indian resilience*', became our North Star.

Building an Ecosystem

Those early years were all grit and *jugaad*. Old employees recall that my grandfather slept barely three or four hours a night, not to rest, but to sketch out the next day's work. He taught by doing: training machinists, mentoring vendors, and even helping skilled workers set up their own small shops to make components.

He created an ecosystem, competitors who were also collaborators, micro-entrepreneurs who supported our capacity when orders surged. For him, enabling others wasn't charity; it was how industry grows. That instinct to empower people became a family trait, one my father carried forward in his own way.

My father, Mr Sanjay Kr Singh, later joined and modernised operations, expanded our reach, and strengthened our reputation, all while preserving the people-first ethos. From him, I learned that while products and markets will continue to evolve, values must remain non-negotiable. Entering the internet age, he infused technology and automation into the business, setting the stage for the next generation.

When my turn came, I realised that joining the family business was about carrying responsibility forward, not just our family surname. I wanted to bring global exposure, technological insight, and new ways of thinking, while preserving the resilience and trust my grandfather had built.

I've come to believe that in a family business, you don't inherit entitlement, you inherit responsibility.

Early Sparks and Subtle Pulls

My path back to the family firm was a series of small, stubborn pulls that grew louder over time. The earliest one was almost embarrassingly simple: In fifth grade, I made school projects for my classmates and earned pocket money. That tiny thrill of creating something people wanted, and being paid for it, stuck with me.

At home, business was a daily part of life. Accounts, discussions about orders, late-night calls on production updates, all of it seeped into my imagination as a child.

What drew me most, though, was watching my father. He wasn't just building machines; he was building lives. Employees came to him not only for work-related issues but also for personal struggles, and he treated them with the same respect and care he showed his own family. That taught me an important lesson: business is not only about transactions, it is about trust. Profits matter, yes, but the purpose behind them is what creates legacy.

Earning My Place in the Business

I didn't feel 'in business' the day I joined the company. That day felt more like stepping into a legacy, not yet into my own role. The shift occurred when I was entrusted to take responsibility, not as the son or grandson of the founders, but as someone accountable for the outcomes.

That moment arrived with my first independent client assignment, a major semiconductor company we had been trying to secure for over a year. The conversation had gone cold, but it also represented a potential new vertical for us. The chances of conversion were slim. My father gave me the lead because there wasn't much to lose, but there was a small risk that a rookie like me could close the door altogether.

Suddenly, there was no one to shadow and no script to follow. It was up to me to make decisions, negotiate terms, and ensure delivery. The project was based in Gujarat, so I decided to work with a local consultant who spoke the same business language as our prospective client. That connection turned out to be the key.

When the deal finally came through, the win meant a lot to me. For the first time, I saw employees, clients, and even my father look at me differently. I wasn't just *the next generation* anymore, I was part of the present.

That moment was both empowering and humbling. Empowering, because I realised I could stand on my own. Humbling, because I understood what was truly at stake: people's jobs, customer trust, and the weight of a 45-year-old name.

That day, I experienced firsthand what it really means to grow in a family business. You don't grow into it through results and accountability. The day people start relying on your decisions, not your last name, is the day you truly step into business.

Learning Beyond the Classroom

I completed a Bachelor's in Business Administration, graduating as a gold medallist. I also earned my Six Sigma and QMS certifications from BSI to strengthen our manufacturing practices. While the degree gave me theoretical knowledge and confidence, I soon realised that classroom concepts don't always translate neatly into business.

Take the 4Ps of marketing: Product, Price, Place, and Promotion. I knew them inside and out and had applied them during my college years in the Entrepreneurship Cell, where I organised events and ran small ventures. It felt exciting, and I thought I had a solid grasp of how business worked.

Stepping into the family business was an eye-opener. I quickly understood that even when the 4Ps are executed perfectly, something crucial is missing: *People*. In our B2B manufacturing context, it is important to understand how the *person* makes a purchasing decision. How do you connect with them? How do you communicate in a way that feels natural and familiar? How do you negotiate or find a *jugaad* solution that makes sense in the Indian context?

In global corporate setups, communication happens through structured emails, presentations, and formal meetings. But in Indian manufacturing and local client relationships, conversations are personal, flexible, and deeply human. Understanding this nuance, where trust and familiarity often outweigh formal credentials, became essential.

That realisation marked a turning point for me. I understood that business involves empathy, relationship-building, and reading people. My corporate experience provided me with a global perspective, but my family business taught me to ground that knowledge in local reality, blending formal strategy with human connection.

Ultimately, that lesson humbled me. Education and accolades are important, but they become truly meaningful only when paired with a practical understanding, adaptability, and genuine care for others. That's when I truly felt I was stepping into business, not just as part of a family legacy, but as someone committed to making it work for people, every single day.

Building Something the World Said We Couldn't

One of the most rewarding moments in my entrepreneurial journey came recently, while working on a highly specialised project for the cable industry, a chamber instrument that not only validated our technical capabilities but also reaffirmed the values my grandfather instilled in our business: trust, perseverance, and the pride of building something meaningful from scratch.

India's cable manufacturers were increasingly exporting to global markets and facing stringent quality standards. Worldwide, only a handful of suppliers, primarily based in the US and China, can provide such precision equipment. Importing these machines was expensive and complicated by freight costs, installation hurdles, and long lead times. Many Indian players imported equipment from China, rebranded it, and sold it locally. The quality and after-sales service often fell short.

Our client, however, placed their faith in us to design and manufacture the entire chamber indigenously. It was both a huge vote of confidence and a daunting challenge. Could we design and build a high-precision, globally compliant chamber in India, utilising limited resources and minimal prior experience?

My father, Mr Sanjay Singh (2nd Gen), with our very first chamber, proudly made in India

The project demanded months of R&D, intense technical calculations, and continuous experimentation. We had to return to the fundamentals, revisiting physics concepts like radiation, AC and DC currents, and machine design, because our engineers had never built something of this complexity. Every component had to be sourced with care, and rare parts, such as specific xenon bulbs, were imported from Japan at a steep cost.

Deadlines were tight. Every day brought new setbacks, delayed shipments, programming errors, and calibration mismatches. At times, it felt like we were failing more than succeeding. We invested heavily from our own funds, often stretching beyond our financial comfort zone. Yet, we meticulously logged every misstep, learned from it, and continually refined our approach. Each failed attempt brought us a step closer to success.

Finally, after countless nights of problem-solving, collaboration, and sheer determination, the machine worked. It passed all tests, met the client's rigorous standards, and functioned exactly as designed. The moment it came alive was electrifying, not just because we had built a sophisticated instrument, but because of the journey it represented.

Our engineers, welders, and programmers had poured their expertise, creativity, and pride into every component. Watching their faces light up with satisfaction was more rewarding than the machine itself.

Soon after, senior executives from the client visited to congratulate us personally. We received follow-up orders for additional chambers. That recognition was deeply fulfilling, not just as a business win, but as validation that a small, family-run enterprise could deliver world-class innovation.

Lessons that Stay with Me

That project taught me lessons that will stay with me for the rest of my life. First, perseverance truly pays off, even when every day feels like failure. Second, success in entrepreneurship is not just about products, it's about empowering people and nurturing talent. And finally, calculated risks, backed by trust, teamwork, and persistence, can lead to breakthroughs that redefine what's possible.

Looking back, that project was far more than a business milestone. It was a moment of personal and professional validation, a reminder of why I chose this journey, and why every challenge we face is an opportunity to grow, innovate, and inspire.

Guarding Quality, Facing Challenges

In recent years, one of the biggest operational challenges we've faced is the growing presence of duplicate and low-quality products in the market. While we source components from trusted suppliers, the rise of substandard alternatives has put added pressure on us. Even after paying a premium for quality materials, we often find ourselves navigating a landscape where dealers discontinue specific models or supply parts that fall short of the durability and reliability standards we promise our clients.

This constant challenge drives us to continually innovate, develop new models, refine existing ones, and ensure that every instrument we deliver remains safe, precise, and dependable. For us, it's important to safeguard the reputation we've built over decades and stay ahead in an increasingly competitive industry.

Reducing Dependency, Reinforcing Self-Reliance

Another major hurdle lies in our dependence on certain imported components, particularly PLCs and semiconductors. Many of these are sourced from China, which adds cost and availability pressures. This experience has underscored a broader realisation for us: there is tremendous potential for Indian manufacturers to produce these critical modules domestically. Building such capabilities within India would not only reduce our dependency on imports but also strengthen our national manufacturing ecosystem.

While these operational challenges can be demanding, they also serve as a motivating factor. They push us to stay innovative, agile, and forward-looking. Above all, they remind us that quality, reliability, and perseverance are what truly distinguish a legacy business from a mere commodity supplier.

Balancing Quality and Competition: *The Dilemma of Value vs. Values*

In our industry, quality has always carried a cost. But the market has evolved, and there are now several products that offer 'acceptable' quality at lower prices, naturally intensifying competition. This has led us to an ongoing internal debate: should we launch a sub-brand or a separate product line aimed at this lower-price segment, perhaps by using alternative materials or offering shorter service guarantees to make it more affordable?

However, this idea brings a unique challenge in a family-run manufacturing culture. Our engineers and technicians take immense pride in what they build, and it's hard to justify letting a product leave the factory that doesn't meet our core standards. Introducing a lower-cost line would require dedicated teams, distinct quality protocols, and careful brand management to ensure our mainline reputation remains untarnished.

For now, we've chosen to stay true to our core values, delivering high-quality, durable products and nurturing long-term relationships with clients who appreciate that commitment. Instead of chasing every low-cost competitor, we focus on innovation, reliability, and service excellence. Over time, we've learned that quality and trust may take longer to build, but they are what truly sustain a business through generations.

The Human Side of Business

Running a family business presents a set of challenges that are uniquely intertwined with human relationships, legacy, and emotion, challenges rarely found in non-family businesses. In such enterprises, the line between personal and professional life is constantly blurred. Unlike in corporate offices, where disagreements end with a meeting, in a family business, the same people you negotiate with, disagree with, or feel frustrated by at work are the same ones you share dinner with at home.

A disagreement with your father over a business decision, for instance, doesn't end at the office door, it lingers, shaping how you interact at home. Likewise, personal emotions such as pride, frustration, or joy flow back into the business, amplifying both victories and setbacks. Successes feel more rewarding, and failures cut deeper, precisely because family is involved.

Intergenerational Perspectives

Intergenerational dynamics add another layer of complexity. My grandfather built a legacy anchored in trust, quality, and relationships. My father, navigating this legacy, often prioritised family loyalty over pure business logic, sometimes letting go of clients or opportunities to maintain harmony among relatives. While this reflected strong family values, it occasionally conflicted with the need for sharper business decisions.

I often felt this tension firsthand. I wanted to preserve our values while ensuring that growth and merit guided our choices. It became clear that sustaining a legacy also meant evolving it, honouring the past while preparing for the future.

Another subtle but significant challenge lies within the father–son dynamic at work. Out of protective instincts, my father sometimes downplayed my suggestions to shield me from risk or responsibility. Though well-intentioned, such instincts could have limited innovation had we not addressed them openly. To balance perspectives, we introduced senior mentors within the organisation who now act as neutral advisors, helping bridge tradition with new ideas and ensuring that every generation's voice is heard.

The Cultural Challenge of Formality

Family businesses in India also face cultural constraints regarding contracts and formal agreements. Historically, signing contracts with relatives has been viewed as unnecessary or even disrespectful. My father, following this norm, often preferred informal understandings with cousins or extended family members, even at the cost of losing business opportunities. While this reflects integrity and trust, it can also lead to inefficiencies that corporate setups avoid.

Through experience, I've learned that respecting tradition must coexist with professionalism. Clear systems, written agreements, and defined boundaries are crucial for maintaining both healthy relationships and business operations.

Ultimately, the unique challenges of a family-run business, emotional overlaps, intergenerational conflicts, cultural nuances, and the balance between loyalty and logic, shape leaders who are not only strategic but also deeply empathetic. This journey teaches patience, humility, and the art of balancing relationships with responsibility. It's both a challenge and a privilege, one that continues to remind me that in family business, success is measured not just in numbers, but in the trust and understanding we build across generations.

When Failure Became My Teacher

One of the toughest challenges I faced in my entrepreneurial journey came during my early months in the family business, around the second wave of COVID. I was deeply involved in upgrading a cable printing machine used in the cable industry. I had contributed to the research, design, and even helped accelerate parts of the manufacturing process. For me, the machine was almost an extension of myself. I was emotionally invested in its success.

After months of development, testing, and painstaking effort, the machine was finally ready for dispatch. The sense of accomplishment was immense, but it didn't last long. Once installed, the machine failed to perform as expected. It ran smoothly at lower speeds but faltered at higher speeds and over long durations, unable to meet the performance standards of our older legacy models.

Our engineers made several visits to the client's site, running multiple tests and adjustments. Despite their best efforts, the issue remained unresolved. With travel costs mounting, we ultimately decided to bring the machine back to Delhi for internal rework. During that period, I handled numerous client calls and emails, each one a painful reminder that we hadn't delivered as promised.

For me, it was a profoundly emotional experience. I had always been at the top of my class, a gold medallist, and someone known for delivering results in every role I undertook. I had never encountered failure on this scale, and now, it was in my own family business. The machine sat in our facility, the team continued their work, my father remained calm, and the office carried on as usual. For me, *it felt like the world had stopped, but for everyone else, it hadn't.*

I can't describe that feeling in words. It was a mix of frustration, helplessness, and self-doubt. And because these were my early months, and I believed in astrology back then, I even joked to myself that maybe it was my 'energy' that caused it!

Eventually, upon re-examining the machine, we discovered the culprit: a tiny set of screws in a small wheel that couldn't withstand high-speed operation over prolonged periods. Something so small had caused such a big setback. That little screw had 'screwed' me mentally more than I could have imagined.

But that challenge became a turning point. I applied Lean Six Sigma principles and a structured problem-solving approach, tracing the issue step by step, learning how to manage technical setbacks, coordinate resources, and, most importantly, maintain composure under pressure.

We documented every lesson learned and refined our internal processes for future projects. Looking back today, that failure stands as one of the most important experiences of my entrepreneurial journey.

The upgraded cable printing machine, a project I was part of, photographed at our facility, which taught me how to handle setbacks

Balancing Innovation with Wisdom: The Plasma Technology Experiment

When I first joined the family business, I was eager to make an impact and bring innovation to our instruments. One of the first ideas I championed was introducing plasma technology for some of our high-precision instruments. The concept seemed simple in theory. Large global corporations were already producing such instruments successfully, and I was convinced we could disrupt the Indian market. I was full of energy and ambition, eager to make my mark, and my father was supportive of my enthusiasm.

However, I soon realised that my approach was naive. I was so focused on creating a new product that I almost overlooked the bigger picture. Our existing product line was already highly specialised, involving complex precision engineering with multiple interdependent processes. These instruments had strong entry barriers, a loyal client base, and a reputation built over decades. In considering the disruption of the current line, I had underestimated the immense value of what already existed.

As we began working on the plasma technology product, I also failed to fully assess the market segment that actually required it, the client channels, and the holistic effort needed beyond just engineering. Something that I missed that time was that, beyond creating the product, it was crucial to understand client needs, build trust, establish distribution, and position the product in the right story and context.

Within a few months, I realised that my youthful ambition had led me into a narrow, almost single-minded pursuit. The project didn't fail, but it entered what I would now call a 'pause phase'. And in that pause, I learned a profound lesson: even the most exciting innovation cannot succeed without considering the entire business ecosystem.

This experience was deeply humbling. I understood that in a family business, especially one with legacy, responsibility is not just about building a cool product. It's about thinking holistically: about operations, client relationships, production capacity, and the long-term impact on the organisation. My father, with his broader perspective, was right in every way. Innovation must complement the foundation of the business, not disrupt it recklessly.

That lesson stayed with me. Ambition is vital, but it must be balanced with perspective, patience, and respect for existing systems. Today, the plasma technology project remains on our roadmap, and I continue to see it as a potential avenue for innovation. However, I now approach it differently, considering market readiness, client adoption, and sustainable growth.

That early misstep taught me to merge my instinct for disruption with strategic thinking, a balance that has since guided every new initiative I undertake in the business.

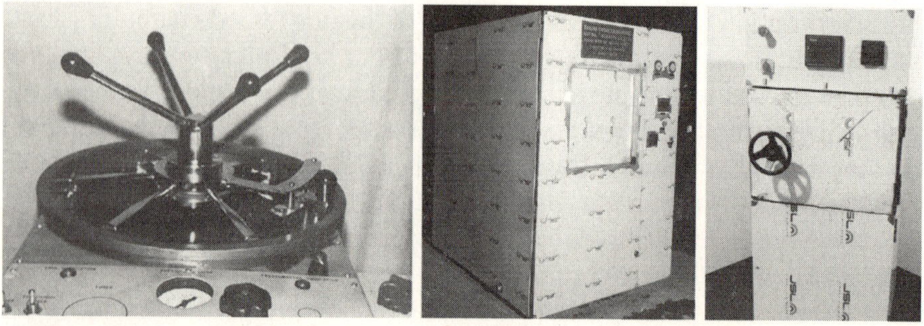

From left to right: the first manual steriliser for healthcare built by my grandfather in his workshop, the first fully automatic model developed by my father in our next manufacturing unit, and the plasma technology model I intended to introduce, currently on hold at our present facility

Redefining Success: Celebrating People, Not Just Profit

For me, success has always been more than profit or performance metrics. It's about giving my full effort and ensuring that the people around me, especially our engineers and team members, see their work truly shine.

Success is when every component, every machine, and every process we create reflects the dedication, precision, and craft of the people behind it. When our engineers' contributions are visible in the final product, when clients trust us with their most critical projects, and when that trust translates into real-world validation, that, to me, is true success.

We should strive to ensure that every person's effort is recognised and valued. When our team takes pride in what they build, when their skills are recognised, and when their work carries meaning beyond numbers, that's when I feel we've truly succeeded.

Moments of Doubt and Renewal: *When Quitting Crossed My Mind*

There have certainly been moments when the idea of giving up felt real. There are days when we work quite literally around the clock, leaving early and returning late, managing last-minute dispatches, and handling logistical challenges that leave little room for rest.

During those nights, I often think back to my corporate days, when I could close my laptop at the end of the shift and switch off. The contrast can be mentally draining. At times, I even found myself briefly considering a return to the corporate world, where responsibilities felt more defined and predictable.

I recall a specific day during a particularly high-stress period when my former director called to check in. For a fleeting moment, I genuinely considered rejoining for the comfort of a steadier schedule. But what stopped me was a more profound sense of purpose, the commitment to my team, the opportunity to solve problems hands-on, and the drive to see our collective effort come to life.

Balancing Generations and Growth

Navigating a family business comes with unique generational expectations. From my father and grandfather, I've learned that one of the most important responsibilities is keeping everyone together, listening to differing opinions, balancing them, and maintaining harmony across both family and business.

This often means making decisions that may not maximise short-term profits but strengthen long-term cohesion. I've seen my father and grandfather let go of clients or even share opportunities with cousins, prioritising family unity over business gain. As one of my professors once said, *'someone has to do it,'* and over time, I've realised that managing these delicate human dynamics is as much a part of the business as designing machines or closing deals.

Balancing modern systems with time-tested values is not easy. It demands patience and emotional intelligence. However, this very connection, the sense of continuity and responsibility, also gives me purpose. It reminds me that our work is not just about machines or products; it's about sustaining a legacy that hundreds of clients' trust, and generations have built with integrity.

Creating Beyond Boundaries

If I weren't leading this family business, I know I would still be an entrepreneur, exploring innovation in other fields. My fascination with electricity, PLCs, and automation continues to fuel my creativity. I often imagine bringing these ideas into home automation or artistic electrical projects, small electronic sculptures and kinetic installations that blend technology with design.

Even outside of business, I find joy in crafting such pieces, some of which I've sold, combining technical skill with aesthetic expression. Ultimately, whether through the family enterprise or other ventures, creation and problem-solving remain at the core of who I am. They are not just what I *do*, they are who I *am*.

Building Legacy and Nation: *Aligning with India's Vision for 2047*

As a third-generation entrepreneur in India, my horizon extends far beyond our family firm. It intersects with the nation's journey toward a Viksit Bharat by *2047*. I believe the most powerful way we can contribute is by aligning our growth with India's manufacturing renaissance, youth empowerment, and global competitiveness.

At our firm, we are preparing for the future by investing in digital tools, adopting cleaner manufacturing practices, and forming partnerships with technical institutions to nurture young talent. By the end of this year, we will partner with a local ITI under the National Apprenticeship Promotion Scheme (NAPS), offering students real-world exposure while bringing fresh energy and ideas into our operations. In doing so, we're not only growing our business but also strengthening India's manufacturing ecosystem.

Honouring the Past While Building the Future

But growth alone isn't enough. I've learned that to move forward meaningfully, we must also look back, to remember where we came from and what built our foundation. To that end, we are establishing an annual tradition called Ranjna Founder's Day (RFD), celebrated every year around Dussehra.

By honouring the past and investing in the future, we aim to continue building a business that makes a meaningful contribution to our people, our industry, and India's broader journey towards 2047.

Walking the Tightrope of Legacy and Innovation: *Lessons from a Gen Z Entrepreneur*

Being a Gen Z and a third-generation entrepreneur comes with its own unique set of challenges. On one side lies the weight of legacy, the expectation to preserve and build upon what your family has established. On the other side is the urge to carve your own path, to innovate, and to prove that you're not just carrying forward the past but creating the future. At times, it feels like walking a tightrope between respect for tradition and the pressure to disrupt.

If I were to give one piece of advice to second or third-generation entrepreneurs, it would be this: respect what your older generation has built. There were times when I wanted to discard old systems or launch something entirely new, driven by excitement and impatience. But over time, I learned that the foundation my grandfather and father created was the result of decades of effort, trust, and learning. Change works best when it is thoughtful, gradual, and built upon what already functions well.

As Gen Z, we live in an age of speed, startups rise and fall overnight, trends shift within minutes, and success often feels like it must be instant. However, family businesses operate differently from startups. Here, you must balance legacy alongside growth. It's not always easy, it won't be easy. You'll face doubt, frustration, and even resistance from within your own circle.

Yet, as Krishna says, 'कर्मण्येवाधिकारस्ते मा फलेषु कदाचन' (you have the right to perform your duty, but not to the fruits of your actions). I try to remind myself of this often: to focus entirely on my work, to give my best to every project, without being consumed by the outcome. Because in the end, when your effort, intention, and integrity are aligned, the results inevitably follow.

—xxx—

SHREE SONIGARA DEVELOPERS

Shree Sonigara Developers is a Pune-based real estate company founded on the principles of trust, quality, and commitment, values that have guided the Sonigara family for over six decades. The business traces its origins to the 1960s, when the family first established itself in Pune through trading and jewellery retail. What began as a small entrepreneurial venture gradually evolved into two thriving verticals, jewellery (Dilip Sonigara Jewellers) and real estate (Shree Sonigara Developers), both grounded in integrity, long-term vision, and deep respect for customer relationships.

Over the years, Shree Sonigara Developers has grown from building small residential complexes to completing more than 25 landmark projects and several plotted developments across the Pimpri-Chinchwad region. The company has built a reputation for timely delivery, transparent dealings, and superior construction quality, becoming a trusted name among thousands of homebuyers. Today, as we expand into new markets, including redevelopment and luxury housing across Pune city, Shree Sonigara Developers stands at the intersection of legacy and innovation, a business rooted in tradition yet forward-looking in its vision for the future.

Tejas Sonigara represents the third generation of our family business. Here, he brings to you the story of his family, their company and himself, and answer all the questions: how the business was built, how it expanded into different verticals, what problems the business faced, why he decided to join in, and what he now aims to execute within the business.

14

Building Beyond Legacy

TEJAS SONIGARA

Our family story has always been intertwined with entrepreneurship. My grandfather moved from Rajasthan to Pune in the late 1950s or early 1960s. Like many Marwari migrants of his time, he arrived with very little but carried an immense belief in the value of hard work and perseverance.

He began modestly, lending small amounts of money against artefacts, watches, or household items. These weren't glamorous beginnings, but they

Three generations of the family still celebrate Diwali together at our oldest store. This 200 sq. ft. store also served as the home for the family in the initial few years

helped him build what mattered most: trust and relationships within the community.

Eventually, my father joined him, and together they ventured into the silver jewellery business. What started as a small operation gradually evolved into a gold jewellery business, and over time, into a full-fledged jewellery store. My father, the eldest among five siblings, shouldered the responsibility of carrying forward the family's growing ambitions. My uncle, on the other hand, chose to explore opportunities in the real estate sector.

For nearly two decades, the two brothers have worked closely, joint in finances but separate in operations. My father focused on jewellery, while my uncle led the real estate ventures. This arrangement, where both had independent decision-making authority, turned out to be one of the smartest moves they made. It allowed each of them to innovate and expand freely, without the bottleneck of collective approvals, while still having the security of shared financial support if either vertical faced difficulty.

The results were remarkable. Over the course of three decades, the jewellery business expanded to seven thriving stores in the Pimpri–Chinchwad area of Pune. Meanwhile, the real estate arm completed over twenty-five residential projects and several plot development ventures. Yet, what stood out most wasn't just the numbers; it was how both businesses became trusted names in the local economy, respected for reliability and integrity.

This was the legacy I was born into, deeply inspiring, yet also intimidating. When you inherit such a strong foundation, the responsibility to sustain and grow it can feel immense.

A Childhood Shaped by Observation and Purpose

Looking back at my journey, my mind often drifts to when I was just twelve years old. At that age, while most kids around me were thinking about cricket, cartoons, or the latest video game, I found myself absorbed in something entirely different, watching my family discussing the complex realities of running a business.

I saw my father, my uncle, and other elders constantly juggling the stress of finances, taxation, and regulatory hurdles. It wasn't just the numbers on paper that caught my attention; it was the frustration on their faces, the countless late nights, and the uneasy conversations around the dining table that left a lasting impression on me.

Even as a child, I sensed that these weren't small challenges. There were cracks in the foundation of our family business that could widen if not addressed. Watching those struggles, I silently made a promise to myself: I would dedicate my life to solving these problems. I didn't want to stand by and watch everyone struggle; I wanted to help bring clarity where things felt messy or stressful.

In our Marwadi culture, it was almost assumed that I would eventually join the family business. But for me, it wasn't about fulfilling an expectation; it was about responding to what felt like a calling. I didn't just want to 'join'; I wanted to *add value.* I wanted to be the one who entered equipped, ready, and confident enough to take the family business to the next level.

Even before I finished school, I had decided on my path: I would become a Chartered Accountant. I had seen how our family CA was respected, how his advice influenced key decisions, and I knew that if I wanted to make a real impact, I had to earn that kind of respect through knowledge, not inheritance.

Education as Preparation and Identity: Learning with Purpose

Recognising the challenges our family had faced in finance and governance, I decided early on to pursue a formal education in commerce. I earned my B.Com from Pune University, but the true cornerstone of my professional preparation was becoming a Chartered Accountant. Additionally, I completed CFA Level 1, which provided me with a broader international perspective on finance and investment.

During my articleship, I got my first real taste of the professional world outside the family business, and it was a humbling experience. As an intern at the bottom of the hierarchy, I was often assigned repetitive work that no one else wanted. At first, it frustrated me. But soon, I realised those moments were teaching me something invaluable: the dignity of labour.

I began to see how the hardest, most essential work in any organisation often comes from those in the lowest positions. Earlier, I might have thought of such people as merely 'workers.' But being in their place changed my perspective entirely. I developed a new empathy and respect for every role in a business, a mindset that later helped me immensely when managing teams in our own enterprise.

I also learned the power of communication and humility. Some seniors, despite their experience, encouraged me to question them freely. Their openness shaped my leadership style. Additionally, I was exposed to how various firms utilised ERP systems and digital tools to streamline their operations. These weren't abstract lessons; I carried these insights back and later implemented them in our jewellery business.

By the time I cleared my CA Final exams in November 2018, I wasn't just academically qualified, I was mentally and emotionally ready to take on the responsibility I had promised myself as a twelve-year-old.

Early Lessons from the Jewellery Business

My first four years after qualifying as a Chartered Accountant were spent in our family's jewellery business. It was the perfect training ground because it blended tradition with scale. On one hand, jewellery in our family was rooted in personal relationships, heritage, and community trust. On the other hand, managing seven stores required strong systems, structured processes, and operational discipline.

One of my first major initiatives was implementing a cloud-based ERP system across all branches. Earlier, each store maintained its own records locally, which were then manually consolidated, a process that was slow, error-prone, and often resulted in discrepancies. The new system centralised everything. From the head office, I could now monitor live sales, inventory, and purchase requirements for each branch in real time. This integration allowed us to centralise purchasing, improve stock allocation, and create stronger coordination between branches.

Initially, there was resistance. Many long-serving employees found the system unnecessary or intimidating. However, once they saw how it reduced manual work, eliminated duplication, and simplified reporting, they quickly adopted it. That experience taught me one of my earliest leadership lessons: people don't resist change; they resist uncertainty. If you help them see how change improves their work, they'll eventually become its biggest supporters.

Working in the jewellery business also provided me with hands-on experience in HR, finance, and backend operations. I was no longer just the 'boss's son'. I was solving real problems, implementing real systems, and making decisions with visible results. Those years built my confidence and shaped my understanding of leadership. Most importantly, they reminded me that respect in a family business isn't inherited, it's earned.

Implementing Systems and Facing Resistance

If the jewellery business was my training ground, it also revealed one of the biggest challenges I would face repeatedly: resistance to change. Most employees had been doing things a certain way for decades, and even the idea of shifting to something new felt threatening.

I remember long conversations with store managers who insisted that their manual Excel sheets were 'more reliable' than any software. I had to explain patiently, and often demonstrate, how automation would reduce errors and free up their time for more meaningful work. That's when I learned that implementing change isn't just about technology; it's about psychology. It's about trust.

The experience also highlighted generational differences within the family itself. My father and uncle preferred informal structures. They liked being the go-to people for every issue, whether it was a sales decision or even a housekeeping problem. They believed this kept them connected to the pulse of the business. And in many ways, they were right. But I could also see how unsustainable it was. For scale, you need systems; for growth, you need structure.

Convincing them wasn't easy. In those early years, I often found myself clashing with them over small but symbolic changes. I'll admit, I made mistakes too. I was impatient. I wanted to modernise everything overnight. This created friction, not just with the older generation, but also with long-serving employees.

It took time and several difficult conversations for me to understand that change in a family business is more like a marathon than a sprint. You can't simply impose transformation; you have to nurture it, one mindset at a time.

Transition to Real Estate and Structural Reform

By October 2022, I transitioned into the real estate business. The shift wasn't merely about changing sectors; it was about stepping into an arena where the stakes were higher, the risks greater, and the opportunities truly transformative.

When I joined, the real estate operations were essentially flat in structure. My uncle oversaw everything, and every employee reported directly to him. Over time, this created decision bottlenecks, limiting growth potential. One of my first moves was to establish a clear hierarchy, a pyramid of responsibility. This wasn't about diminishing my uncle's importance; it was about creating a scalable system where departments could operate semi-independently, with accountability embedded at every level.

The impact was immediate and measurable. In just three years, our workforce grew from 10 full-time employees to over 100. More importantly, while the business had completed around 2 million square feet of construction in its first two decades, we undertook projects totalling 4 million square feet

Left: One of our earliest projects – in the 2000s;
Right: Our latest project – 2025

in my first three years alone. That leap wasn't just a product of favourable market conditions; it was a result of a structure enabling scale. With defined roles, better coordination, and data-driven decision-making, we could handle larger, more complex projects without collapsing under operational pressure.

Simultaneously, I focused on improving our financial strategy. For years, the business had relied solely on internal funds, a cautious but limiting approach. By introducing bank financing, we lowered our cost of capital and leveraged our assets to fuel faster growth. Securing loans at rates lower than those available to established developers was among my proudest moments; it validated not only the credibility of our business but also the trust financial institutions placed in the systems and governance practices we had built.

Scaling Teams and Learning Leadership the Hard Way

Scaling the business meant scaling teams, and that turned out to be one of the hardest lessons I had to learn. Attrition became one of our biggest challenges. At one point, our staff turnover rate was over 70 per cent. I was hiring people, training them, investing time, trust, and energy into their growth, only to watch them leave within months. It was exhausting and demoralising. I often felt like I was constantly firefighting, endlessly replacing and retraining, never able to focus on long-term goals.

At first, I couldn't understand why this was happening. I blamed the market, the employees, and sometimes even my luck. But eventually, I realised part of the problem was me. I was being too flexible, trying to accommodate everyone's preferences, opinions, and working styles. At the same time, I was also over-trusting, assuming everyone would automatically give their best

The Leadership Team of Shree Sonigara Developers and Dilip Sonigara Jewellers – Shruti, Jitendra, Dilip, Tejas and Karan Sonigara

effort. Some did, but many didn't. Over time, I have learned that leadership is about striking a balance. You must be approachable yet firm, friendly yet authoritative, open to ideas yet clear about boundaries. It took me two years of mistakes, conflicts, and sleepless nights to find that balance.

Once I did, things began to change. Our culture stabilised, communication became clearer, and the attrition rate started dropping, first from 70 per cent to 50 per cent, and eventually to under 20 per cent, which now matches industry standards.

That phase taught me that scaling isn't just about expanding projects or profits; it's about scaling people, understanding what motivates them, and creating an environment where they can grow and stay.

The Turning Point: Earning External Trust

One of the most reassuring turning points in my journey came when we were bidding for a redevelopment tender. The society members, who had to choose a developer, specifically requested that my uncle ensure I was present for the presentation. They had seen me speak before; they trusted me to explain the financial planning, funding structures, and to handle the tough questions.

It felt surreal. For years, I had been trying to earn the trust of my own family and employees. And here were outsiders, committee members and stakeholders, insisting that I represent the company. That moment made me realise something important: my efforts were not invisible. People outside the organisation could see my clarity, preparedness, and ability to lead, even before some within had fully recognised it.

A similar moment of validation came later within the company itself. Employees who didn't report directly to me started approaching me with their problems. They saw me not just as the CFO managing finance, but as someone who could help solve execution, scheduling, or operational issues.

When people ten or fifteen years older than me, professionals with decades of experience, came seeking my guidance, it was one of the proudest moments of my career. It reminded me that leadership isn't about age or titles, it's about trust.

The Breakthrough in Branding

For years, our real estate business operated without a clear brand identity. In fact, our name was often confused with several other developers who shared the Sonigara surname. Some of those businesses didn't have the best reputation, and unknowingly, their shortcomings were casting a shadow on us.

This began to change when I teamed up with my cousin, who was leading the marketing team. Together, we pushed for a comprehensive branding exercise, something the older generation had always resisted. Initially, we were allowed to experiment only with a few upcoming projects, and even then, under one strict condition: we had to meet specific sales targets.

Not only did we meet those targets, we surpassed them by a wide margin. The results were dramatic. Customers began recognising our logo and associating it with quality, transparency, and timely delivery. For the first time, we had a distinct identity that separated us from the clutter of similar-sounding names.

The branding initiative went on to play a crucial role in securing a significant redevelopment project in old Pune city, an area where we had no prior presence. Out of dozens of developers, we were shortlisted among the top three, surpassing companies with longer histories and deeper pockets.

That experience reaffirmed a powerful lesson: while history builds credibility, perception builds opportunity. In today's world, how you are seen can often matter as much as what you've achieved.

Operational Challenges and Cash Flow Crises

No story of real estate is complete without acknowledging its biggest challenge, cash flow management. Ours was no different. Real estate demands massive upfront investment, while revenues often arrive much later.

At one point, managing cash flows across multiple special purpose vehicles (SPVs) felt like juggling flaming torches. If one SPV experienced a delay in collections, it immediately affected payments across others. Vendors, contractors, and employees all depended on timely disbursements. Even a shortfall in one project could trigger a ripple effect throughout the organisation.

I made my share of mistakes in this area. There were times I underestimated the timing of inflows, which led to payment delays. Those were some of the most stressful moments of my journey. But they became powerful teachers. Over time, I learned to be more conservative in my projections, always maintaining liquidity buffers, and prioritising payments that would keep the business engine running.

Beyond financial pressures, there were also regulatory hurdles to overcome. On one major project, it took us over a year to secure all the necessary approvals, from local municipal bodies to central government agencies. The list was endless: environmental clearances, land-use conversions, blasting permissions, and even approval from the Ministry of Civil Aviation, since our building was the tallest within a five-kilometre radius and within the airport funnel zone.

That project tested our patience like no other. Yet, it also pushed us to formalise processes, document every step, and build a robust internal system to handle approvals faster in the future. What began as a challenge ultimately became a catalyst for greater efficiency and discipline.

Balancing Short-Term Needs with Long-Term Vision

One of the most brutal balancing acts in business is between short-term goals and long-term investments. In our commercial projects, for instance, our preference has always been to lease out units first, build steady footfall, and then either hold them for rental income or sell them later at a premium.

But at times, cash flow pressures have forced us to sell units earlier than planned. It's never an easy decision. Selling early provides immediate financial relief, but it also reduces long-term returns. On more than one occasion, we've had to liquidate assets or sell land parcels to free up capital. While these decisions were difficult, they ensured the business stayed healthy during uncertain times.

Through these experiences, I've learned that flexibility is key. Business isn't about rigidly adhering to plans; it's about adapting to circumstances without losing sight of the larger vision. The real art lies in knowing when to hold, when to release, and how to keep moving forward, even when the trade-offs are tough.

Mistakes, Lessons, and Growth

I've made many mistakes along the way. In the early years, I frequently clashed with my father and uncle, dismissing their perspectives as outdated. I believed that their caution was a form of resistance to change. It was a course at IIM Calcutta, where I met other family business owners, that genuinely helped me understand the generational gap. I realised that their caution wasn't born of fear; it came from experience. They weren't obstacles holding me back; they were guardians of a legacy built through decades of persistence and sacrifice.

That realisation changed my attitude completely. I stopped seeing disagreements as battles to be won and started viewing them as opportunities to find common ground.

I also made hiring mistakes, bringing in people who were excellent at their technical roles but poor team players. It took time to understand that as an organisation grows, cultural fit becomes as critical as skill. Technical excellence may deliver short-term gains, but shared values and teamwork are what sustain long-term success.

Redefining Success and Giving Back

For me, success isn't defined by profits alone; it's defined by impact. It's about whether employees feel that their lives have improved because of working with us, whether customers continue to trust our brand, and whether society, in some way, benefits from our work.

This belief led me to co-found the *Panraj Pukhraj Sonigara Foundation*, named in honour of my late grandfather. Through the foundation, we focus on education and animal welfare, two causes close to my heart. We've already built a large school in our native village, providing education to over 1,200 students, and contributed to the construction of a new floor at a hospital in Chinchwad. These initiatives remind me that the true purpose of entrepreneurship lies in creating something larger than ourselves.

The school built by the Sonigara group in the native village of Dhana, Rajasthan

संध्या शुक्रवार, दि.८ ऑगस्ट २०२५ पिंपरी-चिंचवड आणि

मोरया हॉस्पिटलच्या विस्तारित मजल्यासाठी सोनिगरा फाउंडेशनकडून एक कोटींचे योगदान

चिंचवड (दै. संध्या) :

स्व. पनराज पुखराज सोनिगरा फाउंडेशन व अश्विन मेडिकल फाउंडेशनच्या मोरया हॉस्पिटल यांच्या संयुक्त विद्यमाने स्व. पनराज पुखराज सोनिगरा स्मृतिदिन सोहळा मोठ्या श्रद्धेने व सामाजिक भान राखत साजरा करण्यात आला.

कार्यक्रमाची सुरुवात सकाळी सत्यनारायण महापूजेने झाली. पाहुण्यांचे स्वागत तुळशीमाळ व गुलाबपुष्प देऊन करण्यात आले. स्व. पनराज सोनिगरांच्या प्रतिमेचे पूजन, नवकार मंत्रजप व आरतीनंतर उपस्थित मान्यवरांच्या हस्ते साध्वीजी विनीतयशाश्रीजी महाराज साहेब व साध्वी निविकल्पाश्रीजी महाराज साहेब यांचा कांबळी अर्पण करून सन्मान करण्यात आला. साध्वीजींनी आपल्या आशीर्वचनात सांगितले की, सोनिगरा परिवाराच्या कार्यातून सामाजिक जाणीव प्रकट होते आणि मोरया हॉस्पिटलच्या इमारतीसाठी दिलेलं योगदान निश्चितच प्रेरणादायी आहे.

या प्रसंगी, फाउंडेशनच्या वतीने मोरया हॉस्पिटलच्या विस्तारित मजल्याच्या बांधकामासाठी १ कोटी रुपयांचे योगदान देण्यात आले आहे. अध्यक्ष तेजस सोनिगरा यांनी आपल्या भाषणात आजोबांच्या आठवणींना उजाळा देत सांगितले की, "आजोबांनी व्यवसायाबरोबरच सामाजिक मूल्यांचे धडेही दिले. त्यांच्या शिकवणीचा वारसा आम्ही सामाजिक कार्यातून पुढे नेत आहोत." श्रुती सोनिगरा यांनीही यावेळी मनोगत व्यक्त केले. कार्यक्रमाचे सूत्रसंचालन मृणाल कुलकर्णी यांनी केले. प्रास्ताविक संस्थेचे कार्यकारी विश्वस्त डॉ. अविनाश वाचासुंदर यांनी करताना संस्थेच्या आरोग्यसेवेविषयीची बांधिलकी स्पष्ट केली. आभार प्रदर्शन संस्थेचे अध्यक्ष डॉ. अरविंद पंडित यांनी केले. या प्रसंगी उपस्थित प्रमुख मान्यवरांमध्ये राष्ट्रीय स्वयंसेवक संघाचे प्रचारक शेखर पंडित, जिल्हा संघचालक विनोद बन्सल, डॉ. रोकडे, जिल्हा कार्यवाह नरेंद्र पेंडसे, विभाग कार्यवाह मुकुंद कुलकर्णी, ज्येष्ठ कार्यकर्ते संजय कुलकर्णी यांचा समावेश होता.

सोनिगरा परिवारातील मोहिनीबेन सोनिगरा, दिलीप पनराज सोनिगरा, जितेंद्र पनराज सोनिगरा, प्रवीण पनराज सोनिगरा, अरविंद सोनिगरा, दर्शन सोनिगरा, करण सोनिगरा, तेजस दिलीप सोनिगरा, प्रवीण कांतिलाल पुनमिया व अन्य सदस्य यावेळी उपस्थित होते. मोरया हॉस्पिटलच्या वतीने या सर्वांचा सत्कार करण्यात आला.

याशिवाय ॲड. अस्मिता वाचासुंदर, डॉ. मुकुंद डिम्गीकर, डॉ. प्रकाश बोराडे, डॉ. अक्षय वाचासुंदर, डॉ. अरविंद पंडित, भगवान तांदे, समीर पाटील, उदय पत्रेवार, सारिका मोरे, रक्षा देशपांडे यांच्यासह मोरया हॉस्पिटलचे डॉक्टर्स, कर्मचारी, ट्रस्ट सदस्य व अनेक नागरिक मोठ्या संख्येने उपस्थित होते.

Contributed towards new development at Moraya Hospital in Chinchwad, Pune – where the family and business are currently based

On a personal note, my dog Ace has been one of my greatest teachers. Having him in my life has made me more empathetic, patient, and attuned to nonverbal communication. He taught me the subtle yet powerful difference between sympathy and empathy, and those lessons have profoundly influenced how I connect with people in both my business and personal life. Through him, I learned that leadership isn't about authority; it's about understanding, listening, and responding with compassion. Whether at work or in life, empathy remains the foundation of every meaningful relationship.

With my dog Ace

Looking Ahead: Vision for the Future

I aim to expand our business into new geographies, undertake larger township projects, and diversify into luxury residential and commercial developments. I aim to professionalise our systems to international standards, ensuring that succession for the next generation becomes seamless, structured, and sustainable.

At the same time, I want our growth to stay deeply rooted in values, quality, trust, timely delivery, and social responsibility. I dream of a time when people hear the name 'Shree Sonigara Developers' and instantly associate it with reliability, excellence, and integrity.

That is the legacy I hope to build, one where progress and principles walk hand in hand, and every project reflects not just what we construct, but what we stand for.

—xxx—

Estd. 1999

Yashraj Biotechnology Limited (YBL) is a research and innovation-driven company, founded in 1999, based in India with sales offices in Germany, the USA and China. The research, development, and production-related activities encompass a wide range of native, recombinant, and cell-derived antigens, monoclonal and Polyclonal antibodies, and services related to iPSC cell lines. With a clear vision and strong values, YBL has grown from strength to strength and has achieved significant growth over the last 25 years. As a Native Antigen manufacturer, YBL has substantially expanded its portfolio over the years to become a premium provider of IVD raw materials and pre-clinical drug discovery services.

Dr Paresh Bhanushali is the Founder, Director and COO at YBL. He holds a PhD in Medical Biotechnology from the MGM Institute of Health Sciences, Navi Mumbai, India, and has published in several reputable national and international journals.

15

Waste to Well-being

Dr Paresh Bhanushali

I was an above-average student during my school years, with a strong aspiration to become a chemical engineer. However, my early college journey did not go as planned. I was barely promoted in my first year of junior college and scored modestly in my 12th standard exams, which left me with no opportunity to pursue engineering. As a result, I enrolled in a B.Sc. program, though my interest in the subject was limited.

Lacking motivation, I took on odd jobs and eventually failed in my first year of B.Sc. It was a challenging phase, but it soon became a turning point. I discovered the JAM examination, a gateway for B.Sc. graduates to pursue M.Sc. at prestigious institutes like IIT Bombay. Motivated and determined, I prepared rigorously and secured an All-India rank of 10. Sensing the potential of the emerging field of Biotechnology, I chose to pursue an M.Sc. in Biotechnology from IIT Bombay, which laid the foundation for my scientific career.

After completing my education, I took a job in the biotech sector and began contemplating pursuing a PhD in the United States. During this time, I was also tutoring the niece of Shree Arvind Bhanushali in mathematics. A

The First R&D and Manufacturing unit Plot C232 Ground plus one facility, constructed and inaugurated on 13th October 2000

YBL Team members, 2003

casual conversation with the visionary Arvindbhai soon turned into a life-changing moment. Inspired by his vision and support, I decided to quit my job and pursue entrepreneurship.

This decision led to the founding of Yashraj Biotechnology Ltd., which initially consisted of a small team of 12. Over the next 25 years, the company steadily grew into one of India's most respected and research-focused biotechnology firms, now employing over 300 people and operating across various domains, including diagnostic proteins, stem cell research, and polyclonal antibody production.

Slow Start, Steady Breakthroughs

The first three years were spent on building our lab and securing approvals from multiple government agencies. Our first sale, ₹2 lakh, came in 2002, and we celebrated it to keep the team motivated. Revenues grew year on year, and we reached break-even in 2007. Until then, Mr Arvind Bhanushali financed the project and kept the company moving forward.

Founder Directors from L to R: Shree Arvind Bhanushali, Mr Bharat Dagha and Paresh Bhanushali

I brought the technical background (M.Sc. Biotechnology, IIT Bombay), while other two promoters were experts in their respective domains: Mr Arvind Bhanushali continued to run his finance business, and Mr Bharat Dagha, a banker who took voluntary retirement at 52, completed a formal biotechnology course to understand the science and lead marketing.

From day one, our vision was clear: make diagnosis affordable and accessible for India. We met with government departments and leading scientists to share this mission. The support we received, even on the regulatory front, pushed us to work harder and smarter. Knowing so many people trusted us made us even more responsible. Our first order of ₹2 lakh in 2002 convinced us we could make international-quality products. In 2003, we received a bulk order for 30 grams of CRP (C-reactive protein), which became one of our flagship products.

Weathering Uncertainty, Building Strength: Validation and Early Challenges

At a major exhibition and conference in the USA, a competitor praised our cancer marker, stating that it would be difficult to match its concentration and quality. When Mr Bharat Dagha called late at night to share this, it felt like a genuine breakthrough, validation that our R&D could deliver internationally accepted quality.

Our business focuses on a niche market with few competitors. A significant challenge has been finding and retaining trained technical talent in R&D and production, as attrition among recruits is high. Demand is also uncertain. Volumes vary by market, and biomedical fluid collection, sourced from large hospitals and healthcare centres across India, can start and stop with shifts in demand. Building and maintaining that collection network takes time. Operationally, we must ensure batch-to-batch consistency despite variable raw-material quality, and we operate with zero tolerance for customer complaints.

Over the last five years, we launched new verticals that are still in the investment phase, with realisations yet to come. Growth in the native antigen segment has slowed, and new native products are lagging. The recombinant vertical has not yet supported revenue. Market pressure comes from uncertain demand and incomplete specifications; most customers engage through distributors. To cope, we produce at defined purity levels and keep products ready "off the shelf," then refine specifications through calls and online meetings so we can deliver quickly once the quantity and quality are finalised.

Family-run firms have several distinct advantages: fewer bureaucratic layers, faster decision-making, and greater alignment with common goals, which is especially helpful when headcount is lean and turnover is costly. But as a family business scales, retaining skilled non-family professionals in critical roles becomes a core challenge.

Turning Point, Growth, and Lessons

The two years before breakeven were the toughest. We had been burning cash for nearly six years; sales were happening, but one customer rejected products that another customer accepted. In 2007, we hired a technical CEO. Around the time of his joining, our marketing team secured a large contract, which was approximately four times our production capacity. We expanded biomedical fluid collection by adding new centres, monitored progress daily (including collections, hospital additions, and approvals), and made on-the-spot financial decisions. We executed on time and reached breakeven in 2007. From there, revenues doubled roughly every five years until 2020. Growth is now flatter, but we have made significant investments in new verticals that are expected to begin generating revenue in the coming years.

One line I hold close is, "This too shall pass." Failures are temporary and teach vital lessons. Early on, I tried to do everything myself, micromanaging, which led to delays in product development, unresolved complaints, and collection bottlenecks. Delegation and building a second line were key, as advised by my partner-mentor, Arvindbhai. Today, team leads handle production, quality control, and biomedical fluid procurement independently while the R&D team stability remains a focus.

Our industry will always carry uncertainty because customers share specifications only when necessary, as they are proprietary. In such a situation, consistent and transparent communication helps reduce ambiguity and builds trust across teams and clients. Another thing that helps is replacing rigidity with flexibility and accepting mistakes instead of justifying them. That shift in mindset helped us design stronger systems and more robust processes for the future.

Our Financial Management

We manage finances with one eye on expenses and the other on revenue, while keeping quality and customer commitments at the centre. Cost is not the priority. By consistently delivering what we promise, on time, we build trust and a strong brand. High customer satisfaction leads to repeat business, enabling us to fine-tune our budgeted revenue and expenses. In our view, healthy margins and sales growth are by-products of meeting customer needs with quality, timeliness, and value for money.

Funding Discipline and Resource Allocation

We track the minimum sales needed to stay afloat and make investments tied to revenue generation. We are disciplined in maintaining a sound debt–to-equity ratio and adequate working capital, both of which are essential for raising funds from financial institutions. We monitor key business ratios and allocate resources accordingly. 50% of the annual budget goes to achieving yearly goals, while 25% is allocated to mid-term goals and 25% to long-term goals.

For us, brand building is a by-product of solving customer problems. Regular communication with clients and staying alert to market trends, through expos and conferences, guides our long-term goals.

From Complaints to Co-Creation: Product Choices and Timing

Our early product development drew on experience, internet research, and competitor websites. The missing piece was customisation. Stability was also a challenge because multiple versions of the same product used different formulations. We faced major failures at the customer end due to stability issues, and management took the bold decision to replace the entire stock, absorbing a revenue loss.

We often slipped into justification mode when complaints arrived. Our certificates of analysis looked fine, but the customer's end use was not what we were characterising. Limited access to end-user teams led to many complaints remaining unresolved. Wherever customers were directly involved, development and rejections were handled correctly, and some blockbuster products emerged from this deep collaboration. Since then, marketing and development have prioritised direct communication to capture the correct characterisation data and deliver the right product.

Not every R&D output earns revenue. Product selection must be grounded in real market inputs, including customer feedback and insights from exhibitions/conferences, and backed by careful planning, as time, money, and people are at stake. Timing is critical – if we miss the window, demand may disappear or a competitor may capture it. The key to launching is choosing the right product and the right time.

We once believed we were the world's largest producer of native antigens. Global exploration showed we were significant, but not the largest. During the COVID-19 pandemic, market inputs suggested that any quantity of CRP, CA15-3, and HBsAg-ay would sell. We scaled biomedical fluid collection and quintupled our capacity, but as infections declined, demand decreased. We were left with over ₹30 crore in stock. The lesson: don't jump on a bandwagon without rigorous market research and analysis.

Success So Far, and the Next 10 Years

The definition of success is personal, but for me, it includes building robust products, forming strong teams, mentoring a capable second line, scaling and customising, and completing my PhD. We now support 350+ jobs, focus on employee well-being, serve a strong international customer base, generate profits, and maintain financial stability. Still, there's more to do: bring new verticals to revenue, stabilise IVD R&D, and speed up development across Native and Recombinant lines. Our value system, which meets the needs of employees, shareholders, vendors, and customers, guides the sustainable building of a legacy. We never gave up, thanks to Arvindbhai's financial and moral support.

10-Year Vision

- Make the new verticals self-sustaining and take YBL to unicorn status.
- Tighten marketing–development coordination; stabilise IVD R&D; and reorganise the recombinant team with a renewed product vision.
- Drive customer-centricity: more first-time-right deliveries and fewer rejections through closer customer interaction.
- Retain talent and build a strong second line.
- Pursue automation and AI-enabled tools wherever feasible.
- Strengthen marketing to build markets in new verticals: goat polyclonal antiserum, Rabbit polyclonal antiserum, recombinant antibodies for control manufacturing, and stem cell services/products.

The Personal Cost and Growth of Building a Business

Starting a business demands time, often at the cost of family and friends. I could not give my family the attention they deserved. Reaching breakeven took seven years, and it wasn't until eleven years later that I took my family on a vacation. A supportive partner is essential to understand these sacrifices. On the positive side, entrepreneurship brings personal growth and confidence, as well as a sense of pride and fulfilment from building something from the ground up and creating a positive impact. Sharing this journey can also inspire family and friends to pursue their own goals. With mindful time management across work, family, friends, and community, achieving a work–life balance is possible, though not always easy.

Day-to-day decisions, operations, staffing, production targets, customer requirements, complaints, and delays create constant pressure. Some days are draining, and stress or anxiety can build up. This is a real part of entrepreneurship. The feeling that there's never enough time adds to the strain. Yet passion for the work and the satisfaction of solving complex problems keep me moving. When you believe in the company's vision and values, some stress becomes energising rather than disabling.

To manage stress, I listen to music, visit holy places, and have candid conversations with my wife. I also enjoy engaging in origami and Ayurvedic research in my free time. These practices help me reset and return to work with clarity.

Founders' Vision, Next-Gen Choices

Ours is a family business founded by first-generation entrepreneurs, including myself, Arvindbhai, and Mr Bharat Dagha, in 1999. Since we didn't have any expectations from anyone, whatever the team delivered excited us. We established our vision and values, on which we based our business. Our children who will follow this will be part of the team. Currently, two of Mr Arvind Bhanushali's sons joined the business in 2020. The initial joining was as a management trainee to understand our value system and align with the vision. My son is currently pursuing a PhD in Biomedical Engineering at IIT Bombay. Mr Bharat Dagha's son is not interested in joining the company as of now.

We have professionals running the business & an independent board to guide us strategically. As shareholders, we are focused on a long-term vision and managing employee expectations by offering market-competitive compensation and investing a substantial amount in staff welfare initiatives. We offer ESOPs/shadow ESOPs to the employee. We are in the process of building a legacy where social good and value systems take precedence over everything else, including commercials.

Self-Worth Intertwined with the Firm

Yes. Since my self-worth and purpose are intertwined with business, our vision is "Be the key player in life science diagnostics and drive innovation for making a healthier world". Since my personal value system is aligned with it, I am comfortable with it.

If not Business...

The turning point to venture into the business was meeting with Shri Arvind Bhanushali and discussing the career path I was pursuing. As mentioned earlier, I joined the industry after my post-graduation in Biotechnology from IIT Bombay to prepare financially for a PhD in the United States. My IIT friends, all of whom were pursuing PhDs in the US, encouraged me to come to the US for my PhD. The environment and the infrastructure were very new in India at that time. I was in the third batch of the Master's program in Biotechnology at IIT Bombay. The meeting with Arvind Bhanushali inspired me to think more critically about the business. It was a mixed feeling, as I was a novice in terms of the business environment and running the show, being the only technical person responsible for driving product development. Additionally, I had high enthusiasm for taking on a project independently and demonstrating my technical skills, rather than working for another company.

If the meeting had not taken place, I would likely have pursued a PhD in the USA, followed by a postdoctoral fellowship, and then perhaps joined a university as a research scientist, as my IIT friends are currently doing. Perhaps I might have joined a Biotechnology Company in the USA as a researcher, working on innovative R&D and Product Development.

Challenges and Opportunities Ahead

I anticipate both the challenges and opportunities that the current business presents. As we are currently established as the native bulk antigen Supplier Company in the international market, the tag makes it really challenging to be a partner in the developmental programs of the end-user companies. Additionally, other portfolios of product supply, such as recombinant antigens and antibodies, are presenting challenges for the research and development teams in preparing and developing market-ready products. This may be due to a lack of understanding of the products by either the development team or the marketing team. Additionally, being established as a Native antigen Supply Company could also be one of the reasons IVD companies have less confidence in us. The other challenge anticipated is that significantly fewer new products have been developed, even in the Native antigen segment. This also makes companies aware of the slow development (Technical competency) or stagnation in the market launch of new products.

Another challenge is the slow performance of the new ventures that the company initiates. The new verticals started in induced pluripotent Stem cell (iPSc) development, Recombinant antibody development using phage display technology, Polyclonal antibody production in goats, molecular diagnostics kit development for blood screening and development of a digitally intelligent stethoscope.

Scaling the native antigen business is a challenge, so we have adopted an appropriate strategy of partnering with end-users to develop new products by demonstrating our capability of collecting biomedical fluids (the basic raw material for Native antigen production) and converting them into customised products. For the overall business, we are developing succession plans for each key position in marketing, R&D, HR, and finance. We are adopting the latest available technology and also integrating all the systems and processes through computerisation and flexible policies/systems to meet business needs. We encourage teams to make out-of-the-box decisions and focus on outcomes rather than assigning blame. We focus on issues, solve them, and move ahead.

Advice for Upcoming Biotech Founders

For new biotech entrepreneurs, adapting and recovering from adversity and stress is a skill that can be learned and developed. One must accept setbacks as they are a regular part of life. See failures as learning opportunities and build a strong support system, including mentors and a diverse team. Be optimistic, focus during challenging periods, and embrace uncertainty as an inherent part of the high-risk, cutting-edge biotech field. Maintain perseverance in the face of scientific and market shifts. Don't take things personally, and understand that the personal and professional aspects of running a biotech business will always be interconnected. Have a positive outlook and avoid giving up too soon. Focus on what you can control and learn from experience. Don't try to do everything alone. The initial years will be tough, and significant breakthroughs can take a longer time to realise. Stay motivated and have faith in your vision. Be prepared to wear many hats, especially in the early stages of your career. Build a team of people who believe in your idea and share your passion for the product and its mission. Hire smarter, not just more experienced, and ensure they are aligned with your vision.

In short, here is some advice: 1. Set a clear vision before one starts a company. Have a value system in place to guide the operation of a business 2. Focus on one thing at a time. In that selection, based on priority and urgency, activities are prioritised using the power of three. Finish that and go to the next power of three 3. Be transparent to all your stakeholders, including customers, employees, suppliers, regulators, investors, and shareholders.

Corporate Office and Stem Cell Research Centre Plot C113

Goat Farm Facility built at Karjat near Mumbai – Aerial View

—xxx—

16

The Soil and the Seed

KINNARI DESAI

My grandfather, the late Shri Anil Desai, was a chemist by education and profession, but more than that, he was a man defined by resilience. His journey toward education was gruelling. His father, my great-grandfather, had migrated from Gujarat to Maharashtra, where he worked in a factory that manufactured utensils. When severe asthma struck him, the responsibility of running the household and raising three siblings fell squarely on my grandfather's young shoulders.

To support his family, my grandfather wrote textbooks, gave private tuition, and took on odd jobs, all while pursuing his M.Sc. in Chemistry and ensuring that his siblings completed their education. It was during these formative years that his entrepreneurial ambition took shape. He leveraged his knowledge to create solutions that improved lives. Inspired by the call of 'Harit Kranti' and 'Jai Jawan, Jai Kisan,' by our late Prime Minister Lal Bahadur Shastri, he decided to build something meaningful. That vision became Sujanil Chemo Industries.

As an entrepreneur, Anil Desai was known for his empathy and compassion. His principles were rooted in fairness, guided by a rule that no person should ever lose money because of their association with Sujanil. He was a perfectionist who set high standards, yet he paired this demand for excellence with encouragement and support, inspiring people to rise to their best.

Guided by the belief that no matter what, it is essential to walk alongside the people who supported you in difficult times, he brought his married sisters and their families from Gujarat to Pune, giving them the responsibility of running the company's printing and packaging unit. This act strengthened family bonds and reflected his philosophy that business was about inclusion and unity. Despite the long hours and endless responsibilities, he was a caring and loving father who made every moment with his family joyful and memorable. He believed strongly that education and passion should never be compromised. Each of his three children was encouraged to follow their paths wholeheartedly, just as he had fought to pursue his own studies against all odds.

The Origin of Sujanil

In 1966, Anil Desai partnered with Sunderlal and Jayantilal Shah, who had the financial resources but lacked technical expertise. Their collaboration gave rise to Pune's very first pesticide manufacturing factory.

However, difficulties soon set in. Agrochemicals proved to be a niche category, with production highly seasonal. Sales peaked for only three to four months a year, leaving the factory idle for the rest of the time. The procurement of active raw materials was largely dependent on multinationals, resulting in frequent delays. Worker retention became increasingly complex, and sustaining operations seemed daunting.

The chemist and entrepreneur in my grandfather began to look for a different path. He noticed that household insect problems, such as bedbugs and lice, were not seasonal inconveniences but year-round concerns, often bringing both discomfort and social stigma. He launched two pioneering products: Nok-99, India's first indigenous bedbug solution, and Licel, a lice treatment oil.

The decision proved visionary. Within three to four years, demand for these products stabilised the business and created year-round employment for workers. Soon after, the Sarabhai Group, one of India's leading distributors, tested and approved Nok-99 for nationwide marketing. At the time, the only alternatives were Bayer's Tick-20 and Pfizer's Dalf, both multinational products. Sujanil's swadeshi offering stood tall against global giants and quickly gained recognition as a homegrown company with homegrown solutions.

The journey was not smooth. In 1971, when his partners faced bankruptcy, my grandfather was advised to close the unit. It was his father who gave him the counsel that became a cornerstone of his business ethics: 'They brought you into this business. It's not right to leave them midway just because times are tough. Run it as best as you can.' Taking this advice to heart, my grandfather chose not to retreat. He brought my grandmother into the administration, entrusted his younger brother with production, and shouldered marketing himself. Together, the family steered the company through stormy waters.

I often wondered what truly motivated my grandfather to develop a lice treatment solution. To me, he was never just a businessman, his problem-solving spirit and boldness made me realise that my love for design was not accidental, but a seed he planted.

Sujanil, founded in 1966, has always been more than a company. It is my grandfather's determination woven into its roots, a man carrying his family on one shoulder and his dreams on the other, never letting either fall.

Late Shri Anil Desai, Founder of Sujanil Chemo Industries, receiving the A.R. Bhatt Entrepreneurship Award

Following Legacy: The Second Generation

My great-grandfather would take my father, Ashish Desai, on daily walks, sharing stories of his migration from Gujarat and the challenges he faced settling and supporting his family. My grandfather also ensured that his son developed an interest in the business and gained an understanding of its intricacies. To strengthen this interest, he encouraged him to attend factory inspections and visits from dignitaries and government officials, even allowing him to miss school so he could be present during important factory visits. Those interactions and experiences sparked his curiosity in managing operations and learning the various aspects of manufacturing and business. Alongside this, my grandfather often shared his own educational and entrepreneurial struggles, and those stories gradually shaped his interest in joining the family business and continuing the legacy.

My father, entered the business earlier than expected. At the age of eighteen, while still in college, my grandfather suffered two heart attacks. He said to him, 'I'm not going to last much longer, and I won't be able to hand over a ready-made business. Do your B.Sc. and focus on business. Studying will help you understand the technical side, and managing the factory will give you experience.' Because his father, Anil Desai, had already instilled in him a genuine passion for business, it was not very challenging to take on the dual responsibility.

My grandfather handed the formulas for Licel and Nok-99 to my father and put him in charge of production. He would work nights at the Chinchwad unit, preparing lots that were then processed and sent to the market, balancing full days of study with full nights of work. Working nights and studying by day was tough, but it gave him early practical experience.

There was also a packaging unit for cartons and labels. During my grandfather's illness, the manager in charge used substandard paper, resulting in consignments being rejected. My grandfather's advice was simple: *"If you want to avoid being cheated, learn the technical side yourself."* Taking this to heart, my father completed a diploma at the Maharashtra Institute of Printing Technology, took charge of the unit, and turned it around. Under the name Besquare Packaging, the unit began supplying not only our own needs but also those of clients such as pharmaceutical firms, SK Bearings, and Bajaj Auto.

Ashish Desai, Chairman & CEO, Sujanil Chemo Industries. Receiving the Best Small Scale Entrepreneur Award from the Government of Maharashtra

The Breakthrough

In a short span of time, my father began to understand the importance of balancing our product profile with business activities. Until the early 1990s, our dependence was primarily on one or two brands and on contract manufacturing, which we had begun using to counter the seasonal fluctuations in agrochemical demand. During this time, we faced stiff competition from multinational giants, but we gave them a tough fight. This period propelled us to develop new and diverse products. We realised that 'me-too' formulations would never help us scale or grow the business to the next level. Instead, we focused on creating niche, customer-centric solutions that addressed real needs and delivered guaranteed efficacy. With this approach, we developed at least twenty-five products that became best-in-class, known for their quality and effectiveness. These products built strong consumer trust while providing good profitability to our channel partners, helping us sustain ourselves against both multinational giants and aggressive local players.

Competition is a Norm

In the early 1990s, competition from multinationals like Bayer and Pfizer was intense. Sujanil couldn't match their advertising budgets, so we focused on strengthening our market presence directly.

Each year, my father would tour the country, sometimes alone and sometimes with the sales team, covering entire regions in just forty-five days. Over the course of four years, he had visited almost every primary market in India and even marketed Licel alone in Tamil Nadu. These tours built direct connections with distributors and retailers, showing the team that he was ready to work alongside them.

Awards and Accreditation

My father kept reminding the team that while we lacked large advertising budgets, we had goodwill and a loyal customer base. Once people used Licel or Nok-99, they returned for more. He urged the team to keep these products visible on counters, even in small numbers. This approach paid off. In 1996–97, we sold forty lakh bottles of Licel, bringing absolute stability to the business.

Financial Lows and Critical Decisions

The late 1990s brought new challenges. After the passing of Jayantilal Shah's son, the business saw increasing difficulties. My grandfather and father were technical partners, but they had little visibility into the company's financial transactions. Liquidity was tight, and it became clear that difficult decisions had to be made.

The partners were offered a choice: either they could take complete control of the company and run it or allow us to continue operating independently. Negotiations dragged on, but the partners were unwilling to let go without securing a liquidity solution. Eventually, my father took on the responsibility of generating the required funds. With the support of my grandmother and my mother, in about 8 months, they were able to create liquidity and amass sufficient capital to buy out the partners. It was a testing period, but it also gave him confidence that this organisation could stand on its own strength.

A New Beginning and a Shock of Loss

By the late 1990s, Sujanil was in fresh hands. After years of navigating partnerships and negotiations, the ropes were firmly in our family's grasp. Just as this new chapter was beginning, life dealt a heavy blow. My grandfather, Anil Desai, passed away suddenly. His absence left not only a personal void but also a question hanging over the business: '*What now?*'

With my grandfather's passing, it felt like the ground had shifted beneath everyone's feet. As the youngest, the responsibility fell to my father. In those uncertain days, my grandmother's quiet strength gave him courage and clarity to move forward.

He soon realised Sujanil couldn't rely on just one side of the business. While our consumer products, such as Licel and Nok-99, defined the company publicly, the roots were in the pesticide manufacturing industry. To survive and grow, the company needed both branded products for visibility and trust, as well as manufacturing for stability and cash flow.

We already worked with Bayer and Indofil, and talks were reopened with Indofil when liquidity was tight. They proposed producing their branded products using our facilities, while they would handle sales and collections. Margins were modest, but payments were assured, keeping our plants active and our reputation intact.

Rebalancing also meant tightening operations. Audit readiness became routine. We built daily discipline around our certifications, including ISO 9001, GMP, US-FDA, and Organic. We reconnected with suppliers to cut lead times, refined production planning, and focused on retaining skilled operators. Gradually, Sujanil regained its rhythm, steady on the floor, stable in the books, and visible in the market.

Building for Growth

Once stability was restored, the question shifted from survival to scaling. For the company and the brand to be taken seriously by both multinational partners and Indian households, we needed capacity, credibility, and consistency.

Our base was at Wanwadi, Pune, where my grandfather had first set up the unit. We upgraded it to meet global audit standards. Then came Gahunje, on the Pune–Mumbai corridor, for better logistics, and Pirangut, in Pune's industrial belt, to balance production and minimise downtime. By 2006, with the assistance of allied units, we had four operating factories.

Growth occurred through two routes: deepening contract manufacturing partnerships with Bayer, DuPont, Rallis, Sulphur Mills, Indofil and others, and expanding our own brands. From Licel and Nok-99, we developed a comprehensive household insecticide range, comprising Nok-99 Gel, Nok Bait, Hunt 100, Nok Lines chalk, Nok-99 Ready-to-Use liquid, and Wood Shield termite solution, with 50 SKUs supported by a team of 250 people.

We followed strict ethics, never launching partner formulations under our own brand and never supplying the same product to two companies. This discipline earned trust and long-term relationships, our strongest asset.

We entered the export market, formed technical collaborations with France and China, and aligned our operations with US-FDA standards. Recognition followed, ISO 9001, GMP, Organic, and US-FDA certifications. Licel won a Gold Medal, Sujanil received the FICCI Small Scale Industries Award, and was even mentioned in the Lok Sabha as a swadeshi company

Left: Production Line – Nok 99 Aerosol;
Right: Sujanil's Manufacturing Unit in Pune

of multinational quality. Maharashtra honoured us with the Best Small-Scale Entrepreneur and Udyog Ratna awards.

Financial Management and Growth Strategy

For my father, financial learning was shaped by trial and error. Much of his career was spent in 'hand-to-mouth' conditions, where every rupee counted and cash crunches were frequent. These experiences taught him practical, disciplined resource management. His guiding principle has always been to ensure optimum surplus without compromising standards.

Our business model is consumer-centric, with zero tolerance for compromise on product quality. This minimises returns, ensures zero defects, and builds both consumer trust and profitability. When one of our flagship products faced tough competition from a multinational giant, a thousand times our size, by staying true to quality and refining our strategy, we not only regained ground but also achieved record volumes and value. That reinforced our belief that uncompromising quality is the best guarantee of cash flow and revenue.

Finance, to me personally, often feels overwhelming. The best way to generate revenue is to create high-quality products and effectively market them. Strong consumer trust has always been our greatest asset, and the goodwill our brands enjoy is a testament to the fact that quality and integrity lead to stability.

For me, progress is measured in two ways: the numbers on a report and the stories from the market. Without revenue, no business can survive, but without customer trust, numbers mean little. Revenue and surplus are essential not just for stability but also for the freedom to expand and scale.

Our goal is to ensure an optimal surplus without compromising standards, a principle I hold dear. To me, money represents growth. I may still be learning the language of finance, but I have come to understand the importance of protecting stability, honouring earned trust, and building for a future where the business grows across portfolios without losing its roots.

The Emotional Landscape of Entrepreneurship

Entrepreneurship shapes not just the business, but also the person. For my father, the impact was felt most in relationships. At times, the demands of work made him seem like a harsh and ruthless father or an irresponsible friend. Endless responsibilities meant that he missed many family moments. The business had a way of claiming all of him, but it helped him navigate the challenges in his personal life.

It also made him deeply empathetic and compassionate toward colleagues and employees. All this at the cost of sometimes watching personal relationships drift. His passion came through most clearly in his love for sports. Growing up, he was a swimmer at the state and national level, even winning medals, and cricket was always close to his heart. When he could no longer compete, he found alternative ways to stay connected by creating corporate platforms for sportspeople, offering them job opportunities, and supporting their training through sponsorships. It became his way of turning passion into purpose and using Sujanil as a vehicle to give back. Coping with stress was never easy, but music was always a refuge. It offered clarity in chaos and calm when decisions weighed heavily.

A large part of who I am today has been shaped by growing up in a business family. Watching my parents devote themselves to this organisation and business sharpened my communication skills and confidence from an early age. Sujanil has always been part of my identity. Still, it is a platform where I can bring together my strengths and contribute in my own way, with flexibility and respect for the legacy.

For a while, I explored other paths, testing my creativity, building my identity outside the family business. Those experiences gave me independence and perspective. They pulled me back to the family business out of a realisation that this platform allows me to combine all my strengths- design, strategy, creativity, and storytelling into a larger, unified picture. On the one hand, I feel excited and energised at the thought of building further, modernising, and leaving my own mark. On the other hand, there is anxiety, the awareness of the high standards set by my father and grandfather, and the question of whether I will be able to match and sustain them.

To steady myself, I often turn to reading and engaging in conversations with others. Listening to their experiences and perspectives provides me with valuable insights that help me grow and develop. It reminds me that while legacy carries weight, it also carries strength.

Legacy, Family and Identity

Navigating the expectations as a leader is never easy. The journey of Sujanil and the growth from a rented factory to eight wholly owned units serves as the strongest testimony to success. Through all this, my grandmother's strength and my mother, Monica's, unwavering support gave my father both courage and clarity during some of the most testing phases. They were a reminder that no matter what the strain of the business, family is what steadies you.

My father always treated inheritance as an honour, never an obligation, where he has been able to provide a livelihood to at least 1,000 families directly or indirectly. Inheritance, for me, is a double-edged sword. It is a privilege that hands you decades of wisdom, values and connections, but it can also feel overwhelming and make you anxious about whether you will ever be enough to carry it forward.

For me, joining the family business is not just about carrying the torch; it is about reimagining the flame. The foundations my grandfather and father built are strong. Now, it is time to let that flame grow, to move away from older modules and create fresh, adaptable models that can thrive in today's world.

Independence, to me, did not come from immediately embracing the family business. It came after I tested other waters, explored my passions in design and creativity, and experienced different worlds on my own. Those detours helped me see more clearly that independence lies in thinking beyond what I already know, trusting myself to bring change, and still staying anchored in the values and culture that shaped us.

If I weren't building the company, I would still be immersed in design and creativity, focusing on well-being and psychology. In fact, I see that as a natural extension of the business itself. The company provides me with a platform to weave together design, storytelling, and creative strategy into a broader picture without restriction, and that flexibility is something I deeply value.

When I receive praise or a critique in the business, the emotions are mixed. There is pride and motivation to keep learning and evolving but also flashes of frustration in the moment. Yet, in retrospect, every word becomes part of my learning curve.

Defining Success

For Sujanil, the most defining moment of success came during one of the toughest challenges in our history: preparing for the US FDA inspection in just four months. The timeline was so tight that we had to practically rebuild everything from scratch. It was the toughest test of our mettle, but years of experience and learning stood by us. Ultimately, we secured approval with only four observations. That achievement gave us a deep sense of accomplishment and the confidence that no challenge is too big when met with clarity and persistence.

Personally, success feels more like a balance between freedom, growth, and impact. The freedom to explore new ideas and apply my creativity, the growth that comes from learning and pushing Sujanil into new spaces, and the impact we can have when our work reaches homes and improves everyday life.

Moving Forward

Our vision for Sujanil is to see the company counted among the top ten manufacturers of health-focused products in the country. To reach that point, our compass must always remain steady, innovative, user-friendly, provide guaranteed service, and, above all, ensure efficacy. These are not just words but the foundation that has carried us this far, and the same will take us further.

Our products have always been born out of well-thought-out, user-friendly solutions. These qualities are not limited to Indian households, they are the fundamental needs of populations worldwide. That is why our future is closely tied to global markets. What we build here, with care and precision, can serve anywhere.

Yet, alongside the challenge, what excites me most is the prospect of exports. India holds a natural advantage here. With our intellectual strength, unique products, and services, we have much to offer the world. Sujanil is well-aligned with these demands, and I see a bright and promising future ahead for us on the global stage. I see our products sitting on shelves not just across India, but across the globe, a synonym for efficacy and efficiency.

The next aim is also about giving back to society, to the environment, and to the generations that will follow. For me, this means embedding sustainability into everything we do while ensuring Sujanil stays at the forefront of technology. It is an opportunity to reinforce the fact that legacy brands can lead the way in both responsibility and growth.

—xxx—

SSA

SSA is a Mumbai-based Architectural firm built on partnership, commitment, and quality, treating design as a strategic tool to achieve impactful results. It is jointly run by sisters Mona Shah and Alpa Shikre, along with Alpa's husband Sandeep Shikre, who is the founder of the firm.

The firm's philosophy, 'Architecture and Beyond,' inspires creative, inclusive, and innovative designs. With a rich portfolio and national and international recognition, SSA offers Architecture, Interior Design, and Construction Management Consultancy Services. The firm's integrated, customised approach ensures a seamless transition from vision to reality, setting it apart from its competitors.

17

Pathikrit: One Who Makes a New Path

Alpa Shikre & Mona Shah

SSA's story begins with a small studio and a big idea: design that puts space, people, and happiness at the centre.

Today, we are proud to say that teamwork and meticulous hard work have been inculcated into our company's very culture, which has helped us build lasting relationships and spaces that perform beautifully for the people they intend to serve.

The Founder

As a Mumbai schoolboy, Sandeep Shikre nearly chose cricket until his father redirected his focus. During a casual chat, his father asked, 'Do

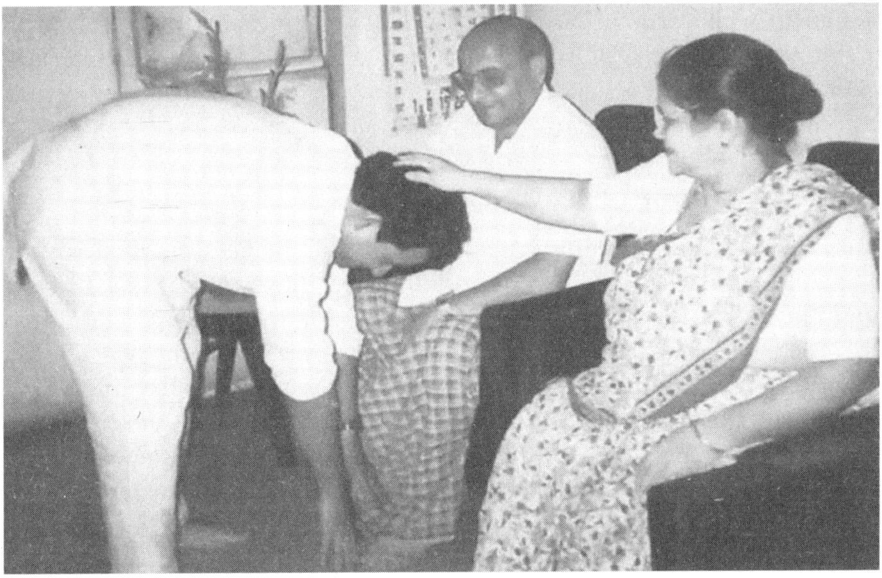

The blessings that drive SSA

you want to be a professional cricketer?' Sandeep said yes. 'Cricket is a 1-in-1000 shot,' his father replied. 'Higher studies are 1-in-10. Choose wisely. And if you ever fail, fail with honesty and diligence. No shortcuts. No compromises.'

That moment reset his compass. Sandeep chose academics, along with a mindset of disciplined effort, calculated risk, and long-range planning, which would later power his entrepreneurial journey. He carried that mindset into architecture. In 1989, he founded SSA, setting uncompromising standards: full compliance, transparent finances, and delivery rigour that won early trust.

SSA believes in empowering specialists, sharing authority, and stepping into whatever role a complex project demands without losing commercial clarity. This approach shaped SSA's identity design for space, people, and happiness, and enabled landmark work like Kohinoor Square.

The Creative Force

The humble beginnings of our company were shaped by ethics and discipline, where teamwork was valued, resulting in promising outcomes. As Alpa joined the business, she brought in the wonderful fusion of design, craft, and operational sense. Her contributions shifted our initial sustainability-centric approach to interiors, making them practical and performance-driven.

The Mudra House and the Kokilaben Dhirubhai Ambani Hospital illustrate her ability to blend creativity with practical, user-focused solutions, earning national and international acclaim. Alpa's commitment to sustainable design is a hallmark of her career. In 2008, she became the first Indian architect to achieve USGBC LEED accreditation for commercial interiors, demonstrating her foresight in prioritising environmental responsibility long before it became mainstream.

The Operational Strategist

Mona's story is one of turning grit into systems. She cut her teeth modernising a mobile-crane business in a male-dominated industry, learning to steer unskilled to highly skilled crews toward one outcome: reliable delivery. In 2004, she brought that edge to our company, co-founding the Project Management Consultancy to bridge the gap between design intent and on-ground execution. Hands-on yet calm under pressure, she pairs risk discipline with empathetic leadership, aligning teams, optimising resources, and safeguarding the vision shaped by Sandeep and Alpa. She led projects like Kohinoor City to the Dharavi Redevelopment, showcasing her problem-solving and planning skills.

The Journey

Founding Years (1989–95)

SSA was founded in 1989 with an initial capital of ₹25,000, a small but dedicated team of three, and a vision to deliver ethical, high-quality design. Early projects were modest but significant, secured through personal networks. The firm's first architectural assignment was the Kohinoor Technical Institute in Aurangabad. This project tested his nascent capabilities, requiring him to navigate client expectations while working within resource limitations, including tight budgets and schedules. We slowly built credibility with clients, contractors, and banks.

Our focus on transparency, compliance, the belief that 'Client is God', and the understanding that we exist because of them is what sets us apart in a competitive industry, where clients have numerous options.

Early Growth and Expansion (1996–2003)

In the late 1990s, we expanded our service offerings to include Interior Design. Alpa's expertise became pivotal in securing institutional, residential, and commercial projects that required both architectural and design insight. The firm navigated its first economic downturn in 1996, when residential projects slowed, testing its operational and financial resilience.

By 1999, we had begun working with international clients, including a partnership with GKK in the United States. A satellite office in Pune allowed the firm to design projects abroad while simultaneously building its domestic portfolio. During these years, we continued to invest in our team, encouraging interns and junior staff to grow within the firm, creating a culture of mentorship and loyalty.

The Era of Collective Leadership (2004 Onwards)

Mona joined SSA in 2004, establishing the PMC vertical. This addition allowed the firm to provide integrated 'one-stop' services across Architecture, Interior Design, and Project Management.

Their first fully integrated project was the 50-acre Kohinoor City development in Mumbai, for Unmesh Joshi. For Kohinoor City, the Architectural and Interior Design, along with Project Management, was seamlessly executed with the support of the 'SSA core team', also known as the pillars of SSA, establishing our brand as a one-stop solution provider. Subsequent projects, such as Kohinoor Square and the BDD Chawls (Naigaon), reinforced the value of this integrated approach.

Innovation and Recognition (2008–15)

By 2008, SSA had over 100 employees and was beginning to receive international recognition. The AIT Award in Germany for the Mudra headquarters and the LEED Platinum certification for Kohinoor Hospital, the first in Asia, positioned SSA as a leader in sustainable and high-performance design. The Dandi Memorial in Gujarat, inaugurated in 2019 as a net-zero energy project, reflected the firm's long-standing commitment to sustainability.

Awards and Accolades

Throughout this period, we emphasised internal growth, offering mentorship, skill development, and career progression. Their culture of collaboration, shared responsibility, and transparent communication has fostered a high-performing and loyal team.

Scaling Operations and Market Leadership (2016–Present)

Subsequently, SSA diversified into urban renewal, high-rise residential, institutional, hospitality, healthcare, and mixed-use developments. Landmark projects include:

Dharavi Redevelopment Project (2022): The largest slum redevelopment project globally, covering 250 hectares and over 120 million square feet of construction. SSA's role includes providing PMC services, statutory compliance, legal and financial advisory services, and socio-economic planning. Kohinoor Square has remained India's tallest mixed-use building for the last decade, incorporating innovative design and project management.

Today, the firm has a team of 425+, with specialised teams in Architecture, Interior Design, sustainability, Project Management, 3D studio, and Revit studio. Every project reflects the team's commitment to exceeding expectations.

SSA's Financial Management

Starting SSA without any seed capital meant that the founders had to focus on the business's fundamentals. Their priority was to deliver exceptional design and architecture while leveraging the collective intellect, creativity, and dedication of their small but determined team. From the very beginning, the emphasis was not merely on completing projects but on creating tangible value for clients. Every decision is rooted in ensuring transparency, integrity, credibility and adhering to financial commitments has become the cornerstone of our financial ethos.

The early years of the firm were surprisingly advantageous in one way: a consultancy practice, unlike construction or manufacturing businesses, did not require extensive working capital to begin operations. Their first major expense was purchasing computers, along with the software licenses, which were funded by savings and borrowings from friends and family.

The firm's meticulous approach to compliance and financial discipline enabled us to maintain impeccable records even when tax returns initially showed a nil balance, which helped build a strong credit profile. Banks and financial institutions soon recognised SSA as a trustworthy, credible entity to whom they were willing to lend and support. As the business gradually grew, profits were reinvested back into the firm, increasing its equity while nurturing a culture of financial prudence. Simultaneously, transparency and credibility inspired confidence among clients, some of whom began providing advances in fees, testament to the trust we had built in our first decade of operations.

Our company's journey, however, was far from linear. The firm experienced multiple economic recessions that tested its resilience and strategic foresight.

The first significant downturn came in 1996, when residential construction slowed, and the team strength was twenty-five.

In 2008, the global financial crisis led to a near standstill in international projects, particularly in Dubai and the USA, at a time when the team had grown to 100. The Mumbai real estate slowdown in 2013 coincided with a team strength of over 200. And most recently, the COVID-19 pandemic in 2020 disrupted the construction consultancy sector, as our team exceeded 300. During these challenging times, the firm made a conscious decision never to lay off a single team member.

Rather than cutting costs by reducing the team, we invested in technology, training, and upskilling its team, ensuring that the organisation was ready to capitalise on opportunities once markets stabilised. This approach fostered loyalty, morale, and trust within the team, which was confident in the leadership's ability to navigate turbulent times. Our strategy embodied this philosophy, ensuring the firm was always prepared to weather such storms.

Understanding that debt is inevitable in a growing business, a careful balance must be maintained between expanding office infrastructure and scaling the team, while avoiding a conservative approach, which is a critical element of our financial strategy.

Financial prudence is complemented by careful project selection. The firm prioritised working with reliable clients, including managing no more than 40 projects at any given time, which has minimised risk and maintained a stable cash flow.

Over its 35-year journey, we have maintained a remarkable record: our company's profitability has never declined from one year to the next. This blend of creativity with business acumen has ensured that financial management was not an afterthought but the core of the company's sustainability and resilience.

Ultimately, our financial strategy rests on a few key principles:

- Integrity in compliance,
- Disciplined reinvestment,
- Risk-aware growth,
- Selective project engagement,
- Prioritisation of people over short-term profits.

Strategy, What We Focus On

We believe strategy is more than a set of directives; it reflects the firm's ethos, values, and lessons learned over decades of practice. Every decision, be it design-related, operational, financial, or strategic, is made collectively, combining the creativity, technical expertise, and operational acumen of the team.

Experience is the greatest teacher, and over more than three decades, we have amassed invaluable insights from every project, every client, and every challenge. From high-rise buildings to urban renewal projects, the firm has developed a deep understanding of what works in the real world versus what looks good on paper.

A critical lesson from early high-rise projects was the importance of integrating facility management teams from the design stage itself. Previously, handovers often faced operational difficulties due to a lack of coordination between design and maintenance teams. We pioneered a proactive approach where facility management considerations were embedded into architectural and interior design workflows, ensuring seamless transitions from construction to operation. We believe in continuously learning from both successes and failures. They institutionalise lessons by incorporating feedback from clients, contractors, and end-users, ensuring that knowledge is transferred across teams. At SSA, lessons learnt are the tools used to create a more efficient, innovative, and future-ready firm.

Being a Team Player: Collaboration is the heart of our organisational culture. Problems are approached collectively, and the culture of assigning blame is actively discouraged. By fostering a solution-focused mindset, the firm ensures that every stakeholder, whether it's the client, contractor, or sub consultant, feels that we is not an external consultant but an integral part of the team.

The core team behind the success of SSA

Sandeep's design vision anchors projects in creativity, functionality, and long-term impact. The design team, under Alpa's leadership, ensures that design excellence is maintained while integrating practical operational considerations. Mona's operational expertise helped to bridge the gap between design and execution.

The synergy of these three perspectives is made possible by our team, which strengthens the firm's approach to problem-solving, enabling us to navigate complex challenges effectively.

Team building is embedded in every operational strategy. Regular workshops, open-door leadership policies, and cross-functional collaborations reinforce trust and loyalty. The leadership invests in people because they recognise that a strong, aligned, and motivated team is the primary reason behind the firm's resilience and success.

Optimising Sustainability Goals

Sustainability is a guiding principle for us. From the earliest green building practices to the latest net-zero energy designs, the firm has prioritised environmental stewardship alongside functionality and aesthetics.

One of Asia's 1st USGBC – LEED Platinum certification for Hospital

Another notable example is the Kohinoor City project, where we convinced the developer to implement organic waste composting at a time when it was not mandatory. This decision now ensures that the 50-acre development efficiently manages massive waste volumes, setting a benchmark for other urban projects. Similarly, the Kohinoor Hospital, built in 2009 in Mumbai, achieved USGBC- LEED Platinum certification, becoming the first hospital in Asia to do so. The Dandi Memorial in Gujarat, inaugurated by the Prime Minister in 2019, stands as a net-zero energy building, a testament to our commitment to sustainable design practices.

By embedding sustainability at every stage from design to execution, the firm enhances both tangible value to the client and environmental responsibility.

Continuous Learning and Innovation: The environment is constantly evolving, and we invest heavily in ensuring that our team remains at the forefront of innovation. Constant learning is both a personal and organisational mantra. The team regularly attends expos, conferences, and workshops to stay up-to-date with the latest trends, technologies, and design philosophies. The team is encouraged to continually upskill, with structured programs available for interns, junior architects, and senior professionals alike. This culture of learning ensures the firm stays ahead of industry trends and equips its people with the tools to deliver superior outcomes consistently.

Internally, we operate a dedicated research cell that pilots new techniques, software, and project methodologies. By adopting advanced software such as Revit, Enscape, and Rhino, as well as exploring AI and machine learning applications in design and project management, the firm ensures that innovation is both practical and scalable.

SSA has long rejected cookie-cutter approaches to design and project management. Every client, every site, and every project is treated as unique. The firm focuses on balancing aesthetics, functionality, and cost efficiency to meet the project targets and client expectations.

An exemplary case is our first internationally recognised Mudra headquarters in Mumbai, which, under Alpa's leadership, reflected India's traditional Warli painting in a contemporary manner, winning the AIT Award in Germany in 2008. Every design element was tailored to reflect the client's brand identity while maintaining functionality, ergonomics, and sustainability. This commitment to customisation has become a hallmark of SSA, helping the firm deliver meaningful, human-centred environments across diverse sectors.

Use of Technology: Technology underpins almost every aspect of our operations. Beyond design software, the firm has developed proprietary tools and workflows to streamline project execution, monitor progress, and maintain quality standards. 3D laser scanning, BIM integration, and AI-driven modelling ensure precision and reduce errors during construction. Technology also empowers SSA to offer value-added services to clients. For example, predictive modelling helps assess project timelines, budget constraints, and environmental impacts, allowing informed decision-making. The seamless integration of technology, design, and management has positioned SSA as a leader in delivering complex projects efficiently and innovatively.

Investing in People: The team is our most valuable asset. From the earliest days, we recognised that investing in talent is essential for resilience. The firm nurtures its team through mentorship, training, and career advancement programs. Interns often choose to join on graduation, while the junior team is groomed into senior leadership roles over time.

Building Client Trust: Trust forms the foundation of client relationships. By serving a limited number of clients at any given time, the firm ensures focused attention, superior quality, and timely delivery. The leadership believes in exceeding expectations, creating experiences that are both 'magical yet measurable.' From fibre lighting innovations in the 1990s to introducing jump-form construction and Compass 360 elevators in high-rises, we consistently pioneer new solutions that enhance client satisfaction. This client-first approach, coupled with transparency and accountability, ensures long-term partnerships and repeat business.

Design, Develop, deliver: By combining Architecture, Interior Design, and Project Management under one umbrella, the firm provides clients with a 'one-stop solution'. This holistic model ensures seamless coordination across structural, MEP, façade, sustainability, and operational disciplines. This strategy not only strengthens client confidence and project success but also positions SSA as one of India's top five multidisciplinary firms, capable of handling projects of unparalleled scale and complexity.

SSA ARCHITECTS — **2002** SSA SANDEEP SHIKRE & ASSOCIATES — **2012** SSA — **2022**

Rejuvenating every decade

The Present, and Looking Ahead

Today, SSA continues to grow across India and internationally. We are committed to mentoring the next generation of Architects, Interior Designers and Engineers, embedding principles of integrity, accountability, and resilience. This vision ensures that the firm remains agile, adaptive, and ready to meet the evolving expectations of clients, millennials, and Gen Z team entrants alike. The succession planning includes the

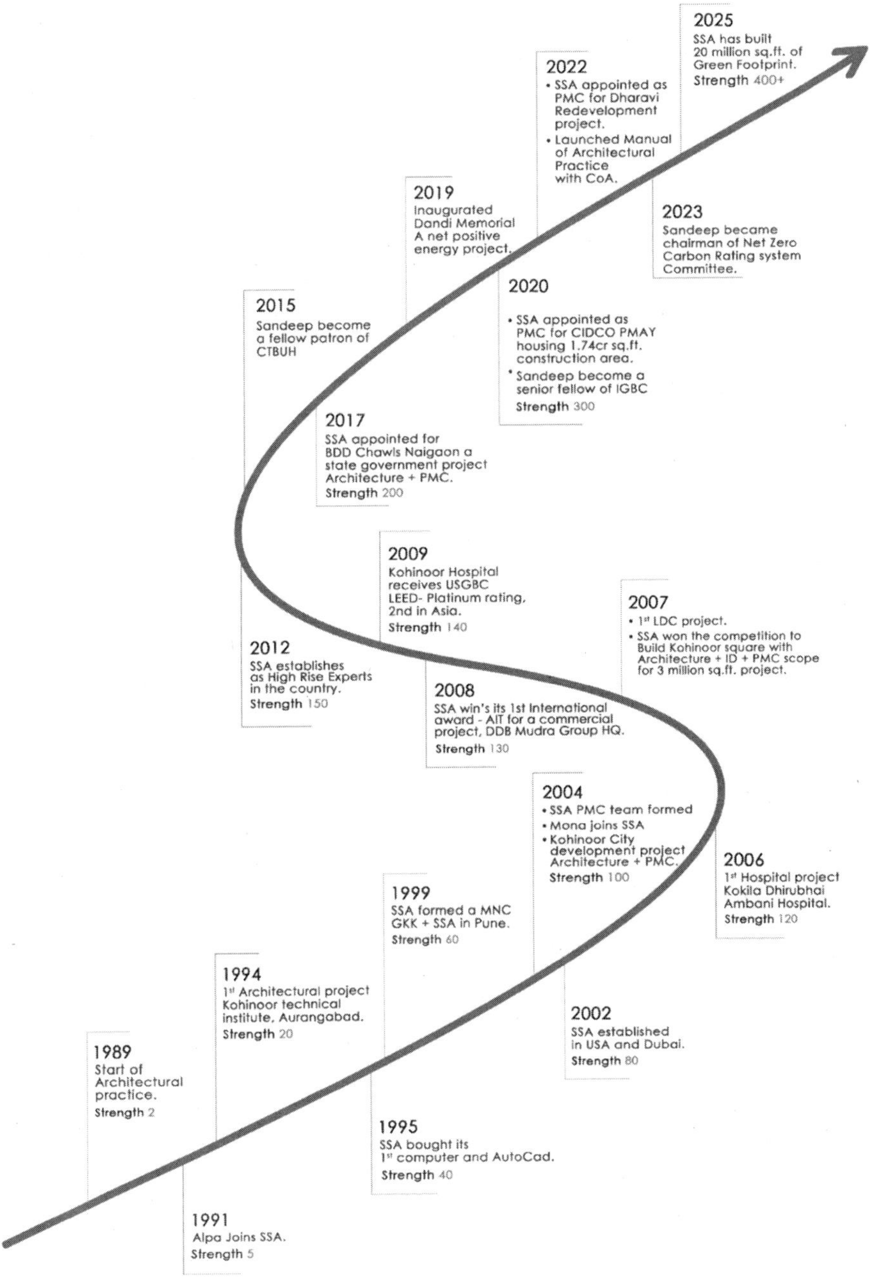

SSA Timeline

next generation team with Alpa's twin daughters, Anisha and Anusha, ensuring continuity of values and innovation.

Future focus areas include:

1. Expanding services across India
2. Leveraging technology for strategic decisions
3. Integrating SSA values in next-gen workforce (millennials and Gen Z)

SSA demonstrates that shared vision and collective leadership create enduring impact, a legacy that makes us a pioneer, ethical, and client-focused consultant, with conviction.

—xxx—

Contributors

Vivek Rajvanshi is a Professor at IIM Calcutta with over twenty-five years of experience in industry and academia. His consultancy and research interests include Investments and Risk Management, PE/VC, M&A, IPOs, and Business Valuation. He believes in making the learning process fun. In his free time, he enjoys playing chess and watching cricket.

Shirsha Guha is the COO of Saint James School of Medicine. She was born in Denmark, raised in the Caribbean and went to school and college in the Caribbean, India, and the United States. She joined her family business in 2003, and has never looked back. She now heads the India operations of the company, with a focus on academics. She holds a master's degree in Molecular Biology and another in Medical Ethics. Her interests include travelling, writing and physical fitness.

Joydeep Chowdhury is the Promoter & Managing Director of Panorama Electronics Pvt. Ltd. He leads the ₹600-crore, diversified Panorama Group. An engineer from the University of Sussex, UK, he drives the group's expansion into Homeland Security, IT, Chemicals, and Defense ventures. An avid golfer and philanthropist he blends innovation, leadership, and purpose in every endeavour.

Ashna Sachdev is a 6th generation entrepreneur from Delhi. She is the Associate Vice President of Corporate Relations at Glossy Color and Paints P Ltd. She has a Master's in International Management from King's College London and an Executive MBA from IMT Ghaziabad. She is currently leading her family's business's sustainability efforts and tie ups with ecommerce platforms.

Saurabh Jain is an entrepreneur, endurance sports enthusiast, and a firm believer in innovation through experience. His journey has been about creating new paths.

Sports has been his lifelong teacher. From tennis to long-distance cycling, he has learned how to channel focus, discipline, and perseverance, the same qualities that fuel his entrepreneurial spirit. He loves experimenting, creating, and reimagining processes to find smarter ways of doing things.

Devvrath Singh is the director of Current Infraprojects Limited and leads the Solar EPC division of the company.

Having graduated from The University of Queensland, Australia, he has led the change in diversification of company's operations from Electrical works into the Renewable Energy sector.

During his free time, he likes to play cricket and tennis. He is also a travel enthusiast and loves to travel around the world.

Prasanth Udayakumar is a 5th generation partner at G Rajam Chetty & Sons Jewellers LLP, a 143-year-old family-run jewellery business in Kanchipuram, Tamil Nadu. As a Chartered Accountant, he began his career at a Big4 Audit firm, before returning to carry forward his family legacy. He brings a blend of financial discipline and modern strategic thinking to a legacy brand.

He is passionate about community building, youth leadership, and fitness, and actively participates in several social initiatives.

Armaan Jaiswal is a Director at Jupiter Infraworks Pvt Ltd. He is the 4th Generation of the family to take forward the legacy. He was born and raised in Kolkata where She completed his Bachelors in Commerce with Honours at St. Xavier's College, Kolkata. He is an ambitious individual who believes in leadership through empathy, transparency and mutual accountability. His hobbies include calligraphy, cooking and baking.

Junaid Patel is a fourth-generation entrepreneur at Patanwala Dairy, a legacy that began in 1949 when his great-grandfather started the company. Over almost a decade, he has immersed himself in every aspect of the business from the farms to brand building, shaping the growth for the next generation. Beyond work, he finds balance through travel, sports, and exploring new ideas that inspire creativity, leadership, and a sense of purpose.

Sukruthi Sanjay is the Managing Partner at Sharada Cycle & Watch Stores, which represents the fourth generation of one of Mysore's most enduring family enterprises. Guided by her father's mentorship and inspired by a legacy that began in 1932, she blends tradition with modern vision. Beyond the business, she is a calligraphy artist—finding balance between enterprise and art, precision and expression. Through both, she continues to honour her family's timeless story while shaping its next century of growth.

Pranav Chaudhari is the Director of Heera Business Group and Yash Wines Pvt. Ltd. He leads liquor distribution, imports, retail, and hospitality. He joined the business in 2018. Business is not just work for him, it's his passion and legacy. He loves building brands, creating concepts, travelling, mixology, and constantly innovating to grow the empire.

Pavan Raju, Director of Sri Sai Siva., holds an M.Tech in AI and Robotics from Amity University. He joined his family's crusher spare parts business in 2022 and he's been modernizing operations through innovation and systems.

Apart from work his interests are in Sanskrit, Vedanta and classical music.

Shobhit Singh is Group Director at Ranjna Engineering Works. He represents the third generation and carries forward his family's 45-year legacy in precision manufacturing in cable and healthcare while championing India's self-reliant manufacturing vision. He is a BBA graduate from Amity University, and beyond business, he finds balance in boxing and caring for strays.

Tejas Sonigara, Director-CFO at Shree Sonigara Developers, brings financial acumen and strategic insight to the family-run real estate business. A Chartered Accountant, he has driven expansion, introduced new technologies, and strengthened internal systems to enhance operational efficiency and performance. Outside of work, he enjoys travelling, trying new cuisines, and listening to music.

Dr. Paresh Bhanushali is the Founder Director and COO at Yasraj Biotechnology Ltd.

He holds a Master's degree from IIT-Bombay and a PhD in Medical Biotechnology from MGM Institute of Health Sciences, Navi Mumbai, India. He carries an extensive knowledge and experience in protein biochemistry, and has published in several national and international journals of repute. He is a follower of Ayurveda and loves reading. He believes in making 'the best out of waste'. He is highly passionate and has an inquisitive mind.

Kinnari Desai is a designer and strategist at Sujanil Chemo Industries, a leading manufacturer of household insecticides, and health and hygiene products. She leads initiatives in design and digital transformation, bringing a modern approach to a trusted legacy business. She holds a Master's degree in Product Design Engineering and Management from ISD Rubika, France. Beyond business, her interests lie in travel, automobiles, fashion, and design, where she continues to explore the intersection of aesthetics, innovation, and human experience.

Alpa Shikre co-founded SSA, an architecture and design firm in 1992, alongside her husband Sandeep, turning a modest three-member start-up into a design powerhouse. With over three decades of experience, she masters sustainability and is the first Indian USGBC LEED-AP in Commercial Interiors. Her human-centric vision continues to shape SSA's enduring legacy of thoughtful design.

Mona Shah is a Cofounder at SSA, a leading architectural firm in Mumbai. She blends her experience from being one of the first woman entrepreneurs in a male dominated mobile crane industry to heading the project management vertical at SSA. Her collaborative strategic approach, which is inclusive and project driven, is what makes SSA unique.

Some participants of the batch enjoying their time during the Kolkata Visit

Interactive classroom session, PGCFBM Batch 06, led by Prof. Vivek Rajvanshi (Programme Director)
Courtesy: IIM Calcutta

Group photograph of PGCFBM Batch 06 (2024–25) with the Programme Directors
Courtesy: IIM Calcutta